Consuming Cities

Consuming Cities

Steven Miles and Malcolm Miles

First published 2004 by
PALGRAVE MACMILLAN
Houndmills, Basingstoke, Hampshire RG21 6XS and
175 Fifth Avenue, New York, N.Y. 10010
Companies and representatives throughout the world

PALGRAVE MACMILLAN is the global academic imprint of the Palgrave Macmillan division of St. Martin's Press, LLC and of Palgrave Macmillan Ltd. Macmillan® is a registered trademark in the United States, United Kingdom and other countries. Palgrave is a registered trademark in the European Union and other countries.

ISBN 0–333–97709–2 hardback
ISBN 0–333–97710–6 paperback

This book is printed on paper suitable for recycling and made from fully managed and sustained forest sources.

A catalogue record for this book is available from the British Library.

A catalog record for this book is available from the Library of Congress.

10   9   8   7   6   5   4   3   2   1
13 12 11 10 09 08 07 06 05 04

Printed in China

Contents

CHAPTER 1

Provide or Divide?

In his book, *The Cultures of Cities* written in 1938, Lewis Mumford distinguishes between "producing cities" and "consuming cities". Since that book was written three quarters of a century ago, consumption has become even more fundamental to the experience of city life. Indeed it could be argued, that at least to some degree all cities are "consuming cities". But is there more to city life than the opportunity to consume? Are cities somehow *determined* by the provision they make for consumers? Does consumption offer our cities and the citizens of our cities a future or does it simply serve to rob them of their past? In this book we aim to present a critical analysis of the impact of consumption on city life at the beginning of the twenty-first century. The consuming city is in some senses a product of a myth that our society has convinced us to consume. Indeed, it could be argued that in many ways the consuming city is nothing more than the figment of the over-active imaginations of town planners, architects and urban idealists. Consumption can offer planners and developers vast financial rewards, but what does it really offer the consumer? You might imagine that the opportunity to consume in cities and to consume cities themselves is by its very definition progressive in nature. But in *Consuming Cities* we aim to illustrate that although in many respects consumption offers a way out, in other ways it can actually create more problems than it could ever possibly solve. A city of consumption is indeed a city of contradiction and a city of paradox, but although some consumers are less victimised by the affluent city than others, all consumers have no choice but to be the subjects of it.

Some of the seeds for this project were sown at a conference the two authors attended in Weimar, Germany in the winter of 2001, entitled, "Consumption and the Post-Industrial City" (see Eckardt and Hassenpflug, 2003). This conference was remarkable for the way in which it appeared to valourise consumption as a, if not *the*, saviour of the contemporary city. The consuming city is mythologised in the sense that there is

a tendency to assume that the expansion of the opportunity to consume is intrinsically beneficial on an economic, social, and even a psychological level. Our position here is that this is not always the case. We
seek to counsel against a fetishisation of consumption and for sobriety
in appraising how the consumer society is actually experienced by
different social groups. It is simplistic to assume that consumption
will always have positive after-effects, simply because contemporary
societies in the developed world deem consumption to be a positive
source of social change. For instance, investment in the cultural economy of the city is often a good thing, but it cannot single-handedly
save the city. Consumption inevitably benefits some consumers, but
only at the expense of others. Consumption has a multi-faceted impact
on our lives: as individuals, as members of groups and as individuals
excluded from groups. Our title reflects this process insofar as we aim to
draw attention to the impact of processes of consumption on the character and form of a diverse range of cities from our immediate locality
to the cities of the future. But we are equally concerned with *how*
human beings consume cities. The increasing profile of consumption in
city life not only alters how we relate to urban environments, but also
how we see ourselves. Consumption has a major role to play in the maintenance of urban living. But ultimately, *consumption divides as much as it
provides* and it is this contention that lies at the very heart of this book.

Consumption has emerged as a key theme of contemporary debate
in both the Social Sciences and the Humanities. Almost every imaginable
issue appears to be somehow implicated by the ability to consume. This
reflects a broader process in which the very nature of our society
appears to be infused with a consumer ethic: politicians arguing that
the consumer needs to have his or her say in how to run an effective
National Health Service; educationalists fretting over League Tables
which parents pour over in order to ensure their children get the education they deserve, and cities apparently reinvigourated by schemes
intended to breathe life into stagnant, lifeless and de-industrialised city
spaces. In his book, *Contemporary Urban Japan*, Clammer (1997) argues
that the study of consumption represents the most insightful means of
revealing cultural patterns and economic organisation which underpin
Japanese social life. In *Consuming Cities* we seek to extend this point in
arguing that a critical analysis of the impact of consumption upon the
city will help us understand the meanings with which that life is
invested.

So, what exactly is the relationship between the city and consumption?
The question of how consumption impacts the urban fabric has been of

particular recent fascination to sociologists, notably since the work of Peter Saunders (1981) who, as Campbell (1995) notes, was one of the first sociologists to identify the need for a new research agenda called "the sociology of consumption" and more importantly perhaps, one of the first to highlight the need to reject a paradigm dependant on production in favour of one that focuses attention on consumption. In other words, Saunders' somewhat controversial position is that the opportunity to consume was a more fundamental factor than class in determining social relations in the city. Saunders (1981) therefore argues that privatised consumption is of increasing social importance insofar as there is a fundamental division in society between people who purchase their services individually through the market and those whose lives are subject to the welfare state. As such, consumption-based divisions are seen to be the main axis of political and social division in contemporary society. For Saunders then, who develops Castells' (1997) original work which we will discuss shortly, the city is a spatial unit of collective consumption. Castells saw the city as the spatial expression of the reproduction of labour power which, in turn, collectivises or socialises the act of consumption. Our collective relationship to the city is, in effect, determined by our collective experience of consumption in the city. In this context, Saunders argues that consumption is not solely attached to the city as a spatial unit. From his point of view the city is not simply a unit of consumption and in this regard, "a sociology of consumption can only be developed once we break with the specific spatial orientation which has characterised urban studies up to the present day" (p. 238). Furthermore, any analysis of consumption in the city needs to be more aware of the ramifications of state provision and the fragmented nature of class relations. In turn, it needs to realise " ... that consumption effects can and must be analysed on their own terms without constantly seeking to explain them in terms of the 'functions' they are held to perform for a system of capitalist production" (p. 238). In considering the impact of consumption on contemporary society Saunders' broad argument is, somewhat controversially, that spatial concerns are secondary insofar as they may or may not influence how particular processes such as class relations develop. Indeed for Saunders, "Today ... the city has ceased to be a significant unit of social, economic or political life" (p. 282). From this point of view consumption is not simply a characteristic of urban life, it is a major factor in determining the nature of that life. But is this really the case at the beginning of the twenty-first century? Can consumption offer cities and those human beings who live within and without those cities what it promises? Or, to paraphrase the words of Horkheimer and Adorno (1973), does the city diner have to be satisfied with the menu? As a result of the intervention of consumption, have cities, in fact, ceased to become a place and emerged instead as an emotional experience, a way of thinking about the world, an idealised perception of experience that may not necessarily reflect the mundane reality?

Ideologies of consumption

Consumption is ideological. In other words, consumption has a key role to play in maintaining social relationships as well as those relationships between people and their physical environments. Ideology is an important cultural concept as Storey (1999) suggests. It is particularly important in the study of urban life, precisely because we live that life in a cultural context. The way in which we "consume" the urban environment is not entirely within our personal control precisely because we are the consumers rather than the producers of that environment. However much consumers' interests are taken into account in urban planning, they are not and cannot be in control of the process. As Storey notes, ideology can be defined as the way in which certain cultural texts and practices present distorted images of reality. As far as the study of "consuming cities" is concerned then, the impact of consumption on the city may be presented to us as citizens of contemporary society in a particular way that reinforces a particular group's way of thinking. In short, ideologies are constructed for a purpose: to fulfil the aims of a powerful social group, at the expense of a less powerful social group.

Manuel Castells

The city is an ideological arena and the contradictions inherent in that arena represent a key concern of Manuel Castells (1977), one of the most important contributors to debates over consumption in the city,

> The city – regarded both as the complex expression of its social organization and as the milieu determined by fairly rigid technological constraints – thus becomes, in turn, a focus, of creation and the locus of oppression by the technico-natural forces brought into being. (p. 85)

It is worth considering briefly Castells' contribution to urban sociology insofar as his interpretation of urban life moved away from common-sense ideas of what constituted the town, the city and indeed, the urban (see Urry, 1995). Castells adopts a structuralist position. He is concerned with the contradictions of capitalist relations and how they are expressed through the city. He therefore identifies cities as sites of consumption, as opposed to production. Castells (1977) defines consumption as,

> the social process of appropriation of the product by people, that is to say, social classes ... From the point of view of social classes, consumption is both an expression and a means, that is to say, a social practice, which is realized according to a certain (ideological) content and which concretizes at the level of the relations of the distribution the oppositions and struggles determined by the relations of production. (pp. 454–455)

From this point of view, consumption is not a free-standing phenomenon. Rather, it is determined by the general rules of production. Collective consumption represents a significant aspect of social change insofar as urban politics becomes focused around this very issue. As such, as Urry (1995) points out, Castells argues against an attempt to understand cities as "culture" or a "way of life". Rather, the social relations of production have developed in such a way as to require labour-power to be reproduced through collective consumption. Castells therefore describes a world of "mass consumption" in which goods that are most profitable are produced rather than those that have a particular use. But most importantly, for Castells, the consumer society is the product of historically determined class practices. Consumption is therefore "the true expression of class practice and of level in the hierarchy of social stratification" (p. 456). A similar point is made by Philo and Kearns (1993) who describe urban form as an ideological project and urban culture as the active project of the urban bourgeoisie who use a city as a means of asserting their social dominance (Philo and Kearns, 1993). From this point of view, the promotion and marketing of cities operates as a form of socialisation which is intended to convince local people that the commodification of the city is entirely positive and that their role within this process is valued. Regardless of the economic implications of a commodity aesthetic, it could be argued that such a process actively pacifies the local population. As Philo and Kearns go on to argue, the relationships people have with a city are often more diverse than a straightforward economic analysis might suggest. The impact of consumption upon the city may give an impression of city life, very different to that which is felt on the ground. But *Consuming Cities* is not a book about the relationship between class and consumption. Our aim is to present a more critical view of the meanings ascribed to consuming cities. We would therefore concur with Philo and Kearns's (1993: 18) suggestion that,

> In . . . [an open market] discourse places do indeed become "commodi-fied", regarded as commodities to be consumed and as commodities that can be rendered attractive, advertised and marketed much as capitalists would any product, and we hence need to appreciate the constituents of this discourse – considering as we do the various turns that the discourse takes for different "actors" in the process – and their various practical consequences.

In this book we therefore regard consumption as a key means by which both the character of our cities is promoted and, in addition, a key factor in determining the meanings with which consumers endow their experience of city life. Urban change is not simply manifested at a physical level. The city is an emotional experience as well as an architectural one.

It might well be suggested that the "evolution" of cities has actually become increasingly "cultural" in nature. Cities may still represent an important focal point for the maintenance of class relationships, but cultures of consumption have come to play what could be argued to be a more subtle role in this process. The impact of consumption on city life is influential precisely because the cultural mode of expression which it adopts gives the consumer the feeling that he or she is in con-trol. A key question with which we are concerned is whether that sense of control is illusory? Does the rhetoric that surrounds consumption simply reflect an ideological imperative in which we are persuaded to assume that a "consuming city" is a desirable city?

For the purposes of this book it is also important to remember that culture is negotiated. Cultures are constructed through the negotiation of meaning, but that negotiation is not always conducted on a level playing field. And neither is a culture necessarily "natural". The key point about a society apparently underpinned by the exchange of the commodity is that that commodity is somehow given unnatural signifi-cance. In a consumer society we are convinced that the commodity represents an absolutely essential means of maintaining our culture. Consumption is good. It is good because it offers us the freedom to choose. But at the same time, at an ideological level, it becomes univer-salised to the extent that we are unable to collectivise our unrest about the ineffectiveness and injustice of that system. In fact, we barely express such unrest at all, precisely because the consumer society gives us the freedom and the opportunity to express our individuality through consumption (whilst we simultaneously and ironically assert our group membership through brands and the like). That freedom is enough in itself. Consumption allows us to be individuals yet remain part of a group. Consumption is particularly important in constructing city life because the city is the primary venue in which consumption takes place. But equally, and what is so often forgotten, it is the venue within which consumption *does not* take place. The city is the primary arena within which consumers can, or quite often cannot, consume. But the city is more than simply an arena. It is,

> a state of mind, a body of customs and traditions, and of the organized attitudes and sentiments that inhere in these customs and are trans-mitted with this tradition. The city is not, in other words, merely a physical mechanism and an artificial construction. It is involved in the vital processes of the people who compose it, it is a product of nature, and particularly of human nature. (Park *et al.*, 1925: 1)

Louis Wirth

It is no coincidence that one of the two authors of *Consuming Cities* has written another book entitled *Consumerism as a Way of Life* which echoes the title of one of the most important articles ever written on the question of urban life, *Urbanism as a way of life* by Louis Wirth (1964). Wirth's contribution is significant insofar as he sought to provide a sociological definition of city life. He recognised that the city was not purely about its physical manifestation, but that it was a cul-tural entity. It is of particular interest that in the editor's introduction to Wirth's article in a recent collection of key texts on the city (LeGates and Stout, 1996), it is suggested that Wirth's work has been criticised for being nothing more than "the social scientific verification of the obvious" (p. 97). We want to suggest that the fact that what Wirth says is in a sense obvious is precisely what makes it so important.

Around half the world's population live in what is primarily an urban culture. Urbanism transfuses every aspect of our lives and we take it for granted. As we pointed out above, the same can be said for consumerism. We take it for granted and that is why it has such a fundamental impact on our everyday lives. But perhaps the world has moved on since Wirth's original article was published in 1938. For instance, Wirth argues that the city can be defined as "a relatively large, dense, and permanent settlement of socially heterogeneous individuals" (p. 98). A key question with which *Consuming Cities* is concerned is whether this is still the case. The hyperbole that surrounds debates concerning consumption would suggest that consumption is inherently liberating: it promotes heteeogeneity. Might there be an argument for suggesting that consuming cities encourage homogeneity – that the affect of consumption of city life is to promote uniformity under the guise of diversity? As consumers, we accept consumption as a positive force in our lives, but what it actually entails is a dominant ideological order inscribed on the urban landscape. Wirth argues that city life produces a particular segmentalisation of human relationships that in turn produce a particular schizoid urban personality. In this context, we have close physical but distant social contact: "We tend to acquire and develop a sensitivity to a world of artifacts and become progressively farther removed from the world of nature" (p. 100). The urban environment is a competitive one of mutual exploitation without any stable core to the extent that "the individual acquires membership in widely divergent membership in widely different groups, each of which functions only with reference to a single segment of his personality" (p. 101). Wirth therefore quite rightly describes the emergence of a mass urban culture in which services are provided for the average person rather than for specific individuals. This is a self-consciously commercial culture,

> Catering to thrills and furnishing means of escape from drudgery, monotony, and routine thus become one of the major functions of urban recreation, which at its best furnishes means for creative self-expression and spontaneous group association, but which more typically in the urban world results in passive spectatorism on the other hand, or sensational record-smashing feats on the other. (p. 104)

Georg Simmel

Wirth's analysis of urbanism highlights the paradoxical nature of city life. But it also indicates the commercial imperatives that underpin that experience to the extent that "there is virtually no human need which has remained unexploited by commercialism" (p. 104). The extent to which that commercialism and more specifically, commodification, represents a positive force for social change constitutes an abiding concern for *Consuming Cities*. Insofar as this is the case, the work of Georg Simmel, notably in his influential analysis of "the metropolis and mental life" is equally useful (see Frisby and Featherstone, 1997). Simmel's work is remarkable insofar as he plots the relationship between the physical landscape and its effect on human psychology. His description is of the psycho-social impact of urbanism. In effect, "The psychological basis of the metropolitan type of individual consists in the intensification of nervous stimulation which results from the swift and uninterrupted change of inner stimuli" (Simmel, 1950: 410). Simmel was concerned with the way in which the metropolis creates particular psychological conditions. In an effort to cope with the over-stimulation of city life, the individual reacts in specific ways. In particular, he or she sees the city through his or her head, as opposed to his or her heart. From Simmel's point of view the city is all about exchange and the money economy. In this environment human beings interact with and use other human beings in a matter-of-fact way. In this sense the urban environment is a less individualistic environment than its rural counterpart. In the city, human relationships are in effect stripped down to their economic essentials. As such, Simmel describes money as "the most frightful leveler ... Money, with all its colorlessness and indifference, becomes the common denominator of all values; irreparably it hollows out the core of things, their individuality, their specific value and their incomparability" (p. 414). Arguably consumption has done precisely the same thing to the city. The "purchasability of things" has indeed been brought to the core of contemporary city life. In this context, Simmel describes a regrettable transition in which the individual's personality is dragged down into an empty pot of worthlessness which sees physical proximity result in social distance. As far as Simmel is concerned, the individual is never more lost than when he or she is in the metropolitan crowd. City life is ultimately a struggle, a struggle that promotes competition at the expense of relatedness,

> It is decisive that city life has transformed the struggle with nature for livelihood into an inter-human struggle for gain, which here is not granted by nature but by other men. For specialization does not flow only from the competition for gain but also from the underlying fact that the seller must always seek to call forth new and differentiated needs of the lured customer. In order to find a source of income which is not yet exhausted, and to find a function which cannot

readily be displaced, it is necessary to specialize in one's services. This process promotes differentiation, refinement, and the enrichment of the public's needs, which obviously must lead to growing personal differences within the public. (p. 420)

What Simmel seems to be implying here is that public needs are being promoted at the expense of private or psychological ones. Developing this perspective we might well ask whether the freedom offered to the consumer through city life represents any sort of freedom at all or whether the freedom to consume is no more than the freedom to help maintain the status quo, to acquiesce in the perpetuation of a consumer society.

The symbolic "nature" of consumption

In understanding the changing city and the role of consumption in determining such change, the increasingly symbolic role of consumption is undoubtedly significant. Indeed, as Baudrillard (1998) suggests exchange value has, in recent decades, undoubtedly extended the sphere of capitalist production. Collective consumption may or may not continue to constitute a key aspect of contemporary city life, but the role of consumption in city life has become increasingly symbolic since Castells', Wirth's and Simmel's work. Perhaps then the impact of consumption on the city is more symbolic than it is spatial. What matters about a product is not so much its utility value or the location in which it is found, but its symbolic value and how we as consumers interpret that product on a symbolic level. In our culture we increasingly appear to find the quality of a product not in its use value or how we consume it as a physical and a geographical entity, but in the meanings and status that we attach to that product symbolically. This reflects a process by which consumption appears to have taken on something of a magical quality. A Marxist interpretation would suggest that the commodity society has become reified to the extent that an abstract concept, in this case "consumerism" has come to take on a concrete existence to the extent that we accept it as a way of life, as *the* way of life. In other words, consumer society is no longer simply social but is so all-powerful, as we suggested above, to become natural. Perhaps more importantly a reified society camouflages the social relations that prop it up. The commodity society creates the impression that social life is about the relatively harmless process of exchange, but that process conceals the social relations that underpin that society. At a symbolic level, consumer goods convince us that they can satisfy our every want and in doing so they help us to forget the fact that those wants are of secondary significance when we compare them to the their potentially destructive origins. The fact that a pair of training shoes, for instance, is produced for a ridiculously low wage in South East Asia is easily forgotten by the consumer. Similarly, the middle classes might gladly consume the fruits of a city's contemporary art gallery without much thought for those people who for all sorts of reasons may be excluded from that environment.

It would of course, be entirely misleading to suggest that consumption constitutes the be-all and end-all of the contemporary city. It would perhaps be more accurate to say that consumption represents the "mental life" or framework within which the contemporary city is constructed. In other words, the experience of city life has apparently, at least on the surface, been reconstituted. Human beings are no longer citizens of the city in which they live, but rather they are *consumers in* and *consumers of* that city. The implication of this process is that the cultural role of the city is more important in the construction of the urban fabric than ever before. But the problem with any discussion of culture is that by its very nature that discussion is imprecise (Mitchell, 1999). Mitchell discusses the increasing incorporation of notions of culture within human geography. It is certainly true to say that urban geographers became more amenable to ideas concerning the human and aesthetic elements in urban change: giving credence to an approach that gives room to human agency and to consumption, as opposed to production. In particular, as Mitchell notes, many authors such as David Ley (1997) have realised the benefits to be had in finding a balance between economic and cultural processes and explanations. Thus, Mitchell (1999: 669) discusses the emergence of the cultural turn within human geography and its impact on the subsequently "fertile period of urban scholarship": "It is thus the very nonfixity and undecidability that I like about the idea of 'culture,' and that I believe has facilitated the establishment of a wider, more curious, more synthetic, and more tolerant community of urban scholars" (p. 669).

There is a danger that the processes we describe above are assumed to be recent in nature. Analyses of social change tend to over-estimate the degree to which the present represents a break with the past. We live in the present and as products of the modern or perhaps post-modern world, we are somehow obliged to assume that the period in which we live is a period of radical change. But the move towards a consumer society is a long-term historical process, as we will go on to suggest in Chapter 2. As Thrift and Glennie (1993) argue, urban contexts have long been central to both the learning of new consumption practices and their pursuit. The historical development of consumerism has perhaps been most effectively described by Colin Campbell (1987) in his book, *The Romantic Ethic and the Spirit of Modern Consumerism*. Campbell argues that prior to the eighteenth century, consumption patterns were limited in nature and simply met very finite needs. But gradually there emerged a culture in which consumption became more and more about desire rather than about the *fulfilment* of a specific need. Campbell therefore describes a world in which we "want to want". We do need specific products to fulfil us, but rather we have developed a more general cultural orientation towards consumption. We have developed a consumer ethic. But this development is not recent in nature. Rather, Campbell sees it as emerging from the late eighteenth century onwards with the emergence of Romanticism which, in turn, was characterised by an emotionalist way of life where an individual's virtues were increasingly expressed through their emotions. The Romantic view of the individual (especially as expressed in the work of the Romantic poets) was all about the emergence of a distinct autonomous being. Romanticism was about the expression of individuality and identity. Consumption appealed precisely because it provided a means of fulfilling a need, yes, but an emotional need rather than a physical one,

> modern hedonism tends to be overt and self-illusory; that is to say, individuals employ their imaginative and creative powers to construct mental images which they consume for the intrinsic pleasure they provide, a practice best described as day-dreaming or fantasizing... The visible practice of consumption is thus no more than a small part of a complex pattern of hedonistic behaviour, the majority of which occurs in the imagination of the consumer. (pp. 77–89)

Consumers do not have an insatiable desire to consume, but rather they seek to experience in reality what they have already experienced in their imaginations. From this point of view, consumers are, above all else, imaginative creatures and "the cultural products offered for sale in modern societies are in fact consumed because they serve as aids to the construction of day-dreams" (p. 92).

It may be worth taking this argument one step further. Perhaps the influence of consumerism on our society, but also our psychology, is so profound that its effect on our urban environment is in turn actually as emotional as it is physical and it is precisely for this reason that it is so difficult to assess the impact of consumption on the urban landscape. Campbell recognises that consumers are in a constantly frustrated state. They find themselves in a constant state of want because their desires can only be consummated on a temporary instantaneous basis. But this state of mind is not something that can easily be escaped because it is the social, and indeed, the psychological norm. The city is the main arena within which these desires are stimulated. The city legitimises consumerism as a way of life. It provides a locale within which the act of non-consumption is deemed to be deviant but at the same time it is trapped within its own geography. Cities are, of course, constantly changing but they are also physically incapable of reinventing themselves as pragmatically as the commodity. This constraint creates the very tension that we intend to capture in *Consuming Cities*.

The move towards a more diverse and sometimes contradictory notion of culture will also be reflected in this book. It is a concern that despite the above sentiments, analyses of consumption tend to be culturally specific in one sense and culturally non-specific in another. When sociologists, in particular, describe consumer society they do so in such a way to suggest that the notion of a consumer society is uncontested and apparently unrelated to questions of space and place. The consuming city exists, but there is apparently no need to indicate where it exists because it is all around us: it is omnipresent. From this perspective, there is an underlying implication that the consuming city is a "Western" institution, or at least that is the implication because specifics are usually hard to come by. In this sense *Consuming Cities* is very much concerned with the broader cultural implications of consumption and how consumerism, far from merely being the product of western capitalism, has a profound influence on cultures worldwide. This is a point well made by Schein (1997) who presents urbanity as an artefact of popular cultural production in post-Mao China. Western capitalism certainly provides a key influence in this respect, but the effect of consumption on the rest of the world is geographically unique. Indeed, for many parts of the world the wonders of consumption are still imagined. The relationship between urbanisation and consumption is not necessarily a healthy one and is as much about the power of the imaginary as it is about consumption itself. As Schein puts it, "What cities have offered in the popular imagination of the postsocialist period is the potential for acquisition, not necessarily its actualization" (p. 225). This brings us back again to the question of desire. Cities and the occupants of cities might well aspire for the joys of a consumer society, but those joys will not always be forthcoming. It is this sense that it is very important to adopt, as far as possible, a place-specific conception of the impact of consumption on the economies and cultures of our cities.

Having reviewed some of the key contributions to debates about the relationship between consumption and the city, a key question raised by Clammer (1997) remains: how do we go about creating a consumption-based analysis of contemporary urban life? In this context, Clammer criticises Saunders' assumption that leisure has replaced work as key focus for contemporary social life. Neither are we seeking to adopt such an extreme position in *Consuming Cities*. Rather we want to argue that consumption has laid claim to being a key proponent of urban social change and as such it is manifested in the urban fabric through both work and leisure. Whether such a relationship benefits the city, and the consumers who live in cities, is the key concern of this book. Is consumption *a* or perhaps even *the* legitimate force behind city life at the beginning of the twenty-fist century?

Before closing this chapter and as a means of addressing some of the above issues and of setting the agenda for the remainder of this book, it might be useful to discuss a case study which illuminates the particular tensions that we will argue are associated with the "consuming city". It would have been very easy to present any number of case studies that "prove" that consumption is the driving force behind contemporary city life and that consumption has therefore transformed what it means to live in a city. World cities such as Los Angeles, Berlin, London or New York might, for instance, have been obvious places to have started. Our feeling, however, is that a case study of Los Angeles cannot help us come to terms with the paradoxical impact of consumption on city life and the fact that many smaller cities have a more contradictory relationship with consumption than the so-called "post-industrial" cities such as those mentioned above. In a sense, consumption is more omnipresent than a discussion of world cities would imply. As such, each chapter of *Consuming Cities* will be elucidated with an extension of a discussion of either a particular city or, as in Chapter 2 (which looks at supermarket shopping), of a particular dimension of the consuming experience. In the case of this chapter, the following discussion of Plymouth, England, in some senses an unexceptional city, serves as a timely, and perhaps unexpected, reminder of both the rich rewards and the unfulfilled promises that are associated with the so-called consuming city.

Consuming Plymouth

Plymouth is the largest city on the South Coast of England with a population of 256,000 and is the major centre of population, west of Bristol. Despite being home to the largest naval dockyard in Europe, Plymouth has undergone an ongoing period of economic decline which has forced the city to reconsider its economic future. In recent years, Plymouth's economic base has become less and less dependant upon the dockyard and nowadays, the city could indeed be more effectively characterised as a regional hub of the call centre industry. Plymouth could not be described by any stretch of the imagination as "post-industrial". "De-industrialised" might be a more appropriate label. Fortunately, the dockyards meant Plymouth was protected by the decline of manufacturing industry experienced by most of the country between the late 1970s and the mid-1980s. However, the dockyards were subsequently hit by privatisation in 1986 and, in addition, by the reduction of the naval fleet. This had severe economic repercussions for the city to the extent that Plymouth found itself struggling to find an economic identity.

Despite the above decline, there is no doubt that Plymouth has genuine attractions as a city and in recent years it has had to seek ways to maximise the benefits of those attractions. It is located on the coast of Devon, is in easy reaching distance of both Dartmoor and Cornwall and it has a considerable historical pedigree, notably to the American visitor seduced by the fact that the Mayflower left here for the New World in 1620. Plymouth is certainly a city rich in maritime history, but a more significant event in that respect and one that has had a more fundamental impact on the character of Plymouth as a city, was undoubtedly the Second World War. During March and April 1941, thirty-one air raids took place over Plymouth and whole areas of the city were obliterated as a result. The urban planners' response to this devastation, was Paton-Watson and Abercrombie's "A Plan for Plymouth 1943" in which they created a vision for a new city; in many respects it was a vision of a consuming city. Even at that stage the opportunity to consume was at the centre of this radical new plan for urban redevelopment, "The Centre of Plymouth is to be that of a modern town, with the beauty and dignity of a city centre still grouped around its ancient Church, and the convenient arrangement of a shopping centre" (Paton-Watson and Abercrombie, 1943: p. 6). This was a grand, even futuristic, vision for a city which would show the world how good city life could be. It was intended that the Plan would not only take Plymouth into a bright new dawn, but that it would also provide a blueprint that would be the envy of cities worldwide.

The City "Fathers" saw the Plymouth Plan as a means to "a new Plymouth worthy of its fame" (see Paterson, 1983; Paton-Watson and Abercrombie, 1943: vi). This was a comprehensive scheme and one that involved a degree of demolition of the urban fabric comparable to the destruction caused by the Blitz. The effect of the Second World War provided the circumstances under which a radical, and arguably overly bold, urban plan could be implemented. The centrepiece of this plan was a sweeping and impressive garden vista that would lead the visitor to Plymouth from the railway station all the way down to the Hoe where Francis Drake finished his game of bowls prior to defeating the Spanish Armada in 1588. However, years after the new city centre was built it was doubtful whether, beyond the stark modernity of the city centre, the above plan really afforded the impact that was originally envisaged. On an anecdotal level many contemporary visitors to Plymouth, though charmed by the location of the city, are often dispirited by the concrete and unwelcoming urbaness of its centre. A key criticism of the Plan is that it failed to give expression to the city's unique history or its maritime geography. It is arguably a landscape bereft of landmarks and bereft of a past (Paterson, 1983). A Plan that offered consumption, but left nothing to consume. In this context, Chalkley and Goodridge (1991) argue that the failings of the plan are less a product of the plan, than a result of the way in which the plan was implemented, and not surprisingly, the limited nature of ongoing investment. This is reflected in the urban morphology of Plymouth insofar as the lack of investment in buildings that form part of the top end of the vista at Royal Parade that runs right through the city centre. The buildings are clearly not of the size or gravitas that the original plans envisaged. In this sense, Plymouth's urban shopping centre failed to produce the goods. The Plan was an ambitious one, but the ideas that underpinned the plan were never sufficiently backed up with the appropriate investment. The City of Plymouth Planning Department Report "Tomorrow's Plymouth", published in 1986, suggests that

> The Plan's achievements are acknowledged and admired, not only in the City but throughout the world. But there is now a need for adjustment – to adapt the City to provide for the needs and expectations of the 1980s and beyond. Other towns and cities which have improved their centres more recently have threatened to overtake

Plymouth commercially...In short the centre needs a "shot in the arm". (p. 7)

In short, the ground-breaking intentions of the Plymouth Plan did not pass the test of time, and the harsh architecture of the 1960s is certainly not, on the whole, viewed with very much affection by the people of Plymouth (Shepley, 1991). The recognition that Plymouth needed a "shot in the arm" reflects a series of proposals that have seen the light since this report was written. Plymouth has indeed undergone at least something of a sea-change, with new developments, typical of many throughout the UK, including the opening of the National Marine Aquarium, the Barbican Leisure Centre at Coxside which includes a multiplex cinema, a bar, a nightclub, bowling alley and a health and fitness club and restaurants. Plymouth Argyle opened their new football stadium in 2002 and the Barbican, the city's historical focus, has undergone a degree of regeneration in recent years including the splattering of a sign of a "cafe society" and the recent opening of the Mayflower Centre which chronicles the history of Sutton Harbour and the Pilgrim Fathers through a series of hands-on exhibits aimed at the family, at a cost of £2.3 millions. On the other hand, a variety of other proposals including the "Mast", a 700-foot-high tower surrounded by a revolving restaurant and a viewing platform, and for a pier, have failed to get off the drawing board either through a lack of capital investment or a failure to accrue planning permission.

Perhaps most markedly, having lain neglected and decaying for decades, Tinside Pool, the spectacular Grade II listed Art Deco lido, on Hoe foreshore, and arguably Plymouth's most immediately recognisable landmark, has in recent years become little more than a political football. Over that last decade or so, local council politicians have ruminated and pontificated over the future of the site, whilst struggling and largely failing to secure the appropriate funds to allow the lido to fulfil its massive potential. Tinside Pool did indeed play a key role in the election of a Conservative council in 1999. Furthermore, it might indeed be argued that in many ways Tinside Pool became symbolic of a sort of historical sentimentality amongst many local people in Plymouth who hankered after the Plymouth of old. What appeared to be emerging was a reaction against the assumption that all change was always positive and a concomitant concern that the commodification of the city, did not always have the best interests of its people at heart (Shepley, 1991). The Plymouth public were undoubtedly beginning to doubt the legitimacy of such schemes, and were increasingly wary of the power games going on behind the scenes. In the words of one member of the public who wrote to the local newspaper, the *Evening Herald*, to express his concern:

> Michel Foucault coined the phrase "the repressive hypothesis" to define institutions which think that they have the right to tell us what we can think, how we should behave and where, in the case of Coxside, we should live. This council is making it clear to the people of Plymouth that we are not welcome in our own place of birth. This is an attempt to cleanse the Sutton Harbour area of local people who in the eyes of the council are nothing more than pawns, to be moved on somewhere else without a thought other than the gleaming pound sign in their eyes. (http://www.thisisplymouth.co.uk/displayNode.jsp?nodeId=98912&command=displayContent&source Node=98821&contentPK=1629962)

The above quotation refers to the Coxside waterside scheme which was intended to transform part of Sutton Harbourside into a world class centre for marine science and, perhaps inevitably, a location for luxury flats. What the partnership between the National Marine Aquarium and the University of Plymouth did not account for was the fact that the treasury department denied a £30 million bid to finance the scheme. Arguably even more telling was the vehement protest by local Coxside residents, many of whom would have lost their home if the scheme had gone ahead as planned. This was apparently a plan too far. More recently, government minister, Lord Falconer visited Plymouth to publicise the South West Regional Development Agency's efforts to regenerate the Royal William Yard, disused shipyard buildings with massive potential that have been the subject of local conjecture for decades (Demianyk, 2002). Lord Falconer was in Plymouth as part of his effort to visit the 24 towns and cities involved in the British government's "Urban Renaissance" initiative which includes £22 millions invested by Urban Splash, a Liverpool-based developer and which in turn compliments the £8 millions already invested by the South West Regional Development Agency. But such plans have not been universally welcomed, as a further letter from a member of the public to the *Evening Herald* illustrates:

> Why is it that every piece of valuable real estate close to the foreshore, especially those with magnificent panoramic views such as Teats Hill [Coxside], the Barbican, the Hoe and Royal William Yard, for example, are being considered or limply handed over, lock, stock and barrel,

for the sole benefit of "yuppies"... I always note that when they build these sorts of places, the developers always state that there will be "some affordable" places for the less well-heeled. Probably a broom cupboard at the rear of the building with nothing but a brick wall to look at. Is it not a sad state of affairs that the magnificent Royal William Yard can have no other future but simply being a playground for the rich. This is Plymouth, not Monte Carlo! (http://www.thisisplymouth. co.uk/displayNode.jsp?nodeId=98912&command=displayContent& sourceNode=98821&contentPK=1540248)

We quote the above comments at length because they represent a telling indictment of the paradoxes and tensions that characterise any move, piecemeal or otherwise, towards the commodification of cities, and in particular, relatively small cities such as Plymouth. Plymouth is not indeed Monte Carlo nor is it Los Angeles, Berlin, London or New York. Like many similar cities, Plymouth has long and genuinely struggled to attract external investment into the city. Unbridled successes such as the National Marine Aquarium tend to be the exception rather than the rule. In fact, the impact of consumption on Plymouth as a city has been tantamount to riding a very expensive roller coaster which never quite comes to a stop, so those riding never actually get to savour the experience. Perhaps the city lacks a sense of itself and no amount of opportunities to consume can solve that particular problem. On a geographical level, ever since the Plymouth Plan, the city has lacked a discernible central focus. The city centre itself virtually shuts down in the early evening when the shops close for business. Any potential developments within the city or around it are treated, in some respects understandably with considerable suspicion, as though Plymouth more than anything needs to be *protected* from the tentacles of consumption. In many respects the opportunities to consume in Plymouth remain limited. Today's Plymouth is a city that has struggled to throw off the shackles of the past and embrace an alternative future in which that past can continue to thrive. In Plymouth at least, consumption cannot and does not offer a new dawn and it seems many of its people are happy that Plymouth has never actually become a consuming city. If indeed, such a city exists.

But perhaps there is light at the end of the consumerist tunnel for the city of Plymouth. At the time of writing Plymouth City Council were considering plans for an ambitious commercial/retail development along Armada Way which is specifically intended to give the city the central focus it currently so lacks. P & O holdings are also developing

plans to invest £200 millions in a new shopping centre in the Drake
Circus area of the city. In addition, the University of Plymouth is in
negotiations to construct a new cultural quarter in the city which
would include cafes, shops, and a revitalised library and museum.
Meanwhile, and perhaps most surprisingly of all, internationally
renowned architect and urban planner David Mackay was poised to
sign a major deal which could transform Plymouth's city centre and
waterfront. Mackay along with his Spanish practice, MBM Arquitectes,
played a key role in reinvigorating the city of Barcelona (see Chapter 4).
The Plymouth 2020 regeneration partnership, the South West Regional
Development Agency (RDA) and private funders, have raised over
£100,000 to secure Mackay who plans to oversee a variety of projects
designed to reinvigorate Plymouth and to exploit its locations
(www.thisisplymouth.co.uk/displayNode.jsp?nodeId=98912&command=
displayContent&sourceNode=98821&contentPK=3836732). But the questions remain: Can a city like Plymouth that has in the past barely
benefited at all from inward investment really meet the challenge? Can it
overcome the hurdles associated with petty bureaucracy and political
infighting? Can it give the consumers of Plymouth the city they
deserve? On paper the consuming city offers a promised land. But the
promised land comes at a price. Above and beyond the massive
financial investment involved here, the irony of the consuming city is
that it may divide the people of Plymouth more than it may actually
provide for them.

The above case study illustrates that consumption has a key role to
play in the way both the producers and the consumers of cities think
about the places in which they live. Plymouth would not be at the top
of anybody's list of cities over-endowed with opportunities to consume.
But this is precisely the point. Consumption has become so fundamental
to the way in which consumers and producers think about the present
and the future (although not necessarily the past) that they have come
to depend upon it as a means of propping up city life. If the city has a
problem, consumption provides or at least appears to provide a potential
solution to that problem as the remaining chapters will illustrate.

Structure of the book

Chapter 2 sets the scene by outlining some of the key historical developments that appear to have provided cities with a long-term legacy of
consumption. After discussing key debates concerned with when, if at

all, the "consumer revolution" came about, the chapter considers the emergence of mass consumption before looking at the impact of shopping on the city fabric and then, in more detail, the specific impact of the supermarket. This chapter raises the suggestion that the commercialisation of the city through shopping may actually rid the city of its sense of place.

Chapter 3 looks at the city as a site of cultural consumption. That is, it deals with the moulding of a city's external perception as a cultural destination, and the relation between cultural representation and a city's symbolic economy. The chapter begins, however, by examining different meanings of the term culture – as the arts, but equally (from anthropology) as a set of values articulated in the habits of daily life. It asks what impact cultural marketing might have on the ways of life of a city's inhabitants, and reconsiders the case of New York City – known since the 1970s for its arts district, SoHo as well as being a hub of international cultural institutions.

Chapter 4 follows the above by examining the consumption of place (the city) itself in tourism. There are overlaps between cultural marketing and tourism, but this chapter concentrates on the ways in which the fabric of a city (its built form), as well as its museums and other cultural outlets, becomes an object of consumption. The case of Barcelona is taken to epitomise many aspects of contemporary European city marketing, combining an increasingly up-market appeal to business and cultural tourism with the city's past reputation for winding alleys and population diversity.

Chapter 5 investigates some of the forms of urban architecture which have arisen in response to recent growth in consumption. This is contextualised by discussion of the arcades of Paris in the nineteenth century, as an early type of architecture designed specifically for consumption. The chapter moves to look in passing at the department store, and then the mall. Parallels are drawn with the theme park. The chapter extends its scope to include the Disney Company's new town of Celebration, Florida, as an example of a "new urbanism" combining aspects of the theme park with heritage design, while subsuming housing to consumerism.

Chapter 6 considers what appears to an increasingly appealing means by which politicians can reinvigourate (and indeed create) the city. On the one hand, gambling can be said to represent a form of consumption that can inject new life into places struggling to survive. On the other, that injection could be said to create a city of gambling conformity and a city without community. This chapter considers the way in which gambling creates "unreal space" which blur the boundaries between risk and reality. The chapter concludes with an in-depth discussion of the particular issues faced by the planet's foremost gambling city, Las Vegas, Nevada.

Chapter 7 seeks to challenge our perceptions of what it is that constitutes the consuming city. Arguing that consumption is having such a profound impact on the way in which we live, that it is reconfiguring what it means to be "urban" this chapter looks at the impact of new visions of the city, whether they be expressed through the cinematic representation or perhaps through our experience of travel. In effect, it is suggested that the city is being reinvented though consumption, perhaps most dramatically in the form of the cruise ship a fortress of consumption which appears to create a situation where cities are no longer bounded by the limitations of space.

Chapter 8 breaks from mainstream concerns in the field of urban consumption to look at aspects of the rise of green consumption, as in organic vegetable box schemes. Environmentally aware consumption is still a small part of the total market in all product categories, yet advertisers increasingly play on support for "green" causes (while membership of campaigning organisations has grown rapidly). In context of a new single-issue campaigning which for many of those involved replaces mainstream politics, the chapter asks to what extent consumers might have a choice about the environment – or might find participation in green consumption a step towards an alternative lifestyle. Looking at a micro-scale case, the chapter concludes by emphasising the importance of localised initiatives within a global scenario.

In the final chapter, we bring the above issues to a head arguing that the city has in effect become "consumed" by consumption. It is suggested that the blind faith producers appear to have in consumption is inherently socially divisive and that the consuming city, makes that sense of social division ever more immediate in people's lives. Arguing that the Chinese experience is particularly telling, we go on to ask whether there can be any such thing as a post-consumer society, suggesting that ultimately the future of the consuming city is dependant upon a political question as to how the apparently destructive nature of consumption can be curtailed.

There is no doubt that many cities worldwide have taken on the challenges that consumerism offers with some confidence and flair. We will consider some of them in this book. But however much local and national authorities embrace the brave new world of consumerism, that world will inevitably bring with it conflict, in some shape or form, precisely because the consumer and the producer can never be equal partners. The consuming city needs the sort of investment and political will that most cities can only ever dream about. The promised land of consumerism is appealing to urban developers because it manifestly produces results, but this book is not concerned with blandly reproducing statistics about the commercial benefits of consumer-cultural initiatives for the city. It is concerned with the fact that for every winner there is a loser and that despite the degree of agency that consumerism provides them in some shape or form consumers are almost inevitably victims of the consumer society. The danger is that, as we will show throughout *Consuming Cities*, the undoubted benefits consumption brings to the city are always likely to be compromised at some level or other. And inevitably, the consumer is always the one who pays the price for compromise. That indeed is the legacy of the "consuming city".

CHAPTER 2

Consuming the Past: Cities, Shopping and Supermarkets

The evolution of the city is closely bound up with that of the consumer society. However, there is considerable debate within the Social Sciences as to when the consumer revolution actually occurred: at some point, apparently, between the sixteenth century and the present day. There is no definitive answer as to when the society in which we live and hundreds of other societies worldwide became "consumer" societies, but what is for certain is that the city, in whatever guise or form, has always and will always play an instrumental role in the process. By illustrating some of the key dimensions of the historical development of the consumer society and its relationship to the evolution of the city in this chapter, we may be one step nearer assessing the historical legacy of consumption upon contemporary city life.

It is very easy to forget in grounding an understanding of the consuming city in the post-modern arena that there are significant historical connections between cities and consumption that lie at the very heart of modernity as Miles and Paddison (1998) point out. Much of the debate over the role of the city in modernity is bound up with a more productivist focus which saw the city as the prime centre of economic accumulation. There is of course no doubt that the city has indeed had a critical role to play as a focus for production. However, an over-emphasis on the impact of production on the city may well create a set of circumstances in which consumption is perceived to be nothing more than an economic by-product which apparently has no genuine impact on the nature of the city in its own right. An alternative viewpoint and the one we present here is that consumption is far more than an economic process but is equally and perhaps quintessentially cultural in nature and as such represents a primary factor in the historical construction of city life.

Locating the consumer revolution

In order to begin to address the above issues it would be useful to consider at this stage the period during which the consumer society came about. Is it indeed possible to pin down a particular period in history? Or to put it in another way, is consumer society simply the product of late capitalism, or does the relationship between consumption and the city suggests an alternative explanation? McKendrick *et al.* (1982) identify a consumer revolution in England as early as the eighteenth century where for the first time it was possible to identify a society within which material possessions became prized less and less for their durability and more and more for their fashionability. Clearly as McKendrick *et al.* point out, the consumer revolution accompanied the industrial revolution in that changes in production were inevitably accompanied by changes in people's tastes, preferences and desires. Yet Braudel (1974) goes one step further than this in arguing that exchange relations had developed in a sophisticated manner even before industrialisation, notably in the guise of the seventeenth century French market, fairs and carnivals being focal points of consumption. Meanwhile, Porter (1990) notes that in the eighteenth century small scale enterprises produced consumer goods such as pottery, jewellery, clothing, buttons and pins. The consumers of such products lived in major cities such as Birmingham, Bristol, Leeds, Liverpool and Manchester as well as London: the point being that all these cities were opened up to the cultural influence of London by the development of canals and roads. In other words, regardless of what may or may not constitute a consumer revolution, cities have long been the product of and the catalyst for a consumer ethic.

So how do we go about charting the emergence of a consumer society? McCracken (1990) provides a useful starting point insofar as he identifies three key moments, or episodes, in the history of consumption: in the sixteenth, eighteenth and nineteenth centuries. The sixteenth century saw the transformation of consumption practices on the part of the noblemen of Elizabethan England. In particular, this was a period in history in which the Queen, Elizabeth I exploited the "expressive hegemonic power of things that has been used by English rulers ever since" (McCracken, 1990: 11). In so doing she obliged her noblemen to fit the bill themselves by bidding effectively, through consumption, for the Queen's favour. Consumption became a competitive arena in which noblemen had to partake or they would effectively perish. Secondly, in the course of the eighteenth century the world of goods expended dramatically while social competition provided a motive force. The consumer revolution according to both McCracken and McKendrick *et al.* was driven by the viciously hierarchical nature of eighteenth-century England (and for McKendrick at least, by the demand for fashion). Meanwhile markets exploded, as did consumer choice in general, and the opportunity to consume was more than ever, on the surface at least, an individualistic opportunity. For many people consumption was no longer a minor aspect of domestic life, but a major activity in its own right. At this time, the field of marketing, as illustrated by McKendrick *et al.*'s discussion of Josiah Wedgewood for example, also showed signs of emerging as did advertising more generally:

> This consumer was the object of more and more sophisticated attempts to awaken wants and to direct preferences. This consumer was beginning to live in an artificially stimulated climate that removed his/her tastes and preferences from the hold of convention and local tradition, and put them increasingly in the hands of the emerging forces of the marketplace. (p. 18)

Of more particular interest at this stage of history is the reconfiguration of space. McCracken argues that in this respect the eighteenth century accentuated earlier trends associated with new building forms and home furnishing, and of course, the need to accommodate new ideas of privacy. It is interesting to note that McCracken dismisses the suggestion that there was a consumer boom as such in the nineteenth century. As far as he is concerned the consumer revolution was by now a structural feature of social life. The nineteenth century was a century of change and consumption played a key role in that change.

In building upon the foundations laid by McCracken, Benson's (1994) chronicle of events in Britain between 1880 and 1980 is especially useful. Benson considers the material changes which served to increase consumers' capacity for consumption during this period. There may indeed be grounds for arguing that the emergence of a consumer society was gradual in nature and therefore does not actually constitute a revolution at all. Benson (1994) focuses on the increased demand produced by a rapidly expanding population between the early nineteenth and late twentieth centuries. These changes in demand were accompanied by changes in supply in an increasingly expanding marketplace which came to direct its goods to the attention of those consumers whose purchasing power was increasing most rapidly. In discussing the same debate as to the origins of the consumer revolution, Storey (1999) refers to the work of Bermingham (1995) in which it is argued that consumption is not simply a product of capitalism, but was an integral part of its long-term historical development. As Bermingham herself points out it is important to understand the history of consumer culture because only then can we hold out some hope as to the positive impact of such a culture in the future:

> if the history of consumption is to be not merely a celebration of the status quo but a progressive tool of social change, then its historical formations within the modern conditions of class, gender and racial inequalities must be exposed and understood. We need new theories of material culture that will promote social justice not by ignoring or wishing away the evidence of consumption, but by understanding its modern history and its political instrumentality. Such intellectual work holds out the promise of reconciliation between what have traditionally been seen as the antagonistic forces of industrialism and the needs of social groups. In short, it holds out the possibility that power may not be the exclusive prerogative of the producer, and that it can also be found dispersed among communities and embedded in their practices of everyday lives. (p. 18)

In considering the above developments, Grunenberg (2002) traces the beginning of modern consumer culture back to the mid-nineteenth century and the rise of "democratic" forms of consumption. The radical development of new material goods in France, for instance, was made possible, as indicated above, through technological advance, mass production, mass transportation, improved communication systems and increased disposable incomes. Williams (1982) argues that the scale of the consumer revolution at this time was best expressed in the guise of the Paris exposition of 1900. The exposition was remarkable, according to Williams for its emphasis on merchandising and for the way it self-consciously appealed to the fantasies of the consumer:

> The 1900 exposition incarnates this new and decisive conjunction between imaginative desires and material ones, between dreams and commerce, between events of collective consciousness and economic fact. It is obvious how economic goods satisfy physical needs such as those for food and shelter; less evident, but of overwhelming significance in understanding modern society, is how merchandise can fill the needs of the imagination. (p. 65)

This point is crucial: the impact of consumption upon the city is clearly as much about the imaginary as it is about the physical, and arguably the more history moves on the more so this is the case. Human beings have long explored the possibilities of imagination, but consumption served to provide an avenue through which that desire was physically manifested. The emergence of the consumer society, as Williams suggests, gave the mass of the population the opportunity, for the first time in history, to activate their dreams during the course of their everyday lives. The city of consumption invited consumers to act upon their desires and as far as Williams (1982: 66) is concerned the Exposition of 1900 had a symbolic and yet significant role to play in this process, "Welcome or not, the 'lesson of things' taught by the make-believe city of the 1900 exposition was that a dream world of the consumer was emerging in real cities outside its gates." Williams identifies three lifestyles that are created by the dream-world of consumption: mass, elitist and democratic (see also McCracken (1990) for a critical discussion). For Williams then, consumption is very much about the need for status, but is also an agent for social change. Mass consumption was itself a product of new marketing techniques. Elitist consumption represented an effort to contend with the excess of a bourgeois society that was preoccupied with goods rather than ideas or standards. Democratic consumption, meanwhile, was about a simplicity of lifestyle and a personal dignity that drew the mass consumer away from an unnatural preoccupation with goods. But as McCracken indicates, such categories belie Williams's tendency to belittle consumption, whilst paying little if any attention to the meanings which consumers ascribe to their consumer experiences. What was certain as Williams argues is that, consumption was no longer confined to the royal court. Consumer experimentation nation was becoming a more widespread phenomenon. But it was also a phenomenon that was far more than purely sociological or historical in nature. The experience of consumption apparently lies at the intersection of the sociological, geographical, historical and the psychological.

What we are suggesting here is that given the imaginary pleasure-seeking nature of consumption discussed so effectively in the work of Campbell (1987) which we noted in Chapter 1, it would be inappropriate to pin down the emergence of the consumer society to a particular point in history, in other words, the emergence of such a society was by necessity gradual in nature. Although, we might accept Campbell's contention that the conditions for the emergence of such hedonistic impulses were particularly rife in eighteenth- and nineteenth-century England, the wants of these consumers are, as Campbell notes, forever changing at both an individual and a societal level. The consumer society did not emerge overnight but as a gradual reflection of a succession of satisfied and unsatisfied needs.

Mass society and mass consumption

The most important concern at this stage are not therefore specific dates (which tell us less than half the story), but a more detailed understanding of the character and social impact of these changes. It is therefore particularly important to discuss the emergence of what many commentators and not least the members of the Frankfurt School might refer to as a "mass society"; the concentration of the population in urban centres exposing urban dwellers to an increasing plethora of consumer goods (see Horkheimer and Adorno, 1973). Authors such as Bramson (1961) point out that nineteenth-century European sociology was preoccupied with the emergence of a large-scale society that apparently implied increasing social disintegration. It is especially interesting to note that social commentators such as Simmel, Tönnies, Durkheim and Weber located this new society in concentrated urban centres. This was a "necessary historical development – an evolutionary movement from the simple to the complex, the homogeneous to the heterogeneous, the undifferentiated to the differentiated" (Bramson, 1961: 321). From the mid-nineteenth century onwards then, the public began to be perceived as a physical presence in their own right. As Taylor (1989) indicates cities as large population centres had existed before, but the sheer numbers of people had not previously poured in and out of the city on such a regular basis. What is for certain is that there was emerging a new mass urban middle class market of professionals and white-collar workers who provided a core market for movies, magazines, sports and other mass cultural industries. But this was not merely a European phenomenon as Young's (1999) discussion of the rise of the new middle class in 1920s Japan illustrates. Urban social economies were dramatically transformed in Japan in the aftermath of First World War. City populations were expanding, often due to rural migration which stimulated the provision of city services. It was the urban middle classes that benefited from these developments. From this point of view urbanisation completely transformed the economic and social landscape. It was this sort of a transformation that evoked a moral response, many commentators championing the values of the small town against the apparent sins of the big city (Bramson, 1961).

Regardless of the above debates there is no doubt that, in the long term, industrialisation was the key influence on the emergence of the consuming city. As production for subsistence came to be replaced by wage labour, people inevitably became consumers as well as producers. As such, from a long-term historical point of view, there emerged evidence of a radically different way of life in terms of social structures, social values and attitudes. Gradually then, a new type of society developed: a society built upon the thirst for novelty; novelty that the economic system became more than willing to perpetuate. But the perpetuation of novelty is equally bound up with broader dimensions of social change and in particular the growth of working class purchasing power. The post-Second-World War years saw the emergence of a mass market based at least to some extent on the principles of Fordism. Fordism refers to the ideas and principles spawned by the American industrialist Henry Ford who is generally accredited as the pioneer of the modern mass production system, notably in the guise of the car assembly line. Fordism was based on principles of size, uniformity and predictability and on the notion that to keep demand high wages need to be kept up, whilst government investment provided an essential means of ensuring full employment and prosperity. As far as the individual consumer is concerned what was crucial about Fordist practice was that he or she was provided with the surplus necessary for him or her to be able to purchase consumer goods. Indeed, Henry Ford proffered the notion that workers should be encouraged to be consumers of the very products they produced.

In this environment, whilst mass production ensured on the one hand that standardised, easily produced goods could be introduced to the market at minimum cost, on the other, the surpluses made available to the workers offset a periodic danger, one that capitalism had up to now always been forced to face: the effect of a slump or depression. A wide variety of large-scale industrial sectors including clothes, furniture and processed food were subsequently transformed (see Murray, 1989). Gradually, luxurious consumer goods became everyday items. The Fordist economy was dependent upon the fact that workers had a surplus or disposable income which they could invest in the increasing diversity of goods that were being made available to them. This was an essential development. Consumption came to play an increasingly important role in people's everyday lives. People were not only offered what they needed but also what they desired. Under these conditions wants simultaneously became needs. Consumer capitalism was able to exploit a situation where the *symbolic* value of consumer goods was being endowed with an increased social significance. It is in this sense that the ideological impact of consumerism was becoming increasingly subtle in nature.

Some commentators saw such developments as inherently liberating for the working classes in that the active nature of consumption meant that the "masses" became incorporated in a society from which they had been permanently excluded (see Bell, 1976). On the other hand it could equally be argued that consumers were robbing themselves of individuality in as much as they were willing to buy standardized undifferentiated "mass" products (Murray, 1989). Either way, the impact of consumerism on modern societies amounted, at this stage, to a qualitatively new experience of society. In this context, Cross (1993) considers various sets of figures that reflect the emergence of a consumer society. He identifies an unprecedented degree of access to durable goods in the latter half of the twentieth century. Focusing in particular on the American example, Cross notes that disposable household income in the United States rose from $15,110 in 1940 to $26,313 in 1970 and $28,607 in 1979, whilst between 1935 and 1970 home ownership nearly tripled for white wage-earning families and doubled for black families. The impact of consumerism was equally impressive in Britain, although tempered slightly, in the first instance, by the need to recover from the Second World War. Generally speaking, however, consumerism appeared to be emerging as a way of life on an unprecedented global scale (Miles, 1998).

As far as sociology is concerned, consumption did not emerge as a serious subject of concern to sociologists until the second half of the twentieth century and most dramatically during the 1980s and 1990s. Despite the general tendency to see consumption as ahistorical, as Gabriel and Lang (1995) note, commentators have increasingly come to acknowledge that the social significance of consumption began to emerge far earlier than that. This may well be the case. Consumption was a key factor in the evolution of city, as the discussion throughout this chapter will go on to illustrate. However, our suggestion in this book is that it was not until towards the end of the twentieth century that consumption came into its own in this respect. In other words, consumption was always bubbling under the surface as it were, but it was not until more recently that consumption actually began to *define* city life. More to the point it was not until recently that cities woke up to the value of investing in or promoting themselves as centres of consumption. Cities did not become consuming cities until the potential of consumption as a means of production in its own right was realised.

Those works that have charted the long-term historical significance of consumption are convincing in as much as they illustrate the infiltration of consumer lifestyles into bourgeois realms (see McKendrick *et al.*, 1982; Williams, 1982). This much can be accepted. But the argument here is that it was not until much later that consumption became a way of life for the majority of the population and in particular, the working classes. Although the long-term implications of a consumer revolution were being felt gradually by an increasing percentage of the population of the western world, the experiential impact of such a revolution was in fact variable. It was not until the 1950s that the accessibility of consumer goods began to transcend social classes and that the status-inferring qualities discussed decades earlier by Veblen (1899) came to have a more general social relevance. More specifically, we agree with Whiteley (1993) who sees the introduction of the credit card in 1950 as a particularly symbolic event. Interestingly, in the United States, as Whiteley notes, short-term consumer credit rose from $8.4 billion in 1945 to almost $45 billion in 1958. Of equal interest is the fact that the production of cars in the United States rocketed from 2 million in 1945 to 40 million in 1950, 51 million in 1955 and 62 million in 1960.

With developments in the economy, post-war workers came to have access to resources that meant that they could consider purchasing new objects such as television sets and cars, as well as providing for their families' more basic needs (Bocock, 1993). Accompanied, indeed encouraged, by the rise of advertising, a whole new world of consumerism was on offer to the working majority, most especially to groups of young people who were able to exploit this new situation as long as the resources were available to them. What was emerging was not merely a consumer society, but a consumer *culture*. What had emerged by the 1980s was a consumer culture where, as Lunt and Livingstone (1992) note,

> involvement with material culture is such that mass consumption infiltrates everyday life not only at the levels of economic processes, social activities and household structures, but also at the level of meaningful psychological experience – affecting the construction of identities, the formation of relationships, the framing of events. (p. 24)

What we can identify during this period is a process whereby the consumer society (a society predicated on a market economy which had been in existence for centuries) was superseded by the consumerist society (an advanced state of consumer society in which private affluence on a mass scale emerged as the dominant force in the marketplace) (Whiteley, 1993).

Bocock (1993) therefore suggests that it was in the aftermath of the 1950s that consumption sectors became ever more specific and focused. As capitalism developed alongside improved technology and management practices, usually discussed in the context of post-Fordism and flexible specialisation (the emergence of a multi-skilled flexible workforce who work on small-batch production runs which are readily adaptable to the whims of the consumer), there was an argument for saying that fixed status groups and social classes were being undermined as consumer lifestyles became the name of the day (see Piore and Sabel, 1984; Featherstone, 1991). Post-Fordist consumption was apparently more volatile and diversified, as market segmentation emerged to serve the interests of the consumer (see Lash and Urry, 1994; Lury, 1996). In this new world, consumption no longer appeared to be determined by the producer. On the contrary the producer was increasingly subject to the demands and tastes of the consumer. What was emerging was a shift from homogeneity to heterogeneity, from principles of size, uniformity and predictability to those of scope, diversity and flexibility.

In this context, the work of Martyn Lee (1993) who talks about the re-birth of consumer culture is of particular interest. Lee's argument is that the consumer society arose out of an economic need to establish commodity consumption as the natural means to need satisfaction. In developing this argument Lee suggests that the urban landscape of the modern world grew out of the basic unit of the new domestic space. In other words, the spaces of everyday life represented a socio-geographic response to the new productive forces of the age. Lee quotes Harvey who in turn refers to the "Keynesian city" "shaped as a consumption artefact and its social, economic and political life organised around the theme of state-backed, debt-financed consumption" (Harvey, 1985: 205–206). The restructuring of space (notably with the emergence of surburbia) ensured that the consumption of particular products such as the car and oil became necessities and not mere luxuries. As Lee points out such changes were dependant upon the emergence of a whole new domestic aesthetic based around domestic labour-saving devices and what might be best described as the cult of the home (something that is especially evident today certainly in the UK with the prevalence of DIY home-makeover TV shows).

Suggesting that consumption represents the point at which eco-nomic practice and cultural practice combine, Lee charts the rise and fall of a mass consumption society in the post-war years, followed by the re-awakening of the consumer society in which we live today. In particular, he identifies the role played in this process by the emergence of a new diversified commodity form. Most markedly, it was during the 1980s that the aesthetics, design and styles of consumption became increasingly diverse, as the marketplace became ever more sophisticated as regards to what it knew and what it wanted to know about its consumers (Lee, 1993). Lee therefore suggests that if there have been any significant changes to the regime of accumulation and its mode of regulation then such changes are revealed not so much in the production side of the equation, but more in terms of the changing composition and design of the symbolic commodity form in the late twentieth century. It is in this sense that consumption came to play a fundamentally formative social role in modern societies. But it was not only consumer goods that were becoming increasingly designer-driven. The city itself was no longer merely the arena in which consumption took place, but a commodity in its own right. The commmodfication of the city can be further understood with a discussion of the role of shopping, and more specific-ally, the supermarket, in the long and short-term history of the city.

Shopping

The history of the impact of consumption upon city life is closely connected with the historical emergence of shopping, an issue that has fascinated commentators from a host of backgrounds. By briefly con-sidering the emergence of shopping from an socio-historical perspective (a discussion that will be developed further in Chapter 5 when we look more specifically at the architectural dimensions of shopping) we can begin to draw out some of the above themes. The recent exhibitions, "Brand.new at the V & A" and "Shopping: A Century of Art and Consumer Culture" at the Tate Liverpool provide a useful illustration of the broader cultural significance of shopping developments. As such, Betsky (2000) discusses the emergence of the open-air market as the "first order" of commercial architecture, "This is the space of appearance of those goods that mediate our relationship with the larger world; and their display is halfway between an abstract order (the rows of stalls) and the collage of individual forms with which, for example, we dress ourselves" (p. 114). For Betsky the marketplace constitutes a stage for the freedom of ideas and experience. But that freedom would gradually be eroded as such spaces become increasingly regularised, notably in eighteenth-century France and England. Indeed the development of consumer society can clearly be associated with an increasingly formal conception of urban space in which goods and services were provided in an increasingly efficient manner. As such, the market stall gradually became redundant in favour of the arcades which were in fact, according to Betsky, the first consciously constructed palaces of consumption (see Chapter 5). The arcade was in time succeeded by the department store under the guise of the Bon Marché which opened in 1852. Corrigan goes as far as to describe the advent of the department store as one of the most important moments in the history of consumer culture. The department store provided a fixed-price system, credit and the availability of a wide range of goods. But more generally, as Williams (1982) points out, it provided a new form of urban sociability based around mass consumption that was intensified by the introduction of large-scale city lighting which replaced the less reliable gas power around 1900.

As far as Chaney (1983) is concerned, urban development was a key factor in the emergence of shopping, and of consumer culture more generally. The increasing cost of rent was therefore an important influence on the development of the department store, simply because it was economical to provide such a range of retail opportunities under a single roof. Shopping was responding to the demands of market forces and in particular to the demands of a mass production system that required a more rational approach to selling. But as Corrigan (1997) goes on to note, it is also worth noting the influence of changes in transport and in the actual physical layout of cities. The advent of railways evidently made cities more accessible as did the redesign of cities which massively cut down on journeys within cities whilst encouraging shoppers to explore beyond their locality. What is certain is that the emergence of the department store, and of shopping more generally, had a real impact on the shape of the city. There is indeed clear evidence of a direct relationship between the location of public transportation and the big store, as expressed by posters that featured shops alongside Hampton Court and Greenwich (see Forty, 1986). In Japan, as well as suburban real estate being developed along the railway line, "terminal department stores" were built by railway companies at urban terminuses of commuter lines between the 1910s and 1930s. As such, Young (1999) points out that from the 1930s department stores without formal links to railway stations subsidised stops in order to secure access to their stores,

> The tie-up with urban rail and subway lines strengthened the import of department stores as central institutions in the urban culture-space. This was symbolized in the depiction of department store icons in

contemporary subway maps, massive structures that towered behind each subway stop and dominated the surrounding urban terrain. Such images conveyed the power of the department stores as commercial anchors of the new urban transportation networks and cultural magnets in the urban entertainment complex. (Young, 1999: 58)

But it is also worth remembering that these Japanese developments had a selective, discriminating impact upon the urban environment (Young, 1999). It was middle-class areas such as Tokyo's Yamanote District that benefited from such developments. Shopping was still primarily a middle class pastime and in this respect the city was still designed to serve the needs of the middle classes.

Add the above geographical changes to the dream-like state of possibility that the department store offered and consumer culture was clearly onto a winner. Although in theory such stores provided freedom of entry and the so-called "democratization of luxury", in reality the department store was not equally accessible by all sectors of society and many unwanted "consumers" were excluded. It was the middle classes who had the resources in this context to actively mark out a cultural identity for themselves (Corrigan, 1997). As such, Lawrence (1992) points out that "Even within the purportedly 'middle-class' realm of the down-town department store, very explicit distinctions of status and class were the norm" (p. 67). Similarly, in Japan, the early days of the department store maintained a system in which customers left their shoes at the shop entrance. It was not until 1923, as Young (1999) indicates, that this practice was removed, thereby addressing the embarrassment of less wealthy customers who were ashamed to check in their soiled and tattered shoes. Such measures apparently promoted an environment of consumerist democracy. This was, however, a democracy of urban entertainment perhaps best characterised by the existence of zoos, rooftop restaurants, exhibition galleries, performance halls and rooftop skating rinks that were more accessible to some consumers than to others. The above process contributed to the creation of a city of spectacle: a city of constant stimulation and of survival of the fittest:

Perception in the modern city thus had a distinctly cinematic quality, occurring in transience as the rushed individual took in the dynamic spectacle unfolding on the street. The shifting gaze of the mobile consumer could not escape the attractions of the commodity spectacle which parasitically took over every surface: shouting from shop fronts and windows, from posters and billboards, in newspapers and illustrated magazines, inscribed on buildings and even projected onto the sky at night . . . (p. 225)

Most importantly in this context, there was more to department stores than the mere buying and selling of goods. They became an urban entertainment and leisure service. They were also a source of cultural authority that played a key role in actively defining what it is that constituted the modern, namely: ceaseless novelty and never-ending progress. The 1920s department store was a pillar of urban popular culture – a "school for the modern" (Young, 1999: 60). Such developments inevitably had a profound impact upon the urban fabric:

> the department store removed leisure activities from the round of yearly festivals and the amusement complex that had grown up around shrines and temples. Moreover, in making leisure space its centrepiece, the department store silenced the transgressive overtones of an earlier notion of recreational space, one that had been produced by the Tokugawa policy of quarantining actors and prostitutes within walled and gated districts in the city. (Young, 1999: 63)

In reality, the market ensured that the department store was a largely middle class reserve because only they could genuinely afford to shop there. The working classes remained tied to the streets, the temple and the shrine.

Although department stores had a major impact upon the reform and renovation of cities, the days of the great department stores were not to last long and the opportunity to consume was gradually subsumed into the city as whole. Gradually the city became a melting pot of consumerist opportunity. Consumer experimentation was becoming a more widespread phenomenon and as such gradually reached the lives of more and more consumers. As such, Taylor (1989) discusses the emergence of the Woolworth "dime store" empire which is partly attributed to Frank W. Woolworth's intense observations of the side-walk behaviour of the population:

> Woolworth had observed the changes taking place in the city, the advent of skyscrapers and the crowds that swarmed through the streets. He therefore elected to build a large store in Lancaster that would clearly be visible some distance away. What occurred confirmed what he had shrewdly guessed . . . (p. 303)

Woolworth managed to transform the fashionability of the street, making the side on which the store was located the more fashionable and that the consumption took within city spaces:

> It was only when the middle class began leaving the city and making a place for itself on the fringes of the city that stores regained their function. They became focal points in the new, artificial landscape the middle classes were making for themselves. The suburb, that place between the city and nature where the middle class constructed its meandering, uncertain and technologically driven homeland, found its heart in the shopping mall. (Betsky, 2000: 121)

The nature of the relationship between the city and retail was not always positive and by the turn of the twentieth century Grunenberg argues there was something of a crisis of consumption: the feeling in other words that such developments may well have reached their saturation point. As a result of the sort of developments Lee describes above, the suburbs of the city became more and more important in terms of the evolution of the city. The suburbs were very much dependant on the development of transport links, as, of course, was the supermarket and later the shopping mall which was designed to service the car culture that emerged from the middle of the twentieth century. The first shopping mall, as Betsky points out, was designed by the Los Angeles-based architect Victor Gruen and opened in Southdale outside of Minneapolis. For Betsky the shopping mall constituted a new version of the city street, "an abstract vision of the city the middle class had left behind", a space entirely determined by the desire for a perfect shopping environment (see Chapter 5). Such spaces may have lacked character and visual allure, but at least they provided something of a focal point for the local community which needed all the focal points it could get in a world apparently increasingly characterised by uncertainty. On the other hand the certainties of the shopping malls served to undermine the urban, not only insofar as it helped to construct a uniform shopping environment virtually the world over, but also in terms of having a negative knock-on effect on the city centre.

It would not be too far fetched to suggest that shopping had a profound impact on city life and in many respects served to invigorate city life. Insofar as it injected a new form of urban vitality. Perhaps this was no more the case than in the UK in the 1960s and 1970s. However, with these developments having reached a zenith it could equally be argued that the vitality that retailing injected into urban environments was just as abruptly withdrawn. The city centre was arguably left to rot to the extent that the Conservative government of the 1980s was eventually forced to put on the breaks on out-of-town developments and only four shopping malls that were proposed in the 1980s were actually built. Those that were built were monotonously uniform and it is hard to present a convincing argument that shopping malls genuinely added to the urban/suburban genesis. But what they did do was create an unreal environment neither entirely public nor private in nature, another illustration of the way in which consumption challenges traditional conceptions of space and place. A short discussion of recent developments in supermarket retailing may help to bring these historical elements into sharper focus.

The supermarket

The emergence of the supermarket in its various guises and in particular the work of Rachel Bowlby tells us much about the changing relationship between the city and consumption. The first supermarkets, novel for the way in which they made shoppers serve themselves, were not planned as such, but were more a by-product of the American depression (Bowlby, 2000). The opening of the "Big Bear" in New Jersey 1932 provided the consumer with huge displays and an invitation that implied that there was no limitation on the desires of the customer. By the 1940s as Bowlby goes on to argue supermarkets had been established as the dominant form of food-selling in the United States. Many commentators, particularly in the 1950s and 1960s, have argued that this was and is a damaging development insofar as the ease of choice that supermarkets promote is in effect anti-creative and anti-cultural:

> Customers are seen as being deprived of the power of critical thought, or as never having had it in the first place; they live in the half-light of deceptive images, which they take for reality, never realizing they are being produced elsewhere; they do not imagine a world beyond the checkout. In the supermarket ... the doors seductively swing round to make the illusion of a self-contained environment and the population either drifts about in a daydream or else is chained unknowingly to a perpetual round of trolley-stacking or shelf-stacking whose logic is beyond them. (Bowlby, 2000: 189)

More recently, the supermarket has actively undermined the commercial profitability of the city centre. The out-of-town supermarket apparently indicates a consumerist nirvana where everything is available to the consumer, including the sense of community that it might be argued was drained from Britain's city centres during the 1980s. The emergence of the "superstore" (and indeed of the retail warehouse) is indicative of the power balance associated with the so-called consumer society and the fact that power is concentrated in the hands of powerful multiple retailers who tend to look more concerned with taking over their nearest rivals than with satisfying the needs of their customer base. In many respects, as Bowlby (2000) points out, the supermarket has come to resemble the department store in contents as well as forms. Supermarkets are no longer simply about "piling it high and selling it low"; they often sell a wide range of lifestyle and fashion goods. They even offer their cafes as a direct challenge to the notion that supermarkets are purely functional spaces. The consumer society is such that even the functional space of the supermarket can actually be fun:

> For supermarkets in Britain have risen in the 1990s to a position of unprecedented prominence in that blur between media representations and actual behaviour that makes up the fabric of our daily life...In their metamorphosis into out-of-town superstores, they have become the focus for a new environmental argument about the decline of urban centres and the growth of a car-dependant culture...The future of supermarkets in the twenty-first century is in one sense anybody's guess, anybody's choice. Yet it sometimes appears that the future itself is envisaged in the image of a great supermarket in which citizen-consumers move about making their more or less informed or random individual choices. Whether that image draws on a hope or a fear depends on the persuasions of the speaker. (p. 152)

There could be an argument that the supermarket is symbolic of the potentially increasingly negative impact of consumption upon the city. Not only do the out-of-town supermarkets take business and vibrancy out of the city, they also create an illusion of urban community that simply does not exist. The out-of-town supermarket actually individualises the consumer and it individualises the city experience. Like consumer society itself the supermarket apparently makes a joy out of what used to be a necessity. Amidst the endless desirous qualities of the supermarket, the individual consumer is convinced of his or her individuality, an individuality apparently purchasable from the deli, fresh fish and bakery counters that ironically recreate the service cultures of the past. Cook's (1994) work on the incorporation of exotic fruits into the supermarket culture is a further indication of the superficial freedoms available to the consumer through the supermarket. This illusion of freedom alongside a sense of belonging only succeeds in constructing a citizen of the consumer society and not as a citizen of the city. The supermarket is illusory. It provides rows of identical products indicating a boundless abundance of endless possibility and availability. Meanwhile, Wildt's (1995) contention that the commodification of food obliterates the physical (and potential exploitation) involved in the production process is probably as relevant today as it was in West Germany in the 1950s. But it is also important to remember that like any other space of consumption, the supermarket is open to a degree of interpretation. It is ultimately a contested space. It is just that the producer has a somewhat stronger control of that space than the simple freedom to consume can ever offer.

In many respects the contemporary supermarket like many of the places we will discuss throughout this book is placeless and faceless. Such places do not indicate place but are nothing more than a microcosm of contemporary consumer society, which offers choice, or at least the pretence of choice at the expense of place and space. The contemporary supermarket is a place to sell, and it sells an ideology as much as it sells products. You only have to consider the fact that superstores are more and more likely to be located near other retail opportunities on the outskirts of the city to realise that they represent an attempt to redefine the city as well as retail. In recent years, in Britain at least, there has been something of a resurgence of the supermarket in the city as the major players experiment with small convenience stores in city high streets. But as Bowlby points out, the advent of internet shopping can add to the perennial speculation throughout the history of the supermarket that the urban street will inevitably suffer.

Conclusion

So what does all this tell us about the nature of the consuming city? Taken as part of a broader analysis of the socio-historical development of shopping, perhaps the most prescient comment on this issue comes from the work of Deyan Sudjic (1993) head of Glasgow's campaign during the City of Architecture 1999, who blames planning controls for encouraging the growth of multiple retail chains which have arguably resulted in our city centres becoming no more than identi-kit shopping centres. This raises a key issue:

> The central question about shops is whether it is the form of shopping that dictates the nature of a city, or if it is the city's nature that dictates how shopping, it's primary communal activity, is carried out. Perhaps the truth is somewhere in between; that the different incarnations of shopping, from the market to the department store, the high street to edge-of-town, are the signals that confirm the direction the city has taken. Vast shopping sheds that serve people from more than one city demonstrate that urbanism has already become an amorphous landscape in which mobility allows anything to happen anywhere. Paradoxically, while the city itself has decentralised, shopping has become ever more concentrated. (p. 25)

Perhaps we can take this argument a step further. Perhaps today it is simply more difficult than it has ever been in the past to define what constitutes the city. And perhaps consumption is the key player in perpetuating this uncertainty. That supermarkets, for example, are not adding to the urban fabric at all, but are rather taking away from it whilst simultaneously undermining people's comprehension or image of the city (see Lynch, 1960). It is worth remembering in considering this point that we live in a world characterised by globalisation. The very meaning of globalisation centres on the fact that people and networks of communications are connecting in ever more unexpected ways. Urry (1998) describes this as the "hollowing out" of traditional societies. Global flows combine and cross to fundamentally alter our experience of time and space. Under these circumstances immediate local space becomes nothing more than transitory and cannot any longer determine who it is we are. Rather we pick and choose elements from the disjointed offerings that confront us from day to day. In this world, inhuman objects are becoming increasingly important to the construction of human identities. Technology, imagery, symbolism, machinery are especially important in this regard. It has recently been estimated that around 40 per cent of the British population own a mobile phone. This is a fantastical figure which illustrates very graphically the way in which place and space has been opened up (and arguably closed down) in a global age. Urry's argument is that in these circumstances any power that human beings do have is less and less likely to be human in nature. Histories might indeed be said to have stripped our cities of their humanity in favour of an ideology of consumption. The consumer society encouraged a situation in which cities are inevitably more and more alike, precisely because consumption has been identified as the resource upon which such an identity can and should be constructed. As such many cities market themselves in ways that have little in common with the reality of life in that particular city. We mentioned, Plymouth "City of Discovery" in Chapter 1. Other examples include Swansea, "Dylan Thomas Country", Doncaster, "England's Northern Jewel" and Durham, "Land of the Prince Bishops" (Brake and Harrop, 1994). Such labels have more to do with creating a superficial cultural legitimacy; they are about constructing an image of a place in the imagination rather than about effectively exploiting with the realities of everyday city life. In this sense, marketing and indeed consumption arguably rids contemporary society (if it still exists) of its sense of place. Similarly, David Clarke (1996) has argued that the contemporary city has been transported into the realms of simulation, an idea that will crop up throughout the remainder of the book. In effect, consumption has become so fundamental to city life that cities have actually lost a sense of place. Cities are no more than simulated centres of post-modern "reality". In presenting this argument Clarke refers to Lefebvre (1996) whose work is especially prescient in this regard: "The city historically constructed is no longer lived and no longer understood practically. It is only an object for cultural consumption for tourists" (p. 148).

In this context, the continued attractions of consumer culture encourage a state of affairs in which the individual is arguably more likely to associate him or herself with a global brand and a lifestyle than the characteristics historically associated with a particular nation, region or city. In short the new global culture "is at present a predominantly commercialized culture, devoid of origins or place" (Dunn, 1998: 135). But the paradox here as Dunn points out is that despite the globalisation of commercialisation, such aspects of social change continue to operate alongside cultural values, traditions and ways of life. Local cultures are inevitably being reconstituted in new ways and this has important implications for the nature of identity. Western cities in particular become increasingly diverse, both ethnically and socially, and identities reflect such cosmopolitism. This in itself can only be a positive thing. And yet, contemporary societies are characterised by a breakdown of authority. We live in a far more eclectic "society" than we did in the past and are therefore increasingly uncertain as to what we should and should not do. We are, in turn, increasingly uncertain what our cities should and should not do. Global consumerism is quite possibly the source of such instability. The irony of all this is that people from all backgrounds and class positions continue to use consumption not only to fulfil their basic needs but also to define their social position. Historically the consumer society has predicated itself on "a world of competition and struggle centre around the everyday act of spending" (Johnson, 1988: 41). This competition can take many forms within classes as well as between them. From this point of view consumption has historically constituted a real life barrier that actively served to prevent any sense of class cohesion. In this sense, although consumption may superficially bring people of similar tastes together it is in actual fact inherently socially divisive. The city is the site in which such struggles take place. The question is, does the consuming city help to calm this struggle or does it simply throw flames on the consumerist fire?

CHAPTER 3

Consuming Cultures: The Symbolic Economies of Cities

In this chapter we investigate the role of cultural consumption in the symbolic economies of cities. We consider how perceptions of a city, rather than wealth production in its manufacturing industries, can be central to its marketing strategies and the attraction of inward investment. In that context, where image tends to dominate, cultural consumption has a particular role as the most visible aspect of a largely invisible and service-based economy. Culture also has the advantage of seeming to be politically neutral, as if outside the socially divisive mechanisms of power and money. This follows from the autonomy claimed for art in modern times, but would be contested by cultural critics today who might point out that the art market is no less an exchange mechanism than the stock market or the fish market. Nonetheless, to promote a city as a cultural hub seems, from the evidence of cities such as Paris, Barcelona, Bilbao, Berlin, New York, and Sydney, among many others, to be an effective way of promoting economic growth. In the UK, cities such as Glasgow, London, Liverpool, Newcastle, and Manchester have employed culturally led urban development strategies, while new cultural institutions such as the Baltic in Gateshead and Tate Modern in London are flagships of a cultural turn in urban development. The models for these developments tend to be drawn from regeneration projects in North America – the importance of cultural institutions in New York, for instance. Increasingly, public-sector investment is seen as a means to attract greater private-sector development in the area surrounding the new cultural institution. Even in cities which lack a new museum or concert hall, designation of a cultural quarter may be seen as a means to economic regeneration. There are several difficulties: first, research (Myerscough, 1988) suggests that models cannot be simply mapped from one city to another, and that existing infra-structures and perceptions of a city are important factors in the viability of culturally led redevelopment schemes. Secondly, the extent to which local publics and their cultures are involved or not in such development varies, which raises a question as to whose culture is marketed in whose interests. And thirdly, it may be impossible to predict outcomes when small shifts in taste or fashion, or in global events, can lead to major changes in patterns of consumption, particularly in cultural tourism.

The case of recent developments in Manchester (O'Connor and Wynne, 1996) demonstrates that cultural consumption has a decisive impact on the urban landscape, and offers opportunities as well as encroachments. But before looking at this specific case, we consider what constitutes a symbolic economy, and, as a way to open questions such as that stated above, what is meant by the term "culture" (or cultures). We begin by contrasting one sense of culture as the arts with another as a way of life. We link the idea of a symbolic economy to Veblen's concept of symbolic exchange in *The Theory of the Leisure Class* [1899] (1970), and see how the idea of a symbolic economy is developed with reference to New York by Sharon Zukin ([1982] 1989, 1995, 1996a,b). Then we reflect on the role of the cultural industries and cultural consumption as driving forces of urban redevelopment in an area of post-industrial Manchester in the late 1990s.

Culture and cultures

Colloquially, we might speak of a cultured person, or the cultured class of a society, to mean an individual or group able to appreciate the arts, and perhaps also certain kinds of food or drink – fine wines along with the fine arts – and fashion. These forms, known as high culture, are differentiated from the mass culture of popular music, Hollywood films, television, and computer games, the enthusiasts of which tend not to be called cultured. High-culture is also differentiated from material culture, defined as useful (as opposed to beautiful) objects produced by craft or industry, or in everyday life (such as the self-build garden shed). Such differentiations denote a social division ingrained in verbal language, a situation which cultural studies has addressed since the 1960s by looking to intermediate cultural forms such as film and jazz, as well as by studying the implicit ideologies of mass culture. But while one meaning of culture is linked to elitist forms, we might in a quite different (anthropological) way refer to the culture of a society or social group as based on a specific and shared set of values. Mary Douglas, for instance, refers in *Purity and*

Danger to "...anthropologists who have ventured further into these primitive cultures..." (Douglas, [1966] 1970: 11) to mean those whose field-work concerned the religious practices of non-European societies. Bronislaw Malinowski writes of anthropology as a science of culture, and defines culture as "...the widest context of human behaviour...as important to the psychologist as to the social student, to the historian as to the linguist" (Malinowski, 1944: 5). One of the first uses of the term culture in this anthropological sense occurs in the work of Edward Burnett Tylor in the late nineteenth century. From his work on non-European cultures, Tylor sought to establish anthropology as a subject at Oxford University (see Coombes, 1994: 125–126). In doing so, those cultures investigated by anthropologists were not only described and codified, but also given value as academic material.

Anthropology has exerted a generally progressive influence on discussions of cultures, drawing attention to the fact that every social group has one. Although nineteenth-century ethnographic collections (such as the Pitt-Rivers Collection in Oxford) claimed white superiority by equating contemporary African tools to those of early European society, as Coombes demonstrates (1994), social anthropologists and ethnographers attributed to the forms of organisation of the societies they studied an intricacy requiring close examination. As an academic discipline, anthropology and ethnography drew the attention of a European and North American audience to the value structures exhibited in the forms of non-European societies. One reason this matters is that a realisation that cultures exhibit difference refutes a notion of a single trajectory of human development – a universal culture – through which to measure the status of a specific culture. The methods applied by anthropologists to the study of non-Western societies can be used, too, to study the complexities and senses of difference of the Western societies from which the anthropologists mainly come, as demonstrated by John Eade's research on the Bangladeshi community of East London (Eade, 1989). Such intra-social anthropology tends to enhance recognition of diversity, so that we refer to the cultures of a city rather than a city's culture.

Parallel to the development of anthropology in the late nineteenth and early twentieth centuries was the rise in Europe of another idea of culture: as distinctive national cultures. This concept differs from that of cultures in an anthropological sense in that national cultures represent a dominant class in society, reinforcing national unity when it is unclear, as when a nation-state has a short or troubled history. Culture in this sense also differs from taste, in that the arts, if conscripted to the

national culture, are used for qualities taken to denote national characteristics rather than seen as the products of a self-contained (or disinterested) aesthetic. An example of national culture is the invention of
Morris dancing, or Scottish tartan, in the late Victorian period, when a
unified national culture, combined with imperial adventure, acted to
draw attention away from home disquiets such as wide divisions
between rich and poor. Similarly, in the economically depressed years
of the 1930s, a vogue for half-timbered semi-detached houses recalled
the Merry England of the Elizabethan period. Despite its ersatz quality,
the idea of national culture has remained durable and has tended to
transmute culture into today's heritage; thus the Elgin Marbles (the
frieze from the Parthenon in Athens which was removed to England by
agency of Lord Elgin) are a vicarious part of British culture because they
are housed in the British Museum, one of the repositories of national
culture. Perhaps more importantly, the British Museum itself stands for
a national or imperial aspiration to be known as a cultured and civilised
state, the citizens of which are suitably educated in the appreciation of
classical values. Meanwhile, the Greek government, seeing the Parthenon
frieze as part of Greek culture, has asked for the sculptures back. There is
no ambiguity as to the moral ownership of plunder from an imperial
past (which may not be the case for legal ownership). Yet the issue
remains hotly contested because values other than those intrinsic to
the objects concerned are at risk.

We find, then, three ways in which to think about culture: the arts, a
way of life, a means to national identity. These categories are not self-
contained. Somewhere between a national culture and culture in the
anthropological sense is what we might mean today by the term "American
culture", associated with globalisation and the global dominance of
certain kinds of entertainment, such as the movies or Disney cartoons
and theme parks, and certain kinds of consumption such as fast food
and dependence on gas-guzzling automobiles. American culture might
also, though, consist at a more everyday level of certain uses of language
or modes of dress, and at an imaginative level of romanticised images of
the open road, the wild west, the picket-fence, or the log cabin, all
reproduced in advertising, film, and architecture. It is also, as Davis
(2000) shows, fractured. The local cultures of minority groups in Los
Angeles, for example, present a distinctive visual style in street art, and
for those who produce them these images painted on walls are empowering – a means to visibility. Further, in contrast to national cultures,
social groups whose collective dress codes, body decoration, music, and
so forth reject the conventions of the dominant society are said to form

sub-cultures (Hebdige, 1979). These are often trans-national, like punk. The above uses of the term "culture" have occurred in English since the nineteenth century. Earlier uses of the term, derived from its Latin root in the verb *colere*, refer to cultivation. These survive in words such as agriculture and horticulture, and culture in the aesthetic sense follows a metaphorical idea of the cultivation of minds.

The main dichotomy, today, is between culture as cultural objects and their appreciation, and as a set of values and their expression in the processes of daily living. There is nothing fixed or natural about this, and both definitions are products of historical circumstances. The appreciation of culture by middle-class publics, for instance, is possible only when public museums and art galleries are established, for the most part in large cities, from the mid-nineteenth century onwards. A society's view of the natural world is also shaped by cultural currents (Smith, 1996a), so that the idea of a landscape is a construct to which perception of the natural world (as the countryside) conforms. So, culture is not nature, and while an argument could be made that any individual has an innate capacity to be moved by musical sounds, critical discussion of music is restricted to those who have benefited from the specific educational and leisure opportunities which provide the vocabulary to engage in such discussion (see Bourdieu, 1979).

A characteristic of liberal society is a broadening of access to high culture, to which adult education classes in the nineteenth century and broadcasting in the twentieth (Willett, 1967: 142) have contributed. Yet access is not the only issue, and an achievement of cultural studies, in the work of Stuart Hall, Richard Hoggart, and Raymond Williams, was to question hitherto dominant cultural categories, demonstrating that a comic strip, folk song, or performance of street theatre is as valid an object of critical enquiry as a painting by Raphael, a Beethoven symphony, or a poem by T. S. Eliot. This does not mean that a comic strip necessarily has the same aesthetic value as a Raphael, but that the concept of aesthetic value itself is socially produced and therefore contestable. By the 1980s, as Conrad Lodziak (2002) argues, cultural studies tended to extend its work of reading things and representations of life to a point where almost anything became text – something to be interpreted rather than questioned according to more basic concerns of power or change; at the same time, cultural studies has not given up its project of exposing the ideological (and hegemonic) content of media representation, and has contributed much to an expansion of the categories of social change – from class alone to race, gender, and sexual orientation as well.

The outline of culture's meanings above draws on Raymond Williams, for whom, in *Culture and Society, 1780–1950* (Williams, 1958), culture is one of five key terms, the others being class, art, industry, and democracy. It is a key term, too, in *Keywords* (1976), which began as an appendix to the earlier book. In *Culture and Society*, Williams emphasises that cultural production embodies social change, seeing the modern separation of art from social issues as reflecting a new relation between writers and their middle-class readers in the nineteenth century, as antidote to the industrial revolution and its divisive social consequences. Williams argues, however, that there is more than one kind of cultural product, stating near the end of *Culture and Society* that

> The working class, because of its position, has not . . . produced a culture in the narrower sense. The culture which it has produced . . . is the collective democratic institution, whether in the trade unions, the co-operative movement, or a political party. (Williams, 1958: 315, cited in O'Connor, 1989: 65)

This makes the connection between art and society pro-active rather than re-active, enabling convergence between the narrow and broad senses of the term when social processes such as trades union activity are seen as elements of the culture (anthropologically) of a social group but also processes of cultural production with characteristic forms such as the banner. Williams' argument is compatible with Emile Durkheim's studies of social institutions such as law and religion. It is compatible, too, with Mark Gottdiener's position, drawing on Durkheim: "the kinds of moral values or sentiments that people held in common and which, in turn, reflected the social bond" (Gottdiener, 2000: 5). But how is the social bond affected (or effected) by a symbolic economy?

Symbolic economies

For Williams' generation in the 1950s and 1960s, cultural consumption rested on a few clear categories of the fine arts and literature, to which they added those of more recent technologies such as film and recorded music, and of more multiple valency such as jazz. Now, amid globalised consumption, the pattern is more complex. So are the ways in which things are consumed or co-opted as cultural objects. The cognoscenti of *film noir* may, for instance, consume Hollywood movies as well, if ironically. In a different but no less aestheticising way the same people may consume city streets which seem like settings for *noir* scenes. Such multi-valency of the image informs advertising as well, some of its images perhaps now more sophisticated than some kinds of art, while some commodities are marketed less for their utility than as bearers of a logo. This applies to both high- and street-level society. Nike, for instance, has in the past paid urban stalkers to gauge imminent trends, recycling street looks as expensive fashion but also selling, in effect, the look not the product which bears it (Goldman and Papson, 1998: 79–81). Angela McRobbie says " ... cultural practices are seen primarily and immediately in terms of commercial opportunities" (McRobbie, 2002: 98); and, in *Cultures of Cities*, Sharon Zukin states that when street styles are recycled as de-contextualised cultural icons, "The cacophony of demands for justice is translated into a coherent demand for jeans" (Zukin, 1995: 9). This ability of the market to co-opt rebellion in areas such as clothing and rock music leads some critics to see contemporary capitalism as able to incorporate almost any oppositional tendency, making itself immune to attack (Seiler, 2000: 221).

As well as crossing the boundaries of cultural category and social class, contemporary cultural consumption uses the spaces as well as objects of culture; and adapts hitherto everyday, perhaps rustic or exotic, objects as signifiers of contemporary urban taste. For example, Jonathan Raban observes on a walk through London in *Soft City*, a shop selling white-painted Moroccan birdcages; the buyers will never keep birds in them, and are probably not Moroccan. Indeed, they are likely to be members of specific social group. As Douglas and Isherwood state: "goods are endowed with value by the meaning of fellow consumers" (Douglas and Isherwood, 1979: 75, cited in Lury, 1996: 14). The cages are de-contextualised in white and re-presented as aesthetic objects for cultural consumption (Raban, 1974: 95). This fashion for expensive junk can be explained in the context of the uncertainty of value produced by factors such as changing patterns of urban dwelling and the demise of predictable career paths, together with the widespread availability of cultural experience in the mass media. Lifestyles tend to become culturally coded devices in the formation of identities, and as such are aspirational – a means to be seen as cosmopolitan, particularly for suburban dwellers perhaps but equally for urban bohemians. So, just as, traditionally, high culture was appreciated by the gentry, cultural consumption now contributes to a process of group identification among young professionals.

The concept of a symbolic economy is related to this culturally coded form of consumption, though not identical to it. While the purchase of cultural goods denotes a self-image on the part of the purchaser, so too does the construction of a city's image as a hub of fashion, film, art, or music. Or, equally, perhaps the image of a vibrant place with an array of designer bars, restaurants, and nightlife is a way to position that city in global markets for financial services, advertising, media, public relations, and tourism – all industries in which the product is either invisible (in the sense of the abstraction of money in an electronic accounting system), or highly visible but non-substantial. New York, in this way, is the Big Apple, or a postcard which says "I Love (in the sign of a heart) New York." The city is removed from its material conditions, an image designed to foster consumption of the city itself. An extreme case of this is Las Vegas, discussed in Chapter 6. The inner city districts of New York may be, in a jaundiced academic account, a new frontier in which squatters are the new pioneers (Smith, 1996b; see also Miles, M., 2003; Miles, S., 2003), but the city as reduced to its sign as the place to be. After the attack on the World Trade Centre in September 2001, the city's mayor urged its inhabitants to go out shopping, eating, and being entertained as a way to return the city to normality. But what is normal about buying things we do not need and which most of the world, and the poor at home who sleep in shop doorways, will never afford? If we ask this, we are moved to look at how else a city or society might be organised, rather than burying our heads in the sands of consumption. The problem is that the image of cities the world over are constructed to be all-consuming.

So, while the concept of political economy goes beyond explaining economic processes to see a possibility of changing them by political intervention, a symbolic economy reverts to a normalisation of the world through certain forms of promotion and consumption. The tendency to universality in a symbolic economy – culture seen as having universal value – is not unlike the false unity implicit in a national culture, and while a city such as New York houses difference, its marketing image tends to be as reductive as the skyline of a postcard view from a distant vantage point. Yet, as John Eade and his co-authors show (1997), patterns of settlement and lattices of communication are, in metropolitan cities today, fluid and global. And as Richard Sennett recounts in *The Corrosion of Character* (1998), the notion of a job for life in a single, patriarchally caring company is now remote, the new insecurity affecting both executives and manual workers. These developments follow the widening of access to high culture noted above (see Taylor, 1994; Duncan, 1995). But social status, though it might in part be gained by the decoration of a domestic interior, now also requires performance, and that needs spaces. In this context the spaces of new cultural institutions such as Tate Modern, the Guggenheim in Bilbao, and Barcelona's Museum of

Contemporary Art have a prime role as facilitators of cultural display and signs of a new urban affluence. Such spaces are central to a symbolic economy as the façades (literally and metaphorically) of a new affluence explicit in leisure and an acquired appreciation of cultural forms. Then the consumption of cultural objects transmutes into that of a cultural ambience provided by the new, aestheticised urban landscape. The gallery becomes a place to meet, its café and shop as important as the spaces in which the collection is hung. Esther Leslie writes of Tate Modern:

> Tate is a brand that niche-markets art experience. Its galleries are showrooms. However, this is still art and not just business. The commodity must not show too glossy a face. The reclamation of an industrial space that provides the shell for the Tate Modern lends the building a fashionably squatted aspect... At Tate Modern a former industrial site becomes home to the new-style 'accessibility-rules' culture industry. (Leslie, 2001: 3)

But – which is part of Leslie's point – to whom is it accessible? Flagship cultural institutions, frequently financed as public-sector investments to attract private-sector renovation of the surrounding area, tend to be engines not of a democratisation of culture but of gentrification. After the institution is inserted, the designer bars and boutiques follow. Newly renovated apartments in warehouses or renovated (privatised) social housing are one side of the coin; while rises in rents and land values are the other. This is not all bad, in that run-down areas can be transformed, but it may displace a residual population unless it is adequately protected, and establishes a connection, not between art and society as intrigued Williams (1958), but between cultural space and wealth accumulation. Tate Modern has, in fact, offered training and employment for local people (Cochrane, 2000), but it remains that such cultural institutions attract as visitors members of what might be thought of as a new, international, high-income bohemia (Wilson, 2003: 210–219). This bohemia does not, of course, include the majority of cultural producers, such as artists, whose work provides the raw material for a symbolic economy but who remain (with some notable and extreme exceptions) poor.

Pierre Bourdieu (1984) devised the concept of cultural capital (differentiated from money capital) for the knowledge possessed by those who have creative or interpretive skills, for whom cultural capital counters a lack of wealth and implies sympathy for other economically unempowered groups. A case of this is the alliance of students, philosophers and workers

in May 1968 in Paris. In *The Field of Cultural Production* (1993), Bourdieu
writes:

> The cultural producers, who occupy the economically dominated
> and symbolically dominant position within the field of cultural produc-
> tion, tend to feel solidarity with the occupants of the economically
> and culturally dominated positions within the field of class relations.
> (Bourdieu, 1993: 44)

He continues that a rapprochement between culture and radicalism is
not without misunderstandings, but that those who produce cultural
meaning are in a position to use it " ... to put forward a critical definition
of the social world" (ibid.). This may seem romantic when so much in
the arts is overtly commodified. His view might appear to be derived
from a nineteenth-century concept of a cultural avant-garde, yet the
construction of categories of perception in the arts is a powerful tool
which might initiate new historical insights. A difficulty is that it does
so from a distance. Justin O'Connor glosses Bourdieu: " ... cultural capital,
while related to economic capital, must stress its distinction from it.
Too obvious a connection undermines the claim of culture to be
disinterested ... " (O'Connor, 1998: 231). O'Connor sees Bourdieu's
position as tied to a modern idea of art's autonomy as implied by the
Kantian idea of disinterested judgement.

Cultural capital is, then, the mutable, multi-valent currency of
a symbolic economy: a signification not by capital but by the altogether
more mutable and aestheticising catalyst of image. Symbolic economies
are to postmodern urban analysis what political economy was to modern,
industrial urban theory, putting signs in place of goods, but draining
that analysis of a critical, socially engaged edge. Cultural industries such
as popular music or graphic design may create employment, and the
restaurants, bars, boutiques, hairdressers, florists, and speciality outlets
which tend to cluster in cultural quarters alongside architect's offices,
television studios, and estate agencies may revive some kinds of urban
economy and street life (though the money usually goes elsewhere), but
the non-manufacturing economy which trades on reputation is also
highly volatile. The stability and accessibility of its economic benefits
are questioned in studies of Birmingham (Loftman and Nevin, 1998),
a city which re-invented its central business district as a cultural district,
and claims (in postcards sold at the railway station) to be a city of
culture, despite not having been awarded the title of European Capital
of Culture.

What is clear from culturally based economies is that the relation between economy and culture is not one of base and superstructure as in a Marxist model, but mutual and dynamic, so that what shapes a city is itself shaped by the arena in which it acts. But a symbolic economy is more specific than this, and Zukin's work on New York shows most evidently how it operates. In particular, Zukin notes the use of cultural reputation by the city's entrepreneurs who populate the Boards of museums, and the impact of cultural (and museum) development schemes on property values, so that the museum board is a useful place to be in terms of networking and making money (Zukin, 1995: 109–133). In part this cultural work lends commerce an aura of universal taste, for which reason developers commission blue-chip art for prestigious commercial sites (Selwood, 1992: 21); and in part it trickles down to a layer of young professionals buying limited edition prints or works by emerging artists. Several groups from artists and students to collectors are seen at gallery openings, and this suspension of class difference offers a vicarious thrill to the new bohemians who amass cultural capital like industrialists made money (see Wilson, 2001: 64–71).

Similarly, a city which invests in a new cultural centre or a major piece of public sculpture by an internationally known (usually north American) artist is putting its flag on an international culture-map to gain a global competitive edge – showing it knows what culture is (cultural capital) and that it is prepared to invest in setting the scene for a cultural life-style. In some cases this may be allied to the designation of a post-industrial zone as a cultural quarter, or an enclave of the new knowledge economy of information and communications technologies. Barcelona has both of these, as discussed in Chapter 4; its image is that of a cultural city of museums, galleries, auditoria, and stylish contemporary as well as nineteenth-century (*modernista*) architecture, which gained prominence from hosting the 1992 Olympic Games but which used the opportunity for investment in its cultural infra-structure. Glasgow's economic upturn as European City of Culture in 1990 is similarly related to the expansion of its cultural institutions and convention facilities, replacing previous images of the city identified with deprivation with one honed by a renewed civic confidence and a critical mass of cultural attractions able to attract international tourism.

The concept of a symbolic economy trades on such culturally led development, but can be understood, too, through an extension of Thorsten Veblen's concept of symbolic exchange. In *The Theory of the Leisure Class* [1899] (1970), Veblen studied emerging patterns of consumption in North America in the late nineteenth century, using but going beyond a Marxist framework to evolve an idea of conspicuous consumption as the purchase of goods of low use-value but high symbolic value, which establish an individual's social status by means other than class. This is allied to a concept of conspicuous leisure on the part of the owners of capital. Mark Gottdiener sees Veblen as having more than anyone "...created the field of consumer cultural studies" by showing that "The laboring and the upper classes are based definitionally on economic distinctions; but their *social differentiation* rests on the visible evidence of consumption practices" (Gottdiener, 2000: 6–8). The spur to this is, Veblen argues, a desire to emulate those in higher social positions. Members of an aspiring bourgeois class thus cease to accumulate money and spend it on things they do not need but which they want because to purchase them shows a cultural awareness which, more than wealth, validates social privilege. The model makes particular sense in egalitarian societies (such as, for some groups, the United States in the nineteenth century) where symbolic forms of differentiation between groups replace those of inherited class. Or, as Gottdiener writes: "For Veblen then, the social positioning that produced the status hierarchy of the United States was the visible evidence of distance from the workaday world" (ibid.). That is conspicuous leisure, but conspicuous consumption shows the same distancing from utility and allows it to be inflected by taste. Examples include consumption in museum cafés and shops, designer bars, or fashionable boutiques and restaurants. The benefits of conspicuous consumption and leisure are, however, not evenly distributed, and as Sharon Zukin's research on loft living (1989), on the co-option of counter culture (1991), and on symbolic economies (1995, 1996a,b) shows, an aestheticisation of space allied to gentrification is socially divisive and has socially excluding consequences (see also Deutsche, 1988; Boyer, 2001).

City managers and marketers, meanwhile, seem increasingly drawn towards development strategies in which cultural goods and experiences are prominent. Zukin writes: "Every well-designed downtown has a mixed-use shopping center and a nearby artists' quarter" just as every disused factory or waterfront site "...has been converted into one of those sites of visual delectation – a themed shopping space for seasonal produce, cooking equipment, restaurants, art galleries, and an aquarium" (Zukin, 1995: 22). The ersatz environment thus produced exemplifies a postmodern world of surfaces. It is not only world cities such as New York and Paris which use such forms of representation, but also smaller settlements such as Disney Corporation's excursion into real estate, Celebration, Florida (see Chapter 5) the motif of which is the white picket fence signifying safety in traditional (white, middle-class) values. Citing Disney's mainstream business in theme parks, Zukin writes "The asymmetries of power so evident in real landscapes are hidden behind a facade that reproduces a unidimensional nature and history" (Zukin, 1995: 59). Looking to cultural institutions, she argues that their rapid expansion since the 1980s has produced demands for space which render them "...no longer... adjuncts to property development projects... [but] development projects in their own right" (Zukin, 1995: 120). An example is the Museum of Modern Art's (MoMA) 1976 design for a 49-floor apartment tower (Zukin, 1995: 130). Prototype of the white-walled art space signifying a separation of art from the world outside, MoMA is the standard-bearer of the new symbolic economy. Emulating the ambience of a private collection too, its management always "...resembled more a business enterprise than an educational institution" (Grunenberg, 1994: 197).

Two cases illustrate the spatiality of the symbolic economy. Battery Park City (before September 11) is a mix of financial service spaces and high-income apartments on reclaimed land on the Hudson river, its squares embellished with public art and its interior spaces with bars and cafés, boutiques, hairdressers and florists. During development, contemporary art was shown in the World Financial Centre, where as Patricia Phillips writes it "...served as one more ingredient in an elaborate coronation that attempted to transform nothing more than a low-ceilinged hallway into a dynamic public space, and a private developer into a public patron" (Phillips, 1988: 94). Christine Boyer argues that Times Square and 42nd Street as redeveloped in the 1990s similarly constitute a triumph of simulation. Comparing it with the representation of reality in nineteenth-century panoramas, Boyer concludes:

> But now... designers bring all of their information-processing abilities into play in order to demonstrate the technical and organizational power of planning regulations and design controls that can turn the material form of the city into such an effective illusion. The result is similar to any successful magic show: spectators are doubly thrilled when the illusion is produced by invisible means... (Boyer, 2001: 50)

Perhaps a third case is Sony Plaza in Manhattan which, according to Zukin, reconstructs the glass-roofed arcades of Paris in the nineteenth century (see Chapter 5), while "...imposing a corporate order on the strolling crowds, transforming the dream experience into a 'Sony wonder'" (Zukin, 1995: 260). These instances have in common the centrality of

image, not simply as elements in a city's symbolic economy and representation to its citizens and others, but as gloss, as a seamless surface
which smothers difference.

But how important is culture in the determination of a city's growth,
compared with money? In *The Cultures of Cities* (1995), and two essays,
"Space and Symbols in an Age of Decline" (1996a) and "Cultural Strategies of Economic Development and the Hegemony of Vision" (1996b),
the latter her clearest exposition, Zukin oscillates between affirmation
of the leading role of culture through major cultural institutions and
individual producers, and that of material factors. In reference to gentrification, she is situated between those who see economic determinants
as primary, such as Neil Smith (1996b), and those for whom cultural
consumption and expression of social status are more important, like
David Ley (1980). The positions overlap, not least in the cultural selling
of inner-city living which drives up property values. In any case, models
evolved in one city do not map easily onto another. In a study of
redevelopment in the City of London and Spitalfields, for instance,
Jane M. Jacobs looks at the contrasting aims and needs of the state,
property developers, and local publics (1996: 70–102). The same inter-
sections are unlikely to be found in the same way in, say, Frankfurt or
Tokyo, though both are financial capitals. Taking a broader scope,
Featherstone suggests that "Rather than conceive postmodernism as the
product of a cultural logic, capital logic or other 'logic' ... we need also to
understand it in terms of the practices and experiences of particular
groups ... " (Featherstone, 1992: 265). The same sentence could apply
to gentrification (a shift from multiple-occupancy, rental to single
owner–occupier use of property, among other definitions). Besides,
Zukin's understanding of the cultural economy is limited by her
tendency to see spaces of consumption as "totally programmed" (Thrift,
1993: 236) or impervious to unplanned uses. She sees cultural intermediaries as knowing or unknowing servants of capital (O'Connor, 1998:
231) rather than independent agents. Nonetheless, a strand which
runs through Zukin's work, and for us lends it a renewed interest, is her
concern for social justice.

In response to the question of whose city has made into a cultural sign,
Zukin writes that "To ask 'Whose city?' suggests more than a politics of
occupation; it also asks who has a right to inhabit the dominant image
of the city" (Zukin, 1996a: 43); and that this relates to geographical
strategies when social groups contend for access to a city's prime sites,
such as its centres. She argues that city power is now the power to
impose a vision of the city: "Those who impose the vision 'frame' space

much as museums frame art historical canons by favouring some repre-sentations over others" (Zukin, 1996b: 226), a case of such struggle being that of homeless people in New York. Seeking to clear them from Grand Central Station, Mayor Koch assumed space to have a single function. Rosalyn Deutsche quotes him:

> These homeless people, you can tell who they are ... We thought it would be reasonable for the authorities to say, 'You can't stay here unless you're here for transportation.' Reasonable, rational people would come to that conclusion ... (cited in Deutsche, 1996: 51)

Koch is adding his voice to the tide of those who emphasise visuality, seeing a cleansed city in the invisibility of those its development disadvantages most. The issues are complex, however, and Zukin cites another space, Bryant Park:

> The design was calculated to repel muggers and drug dealers and encourage sitting and strolling by office workers, especially women. And it has succeeded in making the space safe for many more users, especially women, as well as recapturing it for adjacent office building owners and tenants. (Zukin, 1995: 275)

It is now a venue for fashion shows, and as new public space adds value to the neighbourhood. Zukin's point is that the space has been sanitised rather than revitalised, incorporated into the privatised world of Business Improvement Districts (BIDs) which replace elected authorities (Zukin, 1995: 66–69). BIDs use a voluntary tax to fund improvements which they control, and tend to equate a simulation of space derived from the theme park with social order: " ... simulation is economically productive ... provides opportunities to develop new products ... " (Zukin, 1995: 69). Zukin cautions that inequalities are material, and that cultural strategies denigrate as well as compensate:

> Not only is it important to study processes of deriving representations, but it is also important to study the inequitable results of struggles over aesthetic strategies such as historic preservation, over visual images of urban public spaces, and over the development of cultural consumption such as tourism. (Zukin, 1996b: 224)

Zukin, then, sees culture as driving economic change and the redevel-opment of urban districts. The BIDs are mechanisms for making money as well as taking power over space, and although the cultural industries are effective in promoting themselves, and in promoting city spaces as sites of cultural experiences, cultural intermediaries are, by definition, entrepreneurs.

Manchester

Zukin views the cultural industries as drawn into the operations of capital, just as street style is co-opted as fashion. This makes cultural consumers victims of a cunning industry. A more optimistic approach is taken by Derek Wynne and Justin O'Connor, who see the case of Manchester as indicating that cultural intermediaries have considerable scope for manoeuvre. Their findings, with those of several other researchers in popular culture in Manchester, are published in *From the Margins to the Centre* (1996), and summarised by O'Connor in his contribution to *The Entrepreneurial City* (Hall and Hubbard, 1998). The context Wynne and O'Connor make explicit is deindustrialisation: the loss of manufacturing industries and growth of service industries, particularly the creative or cultural industries, in a new economy. This new economy has been described as post-Fordist, or post-industrial, and Phil Mole, in *From the Margins to the Centre*, draws attention to Manchester's move towards such an economy and embeddedness of conventional patterns in its development (Mole, 1996: 16). The background to this is globalisation:

> No longer the privileged site linking local populations to national and international markets, many traditional cities appear to have been sidelined by some inexorable logic of multinational capital. Visible signs of economic collapse are everywhere evident: dilapidated buildings, derelict land, homeless people, begging, rising crime, racial tensions, riots, and much else besides. (Mole, 1996: 17)

The statement is sweeping, and each of those factors may have their own history, but the difficulty of giving too much credit to inexorable logics is that it puts the problem outside the ability of people to change it.

To be fair, Mole's argument is based on empirical research in Manchester which establishes the character of its cultural industries and emphasises their ability to intervene in a situation left bereft of hope by both conventional economics and conventional city politics. He notes that most cultural businesses are small, have multiple outlets and sources of income in both the public and private sectors, and provide a diversity of flexible employment (Mole, 1996: 33–34). He adds that "They successfully create and occupy their market niches precisely because they are small and informal, and they (and their networks) consume as well as produce" (Mole, 1996: 36). The cultural sector is apparently ephemeral, but far from marginal in its suitability to move into redundant industrial sites, bringing a creative flair and buzz together with attendant high-profile image-making and the delights of new areas of consumption, especially at night. From this association of creative day-work and nightlife comes the notion of a 24-hour city. The cultural economy runs parallel to post-Fordism – the replacement of production lines with flexible patterns of wealth creation – and depends on perception. Given the centrality to it of media-related businesses, this is not surprising. It is an area where nothing succeeds like a perception of success, though the collapse of the market in new technology shares in the late 1990s shows its volatility. And while it could be argued that in cities such as London or New York it is the financial services industry rather than the cultural industries which underpin a new economy, cities such as Birmingham and Manchester are not part of the global circuits of capital. They are not in a position to be districts in what Saskia Sassen (1991) calls a global city of financial enclaves linked by electronic communications.

The opportunities presented by a city in which redevelopment is culturally led differ from those of a city which forms part of the global city of trans-national capital. Zukin sees them as constrained, but Wynne and O'Connor see a high degree of autonomy on the parts of cultural intermediaries. O'Connor states:

> cultural intermediaries are precisely that – intermediaries. They are able to interpret, package, transmit and manipulate symbols and knowledge in a way that produces new value. As both producers and consumers they are able to claim an expertise, a close knowledge of the inner dynamics of the cultural field. (O'Connor, 1998: 231)

Citing his work with Wynne and others (1996), O'Connor claims that cultural intermediaries are both key to redevelopment and perhaps the only actors in the situation able to catalyse a new city image. He recalls how early efforts by developers to import a new vision of inner city living to Manchester failed because they were isolated from the prevailing culture, which was not that of a European-style 24-hour city of diverse uses and sociabilities. And that two other forces – the cultural ambience of raves and independent music production, and the gay scene – were more effective engines of renewal, if later appropriated by developers. This follows a decade or more of advocacy for the arts, and a shift within the arts from public administration to business management. One outcome has been the credibility of the cultural quarter model. In 1988, Bianchini *et al.* wrote that "...major investment in arts projects opens up other possibilities, not least by helping to transform the image of each city" (Bianchini *et al.*, 1988: 49–50). The cases noted by Bianchini *et al.* include Birmingham, of which more below, and Sheffield, the latter less successful than most in its creation of a cultural quarter. Of course, investment in the arts does create jobs and add a new dimension to city life, but to concentrate a city's cultural infra-structure in one quarter may marginalise other districts. There is, also, no guarantee that cultural investment and local democracy have any connection. Julia Gonzalez, writing on Bilbao and the Guggenheim, notes a division between democratic aspirations for participation in broadly based cultural activities, and provision of sites for elite culture. Both may be informed by visions of a regional or national cultural identity, or by trans-national cultural currents. But Gonzalez argues that strategies are still needed in Bilbao to support cultural producers, whose needs are not the same as those of cultural institutions, and that "If a city is primarily run by its inhabitants then the citizens' desire to participate in local public life and culture is one of the city's greatest assets" (Gonzalez, 1993: 86–87). Cities are, however, seldom run by citizens; and cultural producers, such as artists on low incomes, are seldom at the centre of urban cultural policies.

This leads to a more interesting problem in two parts: first, the cultural entrepreneurs whom O'Connor sees as driving economic upturn in Manchester remain exactly that – entrepreneurs in the nineteenth-century sense of people who use ingenuity to make money from the labours of others – and are not themselves those who nudge history by inserting into it new readings and inflections. This happens, if at all, through critical cultural production. Secondly, although a field such as independent music production is outside mainstream capital interests and might be expected to be an arena for new and critical content, those old interests are adept in colonising alternatives as, in effect, a commodification of rebellion which neuters its political force (Seiler, 2000). In Manchester, art seems for the most part, as museum collection or public sculpture, an accoutrement of urban development. The city's cultural entrepreneurs, even in their post-modern, post-Fordist mode of operation, are not a new avant-garde. They construct a new cultural economy but they do not represent a new cultural democracy. Yet O'Connor and

Wynne (1996) are correct in stressing Manchester's difference from New York. In their essay "Left Loafing: City cultures and postmodern lifestyles" (1996: 49–90), which includes a critique of Zukin, they point out that in Manchester's residential developments there was no displacement of a residual population as in SoHo, that the idea of inner-city living was new in Manchester, and that a shift of population to the increasingly 24-hour centre has taken place. They note the place of heritage, especially Victorian architecture, in developers' publicity material, but also a new European ambience in outdoor cafés and bars.

The Castlefield district offers a high concentration of such consumption outlets in an aestheticised post-industrial space. In a gesture of postmodern irony, perhaps, one bar under a railway arch is called "Fat Cats", and another next door "Revolution"; further along the canal is a third called "Choice". But, as Jenny Ryan and Hilary Fitzpatrick in the year 1996 show in a study of the use of bars in Manchester's gay district, consumers imprint their own spatial practices on what is provided, are not passive in their occupation of the new city. O'Connor and Wynne make a more generalised point: " . . . the initiation of the process whereby Manchester was to be culturally landscaped actually created new spaces within which cultural contestation and exploration could emerge" (O'Connor and Wynne, 1996: 75). Their definition of the cultural industries rests mainly on areas of aesthetic, or conspicuous, consumption, while Allen Scott, in contrast, gives 29 categories of employment in a production-based analysis of the US cultural economy, from greeting cards and fur goods to advertising and architectural services (Scott, 2000: 9). In his treatment of the cultural industries in Paris he includes perfumes, cosmetics, periodicals, jewellery, furs, leather, furniture, books, sound recording, and film (Scott, 2000: 194–195). But, as a visit to Manchester confirms, its post-industrial zones are thriving. The Castlefield district, alongside a set of canals and winding between railway arches and dis- or re-used industrial buildings, now stands alongside other waterside developments in European cities, and has adopted a specifically European (rather than North American) ambience. An example of this, though perhaps a little spurious, is the designation of a Catalan quarter around an outdoor café and tapas bar. Most of the re-used spaces seem to be bars of one sort or another, and Castlefield comes alive at night, but there are also television studios, and – in a gesture to the cultural clout of New York – a Loft Shop in which to buy loft-style apartments.

Redevelopment in Manchester has constructed new mixed-use quarters too, and in this way differs from Birmingham's strategy in the 1980s (see Webster, 2001) to invest in a new cultural centre, epitomised by the

Convention Centre and new public squares with sculptures and innovative street furniture. Birmingham's new centre is, it seems, a central business district with a cultural face, and could be seen as rotating around the new Hyatt Hotel and television company offices. A question which applies to both Birmingham and Manchester is the extent to which economic or other benefits have been spread through the cities' populations. In Birmingham, according to Loftman and Nevin (1998), they are not. They write that of the profits produced only a minor part remained in the city, and that many jobs were "low-skilled, temporary, part-time and low-paid" (Loftman and Nevin, 1998: 142); and conclude that the new cultural centre is not very accessible to more peripheralised publics. So, if "The symbolic economy unifies material practices of finance, labor, art, performance, and design" (Zukin, 1995: 9), whose city do they reproduce?

Conclusion

Zukin writes that " ... post-Marxist critique asserts the relative autonomy of culture from economic organization" and that this " ... emphasizes the potency of signs and symbols, including language and visual artifacts, for maintaining both domination and resistance"; she continues "smaller cities all over the world have elaborated cultural strategies of economic development, designed public spaces for social control, and designated large numbers of buildings for historic preservation" (Zukin, 1996b: 224, 226–227). That autonomy is implicit in the construction of modern culture, but this should not inhibit a critical appraisal of its impact. Nor should modern culture's claim for autonomy be taken at face value – again, the art market is a *market* first and art second.

In city after city, meanwhile, the growth of cultural industries or insertion of flagship cultural institutions is seen by civic authorities and businesses alike as a solution to the post-industrial condition. To this there are at least two responses: first, to ask how evenly the benefits are distributed; and secondly, to ask whether there are solutions (as predicted patterns of outcome) at all. The experiences of Birmingham, and in a more extreme way that of SoHo in New York, suggest that old economic patterns are reproduced in culturally led urban development. This does not mean a radical cultural intervention could not have a different effect, but cultural entrepreneurs are not avant-gardists in a politicised rather than stylistic sense. Besides, the dominant images of city marketing are highly selective, tending to reinforce rather than challenge structures of power and to represent a city for an audience of investors not known for an interest in social justice, and of aspirational consumers more interested in status and leisure. As to what can be predicted, complexity theory (Byrne, 1997; Cilliers, 1998) suggests it is less than was thought in the rational-planning regimes of the twentieth century. Deriving from chaos theory, complexity theory sees small changes in conditions as producing large changes in outcomes for the same intervention. Byrne, citing Cilliers (1998: 114) who states that local narratives "are instrumental in allowing [social groups] to achieve their goals and make sense of what they are doing", argues that "These local narratives cannot be combined into an overarching grand theory of everything" because there is no viable universal account, only local knowledge (Byrne, 2001: 33; see also Byrne, 1997). The symbolic economy may trade on place identity, but it has little use for the local knowledges of the unempowered. On the other hand, culture is a mutable medium, and some cultural producers deal with local, resistant narratives (Bird, 1993; Smith, M. P., 2001: 115). What would it be like if a city's cultural life derived from the networks by which "... people are connected to each other, make sense of their lives, and act upon the worlds that they see ... " (Smith, M. P., 2001: 194) rather than from the forms of a dominant culture?

CHAPTER 4

Consuming Place: Cities and Cultural Tourism

In the previous chapter we considered the aestheticisation of urban spaces. In this chapter we extend the discussion by looking at cultural tourism, asking what happens when a city is consumed as a tourist destination. The question as to whose city this entails again arises, but in tourism images are used to appeal to visitors rather than to entrepreneurs. But, remembering the differentiation of culture as the arts from cultures as ways of living, outlined at the beginning of Chapter 4, the question can be interpreted as what impact cultural tourism has on local cultures. Does a city's re-presentation in cultural tourism contradict the daily lives of its citizens, and, to put it bluntly, is the city turned into a human zoo? If authenticity of experience is the attraction of other or exotic places for the tourist, is it in effect destroyed in the commodification of place? Underpinning these concerns is a further issue of the gaze with which tourists regard places other than those from which they come, and the relation of an objectification of place in a tourist gaze to the masculine gaze of late twentieth-century cultural theory.

We argue in this chapter that representations of place in cultural tourism are not transparent. What is seen is conjured from what is there, but it is reconstructed for the tourist imagination and apprehended through a tourist gaze which tends to match experiences to previously received images, the selectivity of which is shaped by marketing criteria. We begin by reconsidering Urry's work, arguing that the objectification of place in tourism acts as a foil to the actualities of ordinary life which tourists leave behind when they go away; and comparing his approach with the construction of exotic others as discussed in ethnography and art (Duncan, 1993; Pollock, 1994). We show, too, that the packaging of tourism links it to the standardisation of product and experience in other areas of consumption such as fast food and theme parks (Ritzer, 1993; Alfino *et al.*, 1998; Rojek, 2000), and that the non-contiguity of tourist experience is similar to that of the mall and theme park (Boyer, 1992; Sorkin, 1992). The negative impact of cultural tourism on a local culture is illustrated by the case of Bergen (Myrvoll, 1999). Finally, the case of Barcelona is investigated as exemplifying planning for cultural tourism today (Dodd, 1999), after a history of liberal city planning from the mid nineteenth century to the city's housing of the 1992 Olympics.

A tourist gaze

In the second half of the nineteenth century, railways allowed families from the British working and lower middle classes to take annual holidays at seaside resorts. Across the channel, they provided access to the coastal and rural scenes depicted by Impressionist painters. For Urry, the railways also restructured urban consciousness by bringing mechanisation into ordinary lives (Urry, 1995: 119). In North America, railways had a more strategic purpose in unifying a nation which was still in formation. In the second half of the twentieth century, package tours and cheap air fares extended the horizon of holidays to the beaches of the Mediterranean, the Caribbean, and the Indian Ocean. Television advertising draws on the idyllic scenery of far away places, heightening it to signify fulfilment of desires: in the land of the Bounty Bar eaters the sun always shines, everyone is beautiful, and no one works, has a mortgage, or goes to the toilet. But while mass tourism in Europe produced rows of high-rise hotels in former fishing villages on the Mediterranean coast, adventure holidays using trucks as overland transport for the young and fit, together with the development of remote locations for the rich, now bring faraway places and cultures to specific publics. At the same time, cultural tourism based on short city-breaks in locations such as Paris, Rome, Florence, Barcelona, Vienna, Prague, Budapest, or New York provides a new kind of educated tourism for the middle classes. Weekend city breaks offer a status differential from mass tourism, indicating that those who take them have the time and money to do so, and the taste to select appropriate destinations in which to substitute the intellectual satisfactions of culture for the sensual seductions of sun, sea, and cheap alcohol.

Urry (1995) approaches tourism from a sociological perspective, adding it to housing, clothes, and furniture in a sociology of consumption. This gives him a methodological base onto which to graft his work on travel:

There is really no sociology of travel. The two most useful kinds of analysis have been the work carried out by social historians, such as on the social impact of the railway in the nineteenth century, and the more recent cultural investigations. (Urry, 1995: 129–130)

He draws attention to a democratisation of travel as it becomes more available, but also to the reproduction of social differences through modes of travel – the differential (income-based choice) of rail or air, charter or scheduled flights, and so forth. Then, writing of the way travel denotes an ability to buy time for non-useful pursuits, he notes Veblen's work on the leisure class, which, he argues, needs to be modified for a world in which most people have leisure. He cites a statistic that 63 per cent of people in the UK see holidays as a necessity (Mack and Lansley, 1985: 54; cited in Urry, 1995: 130), but questions two assumptions found in the literature: that the consumer is a social individual; and that consumption is a matter of purchase only, as if the consumer does not undertake work on the objects of consumption once purchased. Challenging both assumptions, Urry writes:

> much consumption is conducted by social groups ... [and] there is generally a considerable amount of work involved in transforming what is purchased ... into an object of consumption. ... in relationship to tourism it is crucial to recognise how the consumption of tourist services is social. (Urry, 1995: 131)

Emphasising the social aspect of group consumption, he moves on to say that what is actually purchased – the ticket, the hotel room, the meal – is really a means to the consumption of something else: "... the minimal characteristic of tourist activity is the fact that we look at, or gaze upon, particular objects, such as piers, towers, old buildings, artistic objects, food, countryside ..." (Urry, 1995: 131). This suggests a parallel with art appreciation, following John Berger (1972), where the purchase of a painting is, like that of the holiday depicted in the brochure, a means to possess what it represents.

In *Consuming Places*, Urry sees tourism as an antithesis of toil. He defines the tourist gaze as disconnected from ordinary life and routine, and argues that places are selected as objects of the gaze "... because there is an anticipation, especially through day-dreaming and fantasy, of intense pleasures" (Urry, 1995: 132). This anticipation is produced in film, journalism, television, and other elements of the mass media which provide a vocabulary through which to add meaning to the place to be visited. It is then reconstructed to correspond to that meaning, that representation: "...what is then seen is interpreted in terms of these pre-given categories" (ibid.). Images of place become imbued with typicality (not topicality), and can be collected in memory or a snapshot album. But to what extent do tourists do this for themselves, or passively accept packaged dreams? Does advertising engage its publics or dupe them? The shift in recent years from packaged to independent travel suggests a growing dissatisfaction with passivity, though in much independent travel the arrangements are still made by an agent. Perhaps the shift is a measure of affluence, and increased internet access, thus an extension of the differentials cited by Urry so that independent travel to exotic destinations signifies the social distinction of a bourgeois class from that of a petit-bourgeoisie which takes package holidays to more accessible places. The question remains as to whether those tourists who think of themselves as travellers in lands as yet unspoilt by the tourism they themselves import are aware of the contradiction. More broadly, it could be asked how far consumers of travel are aware that marketing has its own vocabulary, in travel as in estate agency, and how much they are critically engaged with it, noticing its potential ironies and playing the market's game on their own terms.

In this respect, a perspective from cultural studies might add to Urry's sociological view. Given the work on the ideology of mass media products for which cultural studies has become known, it may provide particular insights. Perhaps there is another way to think of the tourist, as *flâneur* – the disinterested urban stroller who liminally observes others in Baudelaire's Paris, as described by Benjamin (1997, 1999). In *The Tourist Gaze* (1990), Urry links tourist photography to the actions of the *flâneur*, using Marshall Berman's account – in *All that is Solid Melts into Air* (1983: 146–147) – of Baudelaire's Paris. That account is partly based on Benjamin, and in part on New York. Berman sets Baudelaire in context of the rebuilding of Paris by Baron Haussmann in the 1850s and 1860s, seeing a parallel with New York as reconfigured through freeways by planner Robert Moses. Haussmann destroyed the working-class quarters, driving new boulevards through them to create free-fire zones for troops, and creating major opportunities for property speculators. John Rennie Short, too, sees Haussmann's Paris replicated in post-war New York (Short, 1996: 176–178). Berman notes the admiration for Haussmann felt by Moses, yet acknowledges also that the boulevards beneficially opened up the city:

> Pedestrian islands were installed to make crossing easier, to separate local from through traffic and to open up alternate routes for

promenades. Great sweeping vistas were designed, with monuments at the boulevards' ends, so that each walk led to a dramatic climax. All these qualities helped to make the new Paris a uniquely enticing spectacle, a visual and sensual feast. (Berman, 1983: 151)

Enjoyment of the feast now belongs to tourists, a pleasure which is not innocent. For Urry, tourism establishes a power/knowledge relation: "To have visual knowledge of an object is in part to have power ... over it." His concept is implicitly linked to that of the masculine gaze as constructed in film theory (Mulvey, 1989). Urry makes no reference to this, though a comparison of his work with film theory would be interesting (though outside the scope of this book). We would add, however, citing Doreen Massey (1994: 232), that there is a particular sense of power which depends on the long view afforded by a vista, skyline, or panorama. The tourist postcard uncritically replicates such views as well as offering picturesque details culled from everyday streets, though not from everyday lives (Miles, 2000: 9–35). But there are more nuances in the photographs tourists take themselves than in postcards, and Urry sees photographs as miniature transcriptions of reality which hide ideological content, calling tourists amateur semioticians whose shots of waves on rocks signify wild nature. He does not say if signification is knowing or not, but the point remains that the image stands for a class of actualities rather than a single occurrence, though the function of the snapshot may be not primarily visual but as a catalyst to conversation.

In summing up Urry's work on tourism, two insights can be kept in mind: that photography reconstructs particular places according to a generalised, preconstructed category of place; and, as Urry says at the beginning of *The Tourist Gaze*, that to study tourism is like studying social deviance: it is a way to reveal the norm and its ideological content and thereby to study the workings of a dominant society.

Tourism, cultures, and culture

Urry's work could be extended by relating his theories to insights on the production of otherness from ethnography and cultural studies. Tourists on safari in eastern or southern Africa who talk about getting a good shot no longer mean using a gun, but a camera. Animals and the native population alike are objectified in their gaze as if the animals and the people have been put there for them. Meanwhile, in tourism promotion for faraway places, local cultures are distilled into visual representations which become part of the vocabulary of Western society's culture. There are links between this framing of the exotic in tourism and its representation in art. Similarly, there are links between early ethnography and contemporary tourism advertising. Recalling Urry's point, cited above, that there is work in consumption, to draw an analogy with art while noting the construction of otherness may help us to understand how the work of consuming places is done.

Within white, middle-class suburban society (Sennett, 1970), otherness is perceived as dangerous. Only when removed, distanced by its framing as an equivalent of cultural consumption, does it become safe. James Duncan links long-haul tourism to nineteenth-century ethnography, arguing that early ethnographic collections rendered non-Europeans as either a servant class or fallen savages (Duncan, 1993: 46). Coombes (1994) similarly argues that representations of African society in early ethnography characterise it as primitive (see Chapter 3). But while representations of non-Europeans affirmed a subordinate status, they added a highly coloured strand of exoticism:

> This strand...has, since the middle of the last [19th] century, fed into a burgeoning travel industry. Other cultures are often portrayed as occupying remote places that are rare or unique and therefore desirable, places where one can escape the social and psychological pressures of modernity and retreat into a 'simpler', more 'natural' place and time. (Duncan, 1993: 46)

Nature takes on a Rousseauesque opposition to culture, as it does in Henry David Thoreau's retreat to a log cabin at Walden Pond and in the persisting myth, in North American culture, of the log cabin as a sign of a regained primordial state. Duncan continues that even in the progressive field of cultural anthropology, societies are set in a perpetual present of non-negotiable tradition, thereby vulnerable to external corruption by modernising influences. He also sees ethnography's general silence on its contribution to European colonialism as indicating "...the self-delusion of ethnographers that they are studying a 'pure', uncorrupted and uncontaminated traditional society" (Duncan, 1993: 47).

The uncontaminated, in an industrial society in which even the air and water are contaminated, is dreamlike: distant like a memory from childhood, pure like a sacred place. Michael Pollan, in an account of building a hut of his own, cites Thoreau: "Every child begins the world again" (Pollan, 1998: 17). The world begun again, a new Eden, is a world not yet messed up, a vacant (or evacuated) site (*tabula rasa*) onto which almost anything can be projected. This was the attraction for nineteenth-century salon painters of remote histories and places – Babylon for sensuality and apocalypse, Rome for decadence – through which to escape the social norms and limits to polite subject-matter of their day.

In the 1890s, within an emergent modernist milieu, the world begun again was perhaps what Tahiti, a French colony, gave the artist Paul Gauguin. Before his first departure for Tahiti in 1891, Gauguin wrote of painting that it " ... tells whatever it wants", allowing the spectator to dream (c. 1890, in Harrison *et al.*, 1998: 1022). Returning to France in 1893 as a leading painter in the Symbolist movement (previously a stock-broker, collector, and amateur painter before the stock market crash of 1882), he saw a market potential in images of the exotic. In his writings from Tahiti he capitalises on this, a colonial if now destitute figure representing himself for a European market as living like a savage. Strindberg, in a letter declining to write an Introduction to the catalogue of Gauguin's sale of work before his second departure for Tahiti in 1895, echoes the sentiment: "What is he then? He is Gauguin, the savage ... " (Strindberg, 1895, in Harrison *et al.*, 1998: 1036). Strindberg did not like the pictures: "I have no grasp of your art, which is now exclusively Tahitian" (Strindberg, 1895, in Harrison *et al.*, 1998: 1035), but asked Gauguin to visit on his return. Gauguin died in Tahiti in 1903, his last years there marked by poverty, disease, and a suicide attempt. Yet he wrote: "Night after night there are wild young girls in my bed" (cited in Boudaille, 1964: 214). This might connect to today's sex tourism industry in exoticised destinations in south-east Asia or the Caribbean (Mullings, 2000). In 1893, however, when Gauguin exhibited in Paris, his exoticism was not well received. Georges Boudaille writes that the public " ... visited the exhibition as they would a circus ... to laugh and jeer at the sight of these specimens of an unfamiliar race ... " (Boudaille, 1964: 191).

How might we view Gauguin's exotic images now? Griselda Pollock takes Gauguin's painting of a young Tahitian woman on her bed, *Manao Tupapau* (1892), as a case of "sadistic voyeurism" (Pollock, 1994: 68) which re-orientalises an image previously demystified in Manet's *Olympia* (1863). While Manet presented a white woman with a black maid as a working partnership in the sex industry, Gauguin, in this picture of his 13-year-old Tahitian wife Teha'amana, creates a setting which fuses a European primitivism with narratives of sexuality and death – a naked figure and a dark spirit presence. Pollock sees Gauguin's tropical journey, like others in literature, art, or anthropology, as structured by oppositions: "here and there, home and abroad, light and dark, safety and danger..." (Pollock, 1994: 66). Susan Stewart similarly comments "The exotic object represents distance appropriated; it is symptomatic of the more general cultural imperialism that is tourism's stock in trade" (Stewart, 1993: 147).

The promise of far away tourism remains, then, as unfulfilled as any consumer desire, leaving the consumer wanting more, but holds out a return to Eden. In the suburbs, the presence of "travellers" (gypsies or New Age) causes alarm. David Sibley observes that "Planned settlements for Australian Aborigines, native Canadians and some European travelling people ... express the state's interest in separation and the correction of deviance" (Sibley, 1995: 84). But otherness overseas is allowed, because it is overseas, a licensed return of the repressed. Barry Curtis and Claire Pajaczkowska cite Dean MacCannell (1976) to the effect that "the tourist wants nothing more than a discursive substitute for experience, which nevertheless masquerades as experience itself" (Curtis and Pajaczkowska, 1994: 206). Pollock (1994) cites the same source: "the deep structure of modernity is a totalizing idea, a modern mentality that sets modern society in opposition to its own past and to those societies of the past and present that are treated as pre-modern..." (MacCannell, 1976: 8, cited in Pollock, 1994: 64). Curtis and Pajaczkowska add that travel is mediated by a sensuality absent in life at home, a pre-verbal state enforced by lack of linguistic skills for many tourists (Curtis and Pajacz-kowska, 1994: 207). The primitive is associated, too, with childhood, and Sibley draws attention to its role in television advertising for detergent – children dressed as native Americans with face paint and feathers arrive in the kitchen to be returned to civilisation by the washing whiter than white of their clothes (Sibley, 1995: 64–67).

More could be said of the colonialism which permeates these attitudes, as well as of the psychology of otherness, but we want to focus on one aspect – the function of distance – because it seems to link this kind of exoticism with a mode of perception and representation central to modernity, that of the perspective view, or view of a city from a belvedere or distant vantage point. Such a distancing view, in conventional graphic representation based on a single viewpoint and optic cone, enables the spectator to see all. It is a prerequisite for modern planning mirroring the self-contained space of Cartesian geometry, and begins with Alberti's invention of a device for measuring a city's streets from its circuit of walls. It also informs conventional cartography's view of the land, or a city, seen by an imagined bird's eye, or, in Baroque iconography the eye of god in the sky. Doreen Massey (1994) criticises Edward Soja for assuming a view of Los Angeles from a tall building in *Postmodern Geographies* (1989), and writes of the distant viewpoint in general that it is one which privileges visuality over other senses: "It has been argued to be the sense which allows most mastery; in part deriving from the very detachment which it allows and requires" (Massey, 1994: 224). For Massey, it is a gendered viewpoint. She does not cite Michel de Certeau, but in "Walking in the City" (de Certeau, 1984: 91–110) he contrasts the view from the top floor of the World Trade Centre with an experiential and tactical, if ephemeral, realm of streets. Walking can be mapped but this reduces its presence to a relic: "The trace left behind is substituted for the practice" (de Certeau, 1984: 97). A world reduced to signs like marks on paper, however, produces a blank space onto which to project or imprint almost any fancied place.

To re-read de Certeau today is helpful. His insistence on the tactics of everyday life reminds us that meaning and value are created continuously, including incidentally. Creswell writes of de Certeau's idea of tactics that they "refuse the neat divisions and clasifications of the powerful and, in doing do, critique the spatialization of domination" (Creswell, 1997: 363). Tactics are not organised – unlike strategies – but are not random either. The description of urban walking which de Certeau uses to illustrate tactics can be over-used , yet raises a question as to whether the new breed of independent-minded tourists, not just the urban wanderers of Baudelaire's Paris, employ tactics in discovering the city (as they might see it) for themselves.

Industrialised tourism

Industrialised tourism packages fantasies and sells them. As Urry argues, it depends at least in part on a pre-conceived notion of place, of a specific place, so that the tourist may seek out and photograph scenes which mimic those in the travel brochure and poster. Urry writes:

> The contemporary tourist gaze is increasingly signposted. There are markers which identify the things and places worthy of our gaze. Such signposting identifies a relatively small number of tourist nodes. The result is that most tourists are concentrated within a very limited area. (Urry, 1990: 47)

He adds that this restrictive model of the organised tour is, today, diversifying into several other patterns, allowing more scope for individual discovery. In particular, for Urry, there is scope for a more critical tourism in such sites as industrial museums like Wigan Pier (Urry, 1990: 111–112). But mass tourism in all its forms, whatever the label, still produces a rationalisation of provision through division into standard components which can be operated in the same way as, say, fast food with its strict portion control and homogenisation of product. In other words, travel is McDonaldised.

George Ritzer's *The McDonaldization of Society* was first published in 1993 and has sold as both an academic and a popular title (we use the revised edition, 2000). Ritzer sees the standardisation of food as an extension of the production line in a period of globalisation, which rests on four qualities: efficiency in use of resources; calculability of costs and margins; predictability of product; and control, in the case of food through automated technologies (Ritzer, 2000: 12–14). Ritzer mentions Club Med, chains of campgrounds, and package tourism as cases of a formal rationalisation of leisure (Ritzer, 2000: 25–26); his image of the coach tour with its limited stops for photography may be outdated, though such tours are not extinct, but the wider point that tourism is controlled like many other mass market industries remains valid. It is simply that the forms which mass tourism take have been made more varied, just as some manufacturers customise cars or jeans. There is nothing startling or deep in Ritzer's analysis, and his caricature of a fast food society may, in some ways, construct an elitism attractive to middle-class liberals who bemoan a generalised social decline in mass society while themselves enjoying a sheltered and privileged lifestyle.

Rojek comments on the rapid increase in volume of tourist flows since the 1960s, noting that more than 250 million people are employed in tourism. He adds that "The rationalization and commodification of travel have intensified in direct proportion to the growth in value of the travel business" (Rojek, 2000: 53). He compares the voluntarism of MacCannell's work – the tourist as actor in the situation, or we might say the tactical tourist – with the structuralism of Ritzer's approach; and takes Disney World as an example of a highly structured environment in which set prices are charged for set experiences at set times, all controlled by an organization which employs staff to ensure visitors keep to given paths. This is a dystopian view: "McTourism is part of the disenchantment of the world" (Rojek, 2000: 55). He gives a gloss on Urry (2002) in which postmodernism, not modern objectification, frames the tourist gaze. Does Rojek go further here than Urry in disconnecting the idea of a gaze from its gendered meaning in cultural studies? Urry does not explicitly make that connection, but we take his gaze to be objectifying, using fixed viewpoints and preconceived images which carry a degree of illusory stability, if ironically (unlike the gaze of pornography or cartography). This is an intriguing area for interpretation, and we now give a longish quote from Rojek to encourage the reader to draw her or his own conclusion. Rojek writes on Urry:

> The postmodern tourist gaze greets the landscape of tourism as a limitless horizon in which objects and experiences lack fixed or overarching meanings. Instead the meaning of tourist experience is always conditional and plural and hence associated with diversity and variation. Because the tourist gaze recognizes no privileged reading of tourist sights, it follows that concomitant cultures of tourism are more playful and ironic. The tourist gaze turns to tourist experience to provide contrast rather than truth and momentary engagement instead of everlasting meaning. The tourist gaze acknowledges the processual, relatively open-ended, contingent character of tourism by invoking immanent structural forces. (Rojek, 2000: 59)

Rojek then links postmodern tourism to what he calls the crisis in sociological theory, where feminism, semiotics, Marxism, and ethnomethodology offer incompatible readings of a society, and say different things about how groups or individuals intervene in history. He cautions against applying first-world models universally, and notes that "The expansion of the tourist industry is associated with new forms of social inequality and oppression" (Rojek, 2000: 63). But he accepts that encounters between tourists and hosts today are not marked by the same divide as those of the colonial era, and that tourism may yet rupture boundaries. His final point is that consumers of overtly tourist products and places are aware of what goes on, do not see sites such as the Luxor Hotel in Las Vegas (with its "Egyptian" pyramid) as real (see Chapter 6). In this there is, we suggest, a continuity: escaping from the industrial world, tourists at first sought the artificiality of holiday places, then of far away places; this traded on the exotic, but the exotic is now re-manufactured at home and can incorporate kitsch. The search may not always be, as it possibly once was, for authenticity, but for an artificiality seen through the veil of tourism promotion – a taste for the ersatz as such. But then, Gauguin's primitivism was not authentic either. It was the exoticised cultural production of a European artist manipulating an art market.

Just as the far away takes on a quality of otherness, so does the past in heritage culture. This often forms an element of a city's tourism promotion, and tends to a selective view in which neither unsafe working conditions nor strikes figure in industrial museums, and the insecurities of pre-industrial cottage-based production are absent from homely craft museums. Similarly, Franco Bianchini records that present-day local cultures and conditions were marginalised by the hype of Glasgow's year as European City of Culture in 1990 (Bianchini, 1999: 83). Urry seems wryly amused by the collective nostalgia which arises when industries have died: "As Britain becomes rapidly deindustrialized so a huge industry has grown up around the 'authentic' reconstruction of the workplaces, houses and streets of that industrial era" (1990: 124). More common than industrial museums are heritage sites re-used as cultural sites, such as Albert Dock, Liverpool, while in many north American cities there are commercially led redevelopments of heritage sites. Cases of the latter include New York's South Street Seaport, Baltimore's Harborplace, and Faneuil Hall Marketplace in Boston, all historic sites (though the building in Baltimore is new) redeveloped by the Rouse Company (Gratz, 1989: 318; see also Harvey, 2000: 133–156). All include a range of retail outlets catering mainly to the tourist trade, and themed according to the site's supposed history.

Christine Boyer describes South Street Seaport as a tableau "surrounding the spectator with an artfully composed historic ambience" (Boyer, 1992: 182). She notes the mural which re-figures the site's historic look, and that its purpose may be to deflect attention from more melancholy sites along a partly decaying waterfront. Boyer explains the tableau in relation to earlier, nineteenth-century tableaux such as panoramas and dioramas, as well as to the arcades of Paris. These glass-covered passages appeared, cut through privately owned buildings, from the 1830s to 1860s. They are the object of Walter Benjamin's *passagenwerk* (Benjamin, 1999; see also Buck-Morss, 1989), his investigation of an urban phantas-magoria of consumption in which small objects seen in shop windows took on a magical quality (discussed in Chapter 6). The arcades became outmoded by department stores in the second half of the century, but they provided one of the first places in which conspicuous consumption could be practised. Meanwhile, panoramas re-presented for a mass public who paid to see them a world which changed rapidly, which may have gone by the time it was consumed. Boyer sees the panoramas as having an affirmative appeal: "As old traditions were erased before their eyes, the urban spectators of the nineteenth century drew comfort from the art of replicating a bygone reality" (Boyer, 1992: 185). Panoramas also presented imagined scenes, like the marvels of the ancient world, or mysteries of the Orient. Boyer contends that their equivalents as spectacles now are the walk-about heritage sites of historic quarters (such as Plaka in Athens), specific historic spaces (such as Union Square, New York), and the staged spaces of theme parks, malls, or festival marketplaces. All are simulations: "Both the old forms and the new are arts of commercial entertainment and imaginary travel; both are image spectacles, scenographic visions relying on an art of verisimilitude; and both present a particular re-framing of urban reality" (Boyer, 1992: 187). The Rouse Company who manage several such sites impose strict conditions in their way as controlling as Disney in its theme parks. But the emphasis is on local colour.

At Faneuil Hall Marketplace, opened in 1976, national retail chains were initially excluded (though not permanently) in favour of small shops owned by Bostonians. There were 150 speciality stores, food outlets, gift shops, and the like, catering to conspicuous rather than utility consumption, and all signed-up to 40-page leases. Roberta Gratz writes that the scheme uses the management methods of the mall for heritage tourism, and notes the Rouse Company's formula as including long hours, visible security, good sanitation, design control, public entertainment, coordinated advertising, and tenant support through business advice (Gratz, 1989: 317–318). The success of such sites follows and encourages further growth in heritage tourism, but for Boyer, "...to historicize is to estrange" (Boyer, 1992: 199), and in this respect heritage tourism has much in common with exoticisation. To give Boyer the last word on this before briefly looking to a contrasting actuality: "South Street Seaport can be considered a kind of collective souvenir of travel and adventure, exotic commodities and trade" (Boyer, 1992: 201).

European cities compete to be Capitals of Culture, and many have designated a cultural quarter, such as Rotterdam's Cultural Triangle (Hajer, 1993). As Bianchini writes, civic authorities tend to see cultural resources as "...increasingly important complementary factors in the competition between cities possessing similar advantages" (Bianchini, 1993: 18). This position needs revision now, when flagship cultural investments such as Tate Modern or the Guggenheim in Bilbao have been seen to have a transformative impact on a post-industrial zone. Heritage and cultural tourism do not always offer advantages to a city's dwellers. A negative actuality is found in Bergen, a World Heritage city built around its fishing industry. Today it has 200,000 or so inhabitants and ten times as many annual visitors, many in cruise ships. Siri Myrvoll writes of the fish market's adaptation:

> Fresh fish is becoming scarce in the market, the fishmongers being busy with the more profitable business of supplying smoked salmon

sandwiches to the Germans or vacuum packed smoked salmon and tinned caviar to the Japanese. It has reached the point where fish vendors themselves complain: their regular customers cannot get up to the counters, they lose interest and do not return. . . . selling fish in the fish market after the summer season is over is an unprofitable business, Bergen may be in danger of losing the foundation upon which its cultural heritage was based. (Myrvoll, 1999: 48)

The goose which lays golden eggs, it seems, is plucked and stuffed ready-to-cook for the oven of global commercial interests which override those of local publics.

Barcelona

We now look at Barcelona, a city in which cultural tourism – the city break and the add-on to a business trip, or location for a convention – plays a key role in the city's development. It is a city with a strong cultural infra-structure pre-dating the growth of its cultural tourism, and in which Catalan cultural life predominates over the trends of the globalised art market. Barcelona has a history, from the Cerdá plan of 1859 and the city's northern extension (*Eixample*), of democratic planning – though in the nineteenth century the process itself was not democratic: Cerdá's grid plan was approved by royal support and intervention by the national government while the City Council organised a competition for alternative plans, later grudgingly employing Cerdá to implement his own (Soria y Puig, 1999: 23–50). Yet the ethos of Cerdá's plan is pro-foundly liberal in providing decent housing for all social classes, abundant light and access to green space for all dwellings, services and public transport, and a mix of uses of space and sizes of dwelling. This is rational planning in the good sense, rationality as the pursuit of well-being for all citizens. It is rational, too, in the proportions of its regular grid; and in its articulation of the aspirations of the commercial class after a period of repression under the Bourbon monarchy following Catalonia's loss of independence on 11 September 1714.

The city's liberal planning ethos continued in the urban renewal projects preceding the 1992 Olympics. As well as constructing an Olympic Village on disused rail and port facilities, the city undertook more than a hundred small improvement schemes, many providing new public spaces, throughout the city's residential districts (Ghirardo, 1996: 200). Bianchini writes that the new public squares and parks ". . . became powerful physical symbols of urban renaissance" (Bianchini, 1999: 83), but since 1992 a shift of direction is evident in three zones of redevelopment: the cultural quarter of el Raval around the Museum of Contemporary Art of Barcelona (MACBA); the extension of waterfront renovation from the Olympic Village to St Adriá de Besós at the north–east city boundary in preparation for a World Forum of Culture in 2004; and the site of a knowledge economy zone in the working-class district of Poble Nou behind the waterfront.

Although Barcelona is a European city, it is not without its exoticism for the northern visitor. In the past it was a port city, its medieval districts, the *bari gotic* and *bari chino* consisting of dark alleys which were sites of prostitution and drinking. The eighteenth- and nineteenth-century apartment buildings are tall and crammed in because land was scarce before the demolition of the city walls in 1861. And they are bedecked with balconies providing a transitional space between the domestic interior and the street, in which to store tins of oil, put plants in pots and birds in cages, hang washing to dry, and sit. For the visitor these streets were authentic, and felt mildly dangerous. Authenticity underpins the city's tourism strategy today, playing on its past architectures, from the medieval to *modernista*, and on its present-day revival of Catalan culture. The old alleys are still there, though several have been cleared, as are the bars. The more intrepid tourist can rub shoulders, so to speak, with artists, north Africans, Asians, possibly prostitutes and unfortunately a lot of pickpockets in the old city. This rawness (without the street crime, which is a problem) is not inconvenient to the city's tourism strategy, though the promotion of contemporary culture is probably now more central to it.

Dianne Dodd (1999) describes the strategy, formulated in the late 1980s, as rejecting the mass market tourism encouraged by national promotions based on sun, sea, sand, and sangria, which led to the industrialisation of tourism in coastal resorts. Package tourists, in any case, spend little money in the places they visit, while business tourists and those seeking cultural experiences on short city breaks are likely to be both more affluent and more adventurous in consumption. Instead of subordinating itself, then, to mass tourism the city sought to niche market itself as a cultural destination. The renaissance of Catalan culture coincides with this and figures centrally in it. Local distinctiveness appeals to independent tourists who see themselves as travellers seeking out the "real" Barcelona of local publics, including those who consume culture. The city aided their search for authenticity by making them do work in finding local culture, displaying information on cultural events and public transport in Catalan. Dodd writes:

even if the tourists do not use all the attractions on offer, the knowledge of their presence ... will encourage a return visit. [And] because
these cultural elements are not built for tourist purposes, business or
culturally educated tourists will be more interested in them, because
they tend to search for authenticity (Dodd, 1999: 57–58).

This enabled Barcelona's politicians and public officials to support
investment in a tourist infra-structure which was also a local cultural
provision. There was an element of differentiating Barcelona from
Bilbao in this, with its imported Guggenheim isolated from the cultural
life of that city (Gonzalez, 1993). The flaw, as Dodd observes, is that the
emphasis has been on cultural consumption and not production, so
that making art is not much helped: "There are very few subsidies
available for community arts, arts for the disabled or new developing
arts ... little is invested in the derived creativity ... of the city" (Dodd,
1999: 61). Meanwhile, the cost of living has risen rapidly, and areas
where artists once found low-rent, live-in studios have become gentrified
rather as they did in the 1980s in New York's SoHo. The result is a new
professional-class bohemia in the cultural quarter, el Raval.

Much of the new cultural infra-structure, including a National Theatre
and a National Auditorium, has been provided by municipal investment,
but a notable factor in Barcelona is the financial contribution of savings
banks to cultural and social projects. These are non-profit organisations,
required by their constitution to direct surplus income to projects for
public benefit. Several cultural venues have been provided and maintained by the savings banks, and events supported. The most recent
project in this intermediate area between public and private interests is
the Caixa Foundation's contemporary art gallery in a renovated textile
factory near the site of the 1929 International Exposition, where the
German pavilion by Mies van der Rohe has been permanently reconstructed at the base of the long steps to the National Museum of
Catalan Art on Montjuic. Dodd suggests that the abundance of money
leads to a freedom from the economic constraints which affect the
arts in most cites, but also that "... there is not the same need for
entrepreneurship ... and no blatant efforts ... to attract visitors" (Dodd,
1999: 57). This may enhance the sense of a local cultural life. But, in the late
1990s, a more entrepreneurial ethos emerged in the city's redevelopment,
again trading on cultural tourism.

It is in this context that the *bario chino* (*bari xino* in Catalan), the
old red light district on the far side of the Ramblas from the gothic
centre, has been redeveloped as el Raval, the cultural quarter. The

change of name signifies a change of identity. Although much of the previous building stock of nineteenth-century apartments remains, there are major clearances, too, and insertion of the flagship cultural institution: the MACBA designed by US architect Richard Meier. A few blocks south of MACBA is a new Ramblas, a wide street with a pedestrian centre, seating, palm trees and rusting steel lamp posts resembling Richard Serra sculptures. Unlike the old Ramblas, a series of avenues from the port to the commercial centre, the new one goes nowhere in particular. To create it, three city blocks of low-rent apartments were demolished. Those surrounding the space are being renovated, and many of the residual population have been peripheralised (though by no means all). Planning controls required residents to be offered alternative accommodation nearby, but not all could afford the new service charges for buildings which now have lifts, porters, or improved heating systems. The district has begun to take on a homogenised, slightly sanitised, aspect, and several of the small retail outlets which served local needs for ordinary things have been replaced by art galleries, boutiques, and hairdressers. Not all the small galleries, however, have thrived, and the district retains something of its old character and ethnic mix. The wide square outside MACBA, another clearance, is taken over by youths on motorcycles at night, and is attractive to skateboarders during the day. It is also used by residents as a place to walk their dogs in the early morning. There are plans now, however, for a new luxury hotel to drive a further phase of gentrification in el Raval. It is likely that what remains of the old street life will be drained out in the interests of a homogenised space of cultural consumption framed by the local colour of narrow streets and balconies festooned with plants. But, where new buildings have been inserted, the most visually evident change to the streetscape of el Raval is an absence of balconies.

The new, clean, pale marble facades resemble those of a northern city as perhaps it might be imagined by someone in a Mediterranean city. Monica Degen cites a local journalist:

> they are demolishing the old buildings and constructing new ones. The contrast is brutal. There's the old building with the gas canister on the balcony, an old lady leaning out of the window.... Next to it you have a stone building with glass and metal, perfectly rectangular, geometric, with automatic doorbells, the windows hermetically sealed, without balconies. They are more interested in aesthetics than utility (cited in Degen, 2002: 29).

This is complex, and the new character of el Raval is not due only to its role as a cultural quarter around a major institution. The new residents, after all, come from the city not from abroad. But the perception of the city constructed for visitors, as a cosmopolitan, thriving, cultural space is related to that constructed for the city's own publics. It links as well to the city's position as a hub on two economic flows, one from Lisbon through Madrid to Barcelona, the other from Valencia through Barcelona to Montpellier, Marseilles, and Geneva. The city's claim to be a world-city is evident in its World Trade Centre designed by I. M. Pei, on the new waterfront.

The old alleys are picturesque but their location in a tourism economy trading on authenticity is balanced by another specifically cultural tourism economy based on cultural institutions and cosmopolitanism, in which designer-bars are also important markers of place. As a former el Raval Councillor remarked: "public space resolves two problems ... the function of receiving the residual activities of the city for many years ... [and] opening of the neighbourhood to the city ..." (cited in Degen, 2002: 27–28). Or, as a city planner said, it means that "people like us are moving in" (cited in Degen, 2002: 28). The difficulty, for visitors, is that el Raval seems to be becoming a finished space, its streets set out like the backdrop of a stage for the new cultural and professional elite's performance of their public lives. The evident design of the spaces, their aestheticisation, rather than gradual accumulation of an appearance through everyday occupation and use, renders the stroller's experience – the tourist in such a district still the disinterested observer, the *flâneur* – passive, as if consuming the place but not interacting with it. It is hard to imagine any alternative future for el Raval now than as a cultural zone, and this closure, this passivity, renders it moribund. The difficulty is not that local cultures (in the broad sense, as ways of living) are threatened with erosion as in Bergen's fish market, because in Barcelona the local cultures are probably strong enough and the city big enough to absorb cultural tourism, but that these cultures will be subsumed in high culture.

Conclusion

If the aestheticisation of space which is frequently encountered in urban redevelopment, driven by cultural or heritage tourism and the identification of new markets in consumption, tends to imprint a sameness so that the local colour, or difference, which may be the basis of a city's tourism promotion becomes an increasingly standardised product, then it is self-defeating. When so many cities construct niches through which to market their locally coloured images, the niche may in the end take prominence over its content. The image of the city in cultural tourism contrasts with how cities are spoken of in literature. As Stephen Barber says, for instance:

> The landscapes of the European cities are unevenly textured, apoplexically dense with housing blocks in one quarter, vapidly empty and pitted in other areas; the populations concurrently amass and respire, the streets dense with over-inscription and overuse in one district, under-determined and depopulated in other zones. The presence of the lost populations of Europe is marked into the cities as their counterface, the violent negation which enduringly aggravates the structure of the contemporary city, congesting or voiding it: and haunting it. The surviving European city is a conglomeration of renewed buildings and populations, grafted onto the scorched gaps between the remaining buildings and populations. (Barber, 1995: 37)

He concludes this passage in *Fragments of the European City* by saying that the city either envelops or abjects, its future delineated by the traces of its expulsions. Elsewhere he writes of a demolition site, of the escape it offers from the ordering of life, a counter to institutionalisation and routine.

Somewhere in this is a search for something other than what the dominant society dishes up – hope for a better world. The hope may be attached to representations of otherness, or to religious belief or philosophical conjecture. Its forms in tourism are exploitative yet still denote a hope, if one constrained within what the tourism industry makes available. But there are difficulties: the quest for another world projected onto distanced sites does violence to the places and lives it appropriates, and in so doing distracts attention from the causes of dissatisfaction in social and economic organisation at home. And it does something strange to the subject (self), as Stewart writes in *On Longing*: the souvenir depends on a separation not only from the exoticised place: "It must be clear that the object is estranged from the context in which it will be displayed as a souvenir" (Stewart, 1993: 149). The exotic souvenir is a sign of survival, but it is of "... the survival of the possessor outside his or her own context of familiarity. Its otherness speaks to the possessor's capacity for otherness: it is the possessor, not the souvenir, which is ultimately the curiosity" (Stewart, 1993: 148). The African mask, carved in a village and purchased in a city market or at an airport (Steiner, 1994), signifies the tourist's survival of a journey, not to the interior as was once said, but to the exterior, as in another way does the carrier bag from the Museum of Modern Art, or the snapshot of rough street life in el Raval.

CHAPTER 5

Consuming Space: The Architectures of Consumption

In this chapter we turn to the consumption of goods, with a specific focus on the spaces which house new forms of urban consumption in the nineteenth and twentieth centuries: the arcade and the mall; and we see an extension of a culture of consumption in new forms of real estate. The arcade and the mall are architectural forms specific to new kinds of consumption. Both are enclosed, artificial worlds of consumption in which display is emphasised; both are found in proximity to large centres of population (the arcade in metropolitan cities, the mall in outer urban sites); and both depend on consumption beyond the meeting of everyday needs. Both also relate to other sites of display with which they are contemporary. The array of goods in an arcade, as later in a department store, resembles that found in international exhibitions such as the 1851 Great Exhibition in London, or 1855, 1867, 1878, and 1889 Universal Expositions in Paris. Similarly, the mall uses techniques of display found in the theme park. But the arcade differs from the mall in offering luxury goods to an entrepreneurial class in city-centre sites, rather than a mix of mass-market chain stores and fast-food outlets as well as boutiques in suburban sites. But if consumption in the mall seems democratised, we suggest it is also highly regulated.

We begin, then, by reconsidering the arcades of Paris in the nineteenth century, citing Walter Benjamin's *Passagenarbeit*, or *Arcades Project*, in a recent edition in English (1999). We note the gendering of spaces of consumption (Rendell, 2002), and Benjamin's perception, nonetheless, of a utopian aspect to the arcades. We mention the department stores which replaced the arcades in the 1860s, before looking to Margaret Crawford's critique of the mall (1992) and, in passing, Michael Sorkin's of the theme park (1992). Then, moving from shopping to dwelling, we turn to new urbanism in North America and what we see as the transfer of a culture of consumption and surveillance from the mall to housing. The gated apartment complexes and gentrified urban districts which constitute new urbanism represent the constraints, often presented as opportunities, of a consumerist lifestyle. Our specific focus is on the Disney Company's venture into real estate at Celebration, Florida. We use academic (MacCannell, 1999) and journalistic (Drew, 1998; Frantz and Collins, 2000) sources to ask in what frameworks we can situate Celebration.

A question which arises throughout the chapter is whether consumers can regain any power in a situation which offers seemingly unending choice but where the only available option is consumption itself (often without the goods as such being the site of value, which is found in signs, such as the logo). In Chapter 8 we extend this argument by asking the further question as to how far alternative scenarios to that of relentless consumption might be available today.

The arcades

As it appeared in Paris and other major European cities in the early nineteenth century, the arcade constituted a new architectural space designed for a new form of urban consumption. This was enabled by the growth of metropolitan cities as centres of manufacture and commerce in which an entrepreneurial class provided a market for luxury goods and a growing middle class sought to ape their conspicuous consumption. Metropolitan cities were also hubs of rail networks bringing consumers into the city from suburban and provincial centres, and sites of new kinds of sociation as well as anonymity amidst a kaleidoscopic array of shifting visual sensations – as Georg Simmel argues in his essay "The Metropolis and Mental Life" ([1903] 1990). Among such new sites (before Simmel) is the arcade of luxury shops and restaurants. The new *experience* of consumption, then, is not an act of meeting daily needs. It gives rise to a consuming gaze which ingests visually as it responds to the invitation to locate desire in goods, and is enabled by architectural design as the eye is guided towards parallel lines of window displays (which reflect back the image of the person gazing) in a glass-roofed space set apart from the rest of the city.

The form of a vaulted pedestrian space was not new. Two sides of London's Covent Garden, designed by Inigo Jones in 1640, are lined by buildings with arched galleries at ground level. A similar form is characteristic of the commercial centre of Lisbon rebuilt after the earthquake of 1755, notably Praça de Comércio, designed by the military engineer Eugénio dos Santos (Maxwell, 2002: 34–37). But these arcades, like those of the modern extension of Turin (or Renaissance Livorno, one of Inigo Jones' sources), are open on one side to a street or square. They are spaces of public mixing under cover. What is new in the arcades of Paris, as in the Burlington Arcade in London and the Galleria Vittorio Emanuel in Milan, is that they are enclosed on both sides, roofed in glass, cut through city blocks, and dedicated not to the sociable activities of the public street but to consumption.

The arcades themselves were as luxuriant as the goods displayed in them, and exhibited the most advanced technologies of building and lighting in their glass and cast iron vaults and gas-lamps. Lined by shops faced in marble and polished wood, they constituted a world apart which opened as if magically behind the grey facades of the street. Benjamin cites a Parisian journal of 1852:

> These arcades, a new invention of industrial luxury, are glass-covered marble-panelled corridors extending through whole blocks of buildings, whose proprietors have joined together for such enterprises. Lining both sides of these corridors, which get their light from above, are the most elegant shops...the arcade is a city, a world in miniature... in which customers will find everything they need. (Benjamin, 1999: 31)

This world in miniature was an artificial world engendering artificial behaviour. Benjamin notes accounts of taking a tortoise out walking and of smoking in the arcades before it was customary to do so in the public street. He quotes the photographer Nadar: "In all the shops...the oak counter is adorned with counterfeit coins, in every kind of metal..." (Benjamin, 1999: 41, 44) to draw attention to the artificiality of the arcades as an urban space, an artificiality which is also intriguing.

Many arcades were grouped in an area between Rue Croix-des-Petits-Champs, Rue de la Grange-Batelière, Rue Ventador, and Boulevard Sebastapol. Here the narrow streets were, until the 1870s, crowded by carriages, making the arcades attractive to pedestrians (Benjamin, 1999: 37). Most were built in the 1820s and 1830s, replacing previous rows of shops open to the elements. To give a few examples: Passage Viollet (1820), Passage des Deux Pavillions (1820), Passage des Panoramas (1823, redeveloped in 1831), Passage de l'Opéra (1823, illustrated Benjamin, 1999: 49), Passage Vivienne (in 1825, illustrated Benjamin, 1999: 35), and Passage Véro-Dodat, built by two pork butchers

(1823–1826, illustrated Benjamin, 1999: 34). The last, Passage de Princes, was opened in 1860, though by then the arcades had begun to decline. Some specialised in one commodity – Passage du Caire in lithographic reproductions, for instance – while others contained a mix of outlets. Among trades listed by Benjamin for Passage des Panoramas are a music shop, a wine merchant, a hosier, a haberdasher, tailors, bootmakers, bookshops, a restaurant, and a caricaturist. Although a few catered to everyday needs – Passage du Saumon for fish, site of a confrontation between workers and troops in 1832 (Benjamin, 1999: 46–47) – most dealt in items of fashion or taste, and were fashionable places to promenade. Above hosiers, haberdashers, and milliners shops were rooms where young female assistants finished goods and prepared them for sale. Soon, these upper rooms became, too, and remained into the time of Benjamin's researches, spaces of erotic encounter. Benjamin reproduces a card: "Angela – 2nd floor, to the right" (Benjamin, 1999: 40).

When Benjamin began to study them in the 1920s, the arcades were semi-derelict or, like Passage de l'Opéra, listed for demolition. Those in use contained second-hand and curio shops, toy shops, and detective agencies rather than milliners or boutiques. In their decay, Benjamin saw the arcades as dreamworlds in which layers of past time remained present. This is what he documents in the *Arcades Project*, using a method of organisation as systematic as the indexing of a library or museum collection. Yet the project was also a commentary, if largely in the words of others collected as if in a scrap-book. It owes something to Surrealism, which Benjamin saw as an interesting failure, and to Louis Aragon's novel *Paris Peasant* published in 1926 (Highmore, 2003: 55–62). Aragon's sense of "the marvellous suffusing everyday existence" (Aragon, cited in Highmore, 2003: 56) is like Benjamin's perception of the poetic or dreamlike in incidental appearances. Writing on the use of mirrors in the arcades, and citing the French Symbolist artist Odilon Redon, he says, "The whispering of gazes fills the arcades. There is no thing here that does not, where one least expects it, open a fugitive eye ..." (Benjamin, 1999: 542). One thing shifts into another, its outward form mutable as its context changes (as in Surrealism): "If a shoemaker's shop should be neighbour to a confectioner's, then his festoons of bootlaces will resemble rolls of liquorice" (Benjamin, 1999: 872). A sense of interpenetrating layers of time and meaning is, too, contextualised by a refusal of the linear notion of Progress in Baudelaire, on whom Benjamin writes extensively (Benjamin, 1999: 228–387, see also "Critical Method – on the Modern Idea of Progress as Applied to the Fine Arts",

Baudelaire's review of the 1855 Paris Universal Exposition, in Harrison *et al.*, 1998: 485–489).

Because pasts remain present, they awake dreams which do not go away. One such dream is utopian: a collective dream awakened by encounters during ordinary life. Susan Buck-Morss notes Benjamin's "secular, sociopsychological theory of modernity as a dreamworld... [a] collective 'awakening' from it as synonymous with revolutionary class consciousness" (Buck-Morss, 1989: 253). The idea is taken further by French Marxist philosopher Henri Lefebvre in his *Critique of Everyday Life* [1974] (1991). Lefebvre sees breaks from routine, as in leisure, as subverting productivity so that, as Rob Shields puts it, "in the spaces of leisure, resistance through folly and unproductiveness, escape and denial, are normalised in a perpetual Mardi Gras..." (Shields, 1999: 98). For Benjamin, drawing on nineteenth-century sources such as the utopian socialist Charles Fourier, the imagined better world is a realm of plenty available to all. The array of goods in an arcade conjures an intimation of plentifulness as well as the desire for consumption the sellers intend. This imagined plenty is not mere fantasy because, as utopian socialists argued, mass production has a capacity to solve the problem of scarcity. In a commentary on Benjamin, Richard Wolin writes that "... with capitalism's tremendous unleashing of productive forces, utopia has become a real possibility" (Wolin, 1994: 176); and Esther Leslie that "Utopias – for Benjamin their devising is a constant in history – always appear as in the form of fantasies about the deployment of technology to humane ends" (Leslie, 2000: 157). Wolin continues,

> In Benjamin's eyes, the tremendous productive capacities of capitalism could not help but call to mind the deficient state of the *relations of production* in which those capacities remained shackled, relations which led to a growing polarization of wealth ... (Wolin, 1994: 177)

Utopia, then, is in the eye of the beholder but remains a real possibility. The experience of consumption in the metropolitan setting of the arcades allows a collective dreaming which activates a buried desire for a more luxurious and relaxed existence. The refusal of productivity by types such as the poet and the dandy, or the idler – exemplified by Baudelaire – add to a sense that another kind of world is possible even if denied by capitalist exchange.

Benjamin did not develop his understanding of utopian thought as a fully articulated theory, as Ernst Bloch did in *The Principle of Hope*

([1959] 1986). But he and Bloch had many conversations during the 1920s, and Bloch writes of a Land of Cockaigne where "All human beings are equal...there is neither effort nor work. Roast pigeons fly into people's mouths" (Bloch, 1986: 472); and Benjamin of "images in the collective consciousness...[in which] the collective seeks both to overcome and to transfigure the immaturity of the social product and the inadequacies of the social organization of production" (Benjamin, 1999: 4, in Wolin, 1994: 175). He says, too, that "...what Bloch recognizes as the darkness of the lived moment, is nothing other than what here is secured on the level of the historical, and collectively" (Benjamin, 1999: 883). Wandering in the arcades, reading the traces of Baudelaire's Paris, Benjamin dreams of an awakening. If, as he says, "Capitalism was a natural phenomenon with which a new dream-filled sleep came over Europe, and, through it, a reactivation of mythical forces" (Benjamin, 1999: 391), the task was (is) to excavate the content of utopian consciousness glimpsed in the display of commodities.

Commodities take on meanings projected onto them by spectators. These are outside utility and outside the mechanism of exchange, unlike transactions in a marketplace. Alluding to this, Graeme Gilloch describes the arcades as "theatres of purchases" which served as "...the home of the dream-objects of the modern metropolis...the setting, or rather the stage, for the display and exhibition of the commodity" (Gilloch, 1996: 126). Consumers are actors, and the goods displayed, like the painted signs over the shops, figure in the vocabulary of a dreaming collectivity. But that display, the spectacle, has another aspect in the fetish character of commodity display. While a utopian desire can be awakened, commodities can also draw the spectator into a dreamy mystique which arises from the separation of the gazing observer from the object gazed upon, so that the gazed-upon object begins to stand for, or embody, the gazers' desires. Benjamin may have derived his thinking on this in part from Simmel. In *The Philosophy of Money*, in a passage which could be compared to texts by both Benjamin and Bloch, Simmel states that

[o]nly a new process of awareness releases those categories [subject and object] from their undisturbed unity; and only then is the pure enjoyment of the content seen as being on the one hand a state of the subject confronting an object, and on the other the effect produced by an object that is independent of the subject...In desiring what we do not yet own or enjoy, we place the content of our desire outside ourselves...We desire objects only if they are not immediately given

to us for our use and enjoyment, that is the extent that they resist our desire. The content of our desire becomes an object as soon as it is exposed to us...as something not-yet-enjoyed. (Simmel, [1907] 1990: 66)

Money makes distances, and is the means of exchange in which anything can be compared in value to anything else. It is a cold medium – David Harvey cites Emile Zola's *L'Argent* (1885): "It is very difficult to write a novel about money...cold, glacial, devoid of interest" (cited in Harvey, 1989: 166) – but the operations of a money economy become charged when the price of an item represents a consumer's desire for it rather than a reflection of its cost of production or use value.

Money separates producers from consumers, and decrees who can or cannot purchase goods. It facilitates a separation of subject from object, or consumer from that which is or might be consumed. Veblen's [1899] (1970) theory of conspicuous consumption by the leisured class is relevant here, but Simmel and Benjamin add to it an understanding that the attraction of commodities, the hold they exert over consumers and would-be consumers, is psychological as well as social. Harvey hints at this fusion of object and a desire produced independently but imprinted on it: "Money and exchange across the world market turn the metropolis into a veritable bordello of consumer temptation..." (Harvey, 1989: 176). The operative word is "bordello". Benjamin writes: "Love for the prostitute is the apotheosis of empathy with the commodity" (Benjamin, 1999: 511).

Desires can be consuming when external stimuli connect to drives striving for expression in what Freud calls the *Es* (translated *id*, though Freud does not latinise his terms) regulated by the *Ich* (*ego*) in consciousness (Freud, [1926] 1962: 100–109). The *Ich*, however, is open to manipulation by the market, so that fetishised commodities appear to market themselves. More can be said of this, as in Rachel Bowlby's Freudian interpretation of literary representations of consumption and pleasure in *Shopping with Freud* (1993), but that is outside our scope. Benjamin, in any case, makes few references to Freud in the *Arcades Project* – and those only in relation to Proust and gambling, not the consumption of goods. His view of commodity fetishism derives more from Marx, whom he quotes at length (Benjamin, 1999: 651–670), and from historical accounts of the arcades and his own experiences in them. He notes a set of nineteenth-century lithographs: "...women reclining voluptuously on ottomans in a draperied, crepuscular boudoir...*On the Banks of the Tagus, On the Banks of the Neva, On the*

Banks of the Seine . . . It was up to the . . . caption inscribed beneath them, to conjure a fantasy landscape over the represented interiors" (Benjamin, 1999: 213). Perhaps the standardisation was, anyway, appropriate since all the images took the same imprint. Detached from the genres denoted falsely by the captions, then, they correspond to what Adorno terms phantasmagoria: "a consumer item in which there is no longer anything that is supposed to remind us how it came into being . . . a magical object, insofar as the labour stored up in it comes to seem supernatural . . ." (Adorno, 1939: 17, in Benjamin, 1999: 669). Benjamin sees the autonomy claimed for modern art in this concealing of the work which makes the thing (Benjamin, 1999: 670), but its principal form – in the twentieth century as in the nineteenth – is the commodity.

Robert Witkin gives a summary of the Marxist position:

> Capitalism is portrayed by Marx as a system that progressively destroys the individual's sense of himself [*sic*] as participating, ordering, shaping and making his world. To that extent, the world is opaque to the subject. What stands apart from us in our consciousness . . . appears self-possessed . . . it becomes a fetish-object. Its qualities and powers are projected onto it by individuals who then submit to them as though they truly were powers originating outside themselves . . . From here it is easy to move into the Freudian realm of psychopathology and to see . . . that psychoses . . . can be assimilated to a discourse of capitalist economic relations . . . (Witkin, 2003: 4)

The commodity thus puts the consumer in a disempowered, dependent relation to it. And just as glimpses of a utopian realm might be gained in the arcades, or in everyday life, so arrays of commodities which suggest plenitude may also exhibit a standardisation of form to suit the market. For Adorno this is the character of mass culture: " . . . Adorno believed that all these media helped to reinforce the regressive and dependent personality" (Witkin, 2003: 5). But for Benjamin there is a social as well as cultural dimension: "The property appertaining to the commodity as its fetish character attaches as well to the commodity-producing society . . . as it represents itself and thinks to understand itself whenever it abstracts from the fact that it produces precisely commodities. The image that it produces . . . corresponds to the concept of phantasmagoria" (Benjamin, 1999: 669).

Benjamin's view of commodity consumption is that it evinces utopian ideas but also dependency. This complementarity runs through his work in juxtapositions of past and present, construction and demolition, flâneurs and pickpockets, dream and reality, history and trace. A model of conscious and unconscious zones of psyche is reflected in the duality of the arcades above ground and subterranean passages, springs, and catacombs below: an underworld "full of inconspicuous places from which dreams arise" (Benjamin, 1999: 84). But the arcades and the dark labyrinth beneath the city are disjoined and cannot simply be connected. The fetish gives form to a desire which remains impossible to grasp (like Eurydice in the myth of Orpheus). This is evident in the inversion of eros in sexual fetishism:

> In fetishism, sex does away with the boundaries separating the organic world from the inorganic. Clothing and jewelry are its allies. It is as much at home with what is dead as it is with living flesh. The latter, moreover, shows it the way to establish itself in the former. (Benjamin, 1999: 69)

and in contrast to the real-potential of utopian aspirations, which Bloch seeks to establish as like a Freudian drive ([1959] 1986).

The arcades became identified as sites of sexual transaction and transgression, their gaslight lending such transactions a warm glow. Jane Rendell writes that in fiction and non-fiction, "arcades feature as sites of dangerous sexualities in the city...depicted as places of trans-gressive sexual activity" (Rendell, 1999: 169). She refers here to the Burlington Arcade in London, but the point can be applied to those of Paris, too. In Emile Zola's novel *Thérèse Raquin*, for instance, an erotic encounter is set in a room over a haberdasher's shop in Passage du Pont Neuf: "As soon as he set foot in the arcade, he felt a strong tinge of anticipation...(Zola, *Thérèse Raquin*, in Benjamin, 1999: 875; Rendell, 1999: 168). But the arcades were also places where women could mix and consume outside the constraints of the domestic interior. Elizabeth Wilson (1991: 156) argues in *The Sphinx in the City* that "...life in the great city offers the potential for greater freedom and diversity...This is particularly important for women" and Rendell in *The Pursuit of Pleasure* (2002) that "through the development of commodity capitalism... women were encouraged into the city as consumers, both for the home and for themselves". Of course, these were mainly middle-class women while the sex workers were mainly lower class. Women's freedom in the city was compromised, too, by their roles as sellers of goods, or as pur-chasers for others in patriarchal families. Shops hired female assistants to finish goods, wrap and deliver them, and deal with customers. They were required to dress well and be knowledgeable, paid less than factory workers (Wilson, 1991: 49), and seen by men as among the arcade's gazed-on attractions. As Rendell says, women are represented as objects of visual pleasure "in order to sell goods". But she continues that historically it was in sites of consumption as "legitimated zones of pleasure" that "women's presence (as consumers) was most obviously felt in the city" (Rendell, 2002: 17), while social codes restricted them otherwise to sites of production or reproduction – the mill or the domestic interior. Perhaps, then, there is another utopian potential in the arcades, apart from that of plenitude seen by Benjamin.

The department store and the mall

By the 1860s, the arcades had been replaced as principal sites of bourgeois consumption by department stores. During the same period, under Napoleon III (elected Emperor in 1851), the centre of Paris was remodelled by its prefect, Baron Haussmann. Wide streets cut through the old working-class quarters of the inner city to act as free-fire zones in the suppression of unrest, a new central market hall was built, and the new boulevards which eased circulation through and out of the city were lined with middle-class apartment buildings. Speculators made fortunes by lending money to the city, the government, and the middle-class owners of the new apartments (Short, 1996: 176–179; Pile *et al.*, 1999: 110–116). The poor were peripheralised, and the sex-workers banned from the arcades (though they had returned when Benjamin carried out his work).

Inside, the department stores were designed like exhibition halls, with goods of each kind collected in one place, or department. They had window displays on the street but human interaction in conversations between shoppers and assistants and the appearance of assistants was seen as being at least as important as that of the displays of goods. The stores were managed to maximise consumption, and conveyed an impression that assistants were informed and interested collaborators. Margaret Crawford writes of the contrast between a shopper's dream-world, as in Zola's *Au Bonheur des Dames*, and the actualities of economic relations necessitating a constant turnover of goods, standardised modes of organisation, and regulation of staff: "A strict hierarchy separated the sales clerks, drilled in middle-class manners and housed in attic dormitories, from the proletariat that staffed the workshops and stables and slept wherever they could" (Crawford, 1992: 18). This rigid organisation persists into the twentieth century, without the dormitories and the stables. A 1921 US handbook for assistants states:

> In a retail store, you have a wonderful chance to study human beings. Don't you think it is interesting to look at men and women and to wonder about them? Who are they? What are their chief characteristics? Why do they act and talk as they do? Where are they going? For what purposes do they buy various articles? (Leigh, 1921: 110, cited in Bowlby, 1993: 97)

Benjamin notes that with department stores "...consumers begin to consider themselves a mass" while the goods are seen as unique – "With the appearance of mass-produced articles, the concept of speciality arises" (Benjamin, 1999: 43). James Carrier argues that "Mass...marketing appeared as shopkeepers increasingly sought individual transactions with unknown buyers" (Carrier, 1995: 75, in Finn, 2001: 90). A similar trajectory can be seen today in themed restaurants and fast-food outlets, where a completely controlled product, and one which hardly differs between competing chains, is made to seem distinctive by the theme used in the environment. Increasingly, the themes reflect current interests in the entertainment industry and mass media (Gottdiener, 2000: 271–274), creating an illusion that standardised products partake of the mystique of a world of film stars and fantasy narratives.

Department stores gave an impression of affluence through opulent modern architecture. Crossick and Jauman point out that,

> The department stores were highly visible, through their architectural presence and their ostentatious publicity, and this very visibility was one reason why they became a symbol of modernity...modern in design, in sales methods, in the application of new technology to the act of retailing and to the art of attracting customers" (Crosswick and Jauman, 1999, in Finn, 2001: 89).

Similarly, Gail Reekie describes the interior of McWirter's store in Brisbane, Australia, during the Edwardian period as having fittings of polished wood, glass showcases and cabinets, expensive carpets, lavish mirrors, and small parlours where women could contemplate the arrays of fashion goods on offer. Through subsequent evolutions of retail trade, the department store retains a feeling of a (middle class) shopper's utopia. Its goods appear as emblems of a desired lifestyle, in its way an aspired-to culture. Large department stores still occupy key sites in shopping streets such as Oxford Street in London, employing artists to provide vibrant and today sometimes challenging (but highly visible) window displays. It is still common for a new development to seek to attract a branch of one or more well-known stores as a magnet for other less prominent outlets. This applies, too, in the mall, most frequently an architecturally indifferent construction though one of the first, the Southdale Centre at Edina near Minneapolis (1956), was designed like the Galleria Vittorio Emanuel, Milan.

The development of malls parallels that of heritage culture sites such as Faneuil Hall Marketplace, Boston and South Street Seaport, New York (Boyer, 1992) noted in Chapter 4. Margaret Crawford sees the key period for mall development as 1960–1980 when developers "methodically surveyed, divided, and appropriated suburban cornfields and orange groves to create a new landscape of consumption" according to regional demographies (Crawford, 1992: 7). A regional mall serves a twenty-mile radius, with at least a hundred outlets including two department stores. Just as the arcades attracted strollers through display, malls draw in consumers through choice. Typically there is a large number of outlets, though a chain may have more than one shop in the same mall, and mix of stores catering for high and middle incomes. The critical mass may include a cultural attraction, such as a museum display or art gallery, or a theme park, alongside more overt sites of consumption.

Crawford writes of the West Edmonton mall as "...an ungainly pile of over-sized boxes plunked down in the middle of an enormous asphalt sea" when seen from above. But it contains in its 5.2 million square feet "a dizzying spectacle of attractions and diversions..." where "past and future collapse meaninglessly into the present; barriers between real and fake, near and far, dissolve as history, nature, technology, are indifferently processed" (Crawford, 1992: 3–4). West Edmonton is international in its catchment, with over 800 retail outlets (only a few of which are local), 110 food outlets, twenty cinemas, thirteen nightclubs, eleven department stores, a hotel, an ice-rink, a lake, a replica of Columbus' *Santa Maria*, an automaton jazz band, real wildlife including penguins, and a chapel. Architecturally, its interior facades mimic those of nineteenth-century New Orleans and Paris, but in one place. The goods offered for sale, as they were in the arcades, are said to be the best available and the range of consumer choice is crushing. Yet it is also very limited. For the most part, at West Edmonton, "...the mall's mixture of American and Canadian chains...rigorously repeats the range of products offered at every other shopping mall" (Crawford, 1992: 4). Perhaps, then, the mall offers less than the arcades. At the same time, the mall borrows from the architectural model of the international exhibition or trade fair, just as the arcade echoed some aspects of the international expositions of the nineteenth century.

Penelope Harvey (1996: 135) sees recent international exhibitions such as the 1992 Expo, Seville as adapting the model of universal exhibitions for a globalised economy, actualising "principles of spectacle and surveillance simultaneously" while inducing in Foucault's terms, as she says, a disciplined reflex from consumers. The reflex is facilitated in part by the physical environment of the mall. In one of the earlier North American malls, at San Diego, the exterior wall is a blank facade. Pedestrian entrances are hard to find, and inside there are many levels connected by diagonally leaping escalators. The effect is one of disorientation, the city visible at all only from the highest level, as space is fragmented and the same chains make repeat appearances in different visual styles. The architecture is neon but also postmodern-eclectic, with references to Italian piazze as well as south-west adobe. Everything is designed to retain the consumer for as long as possible, as if shopping were leisure. Crawford writes (of malls generally): "Sealed off from the tasks of everyday life, shopping became a recreational activity and the mall an escapist cocoon" (Crawford, 1992: 22).

The Mall of America at Bloomington, Minnesota, developed by the same company as the West Edmonton Mall, opened in August 1992, with more than 4 million square feet of interior space, 2.5 million of which is given over to retailing. There are more than 400 shops, 45 food outlets, four department stores, three hotels, a convention centre and a 14-screen cinema, nightclubs, bars, and a seven-acre theme park with living vegetation in a controlled climate. The theme park has its own 14 restaurants and 23 amusement rides. Gottdiener cites the mall's promotional literature as saying it could contain 88 football fields, 20 basilicas the size of St Peter's in Rome, or five Red Squares; and notes the designation of its four main sections using downtown-like terms: Main Street USA (in the north), West Market, South Avenue, and East Broadway (Gottdiener, 2000: 276). This draws attention to the city-centre shopping districts that malls have tended to render defunct, relocating centres to suburbs in keeping with the shift of middle-income publics through the post-war period. The mall also, as Crawford remarks, adds to its suburban ambience the one thing suburbs never have – the cosmopolitan feeling of a city centre. The city is thereby re-constructed, minus the ordinary and the awkward bits, as a zone of safety which has, in simulation, the variety of space and function of downtown. In some cases, high-rise apartment blocks, office parks, and hospitals have been located in proximity. But there are two crucial differences: first, the mall is private not public space: Crawford cites signs reading "Areas in this mall used by the public are not public ways . . . Permission to use said ways may be revoked at any time" (Crawford, 1992: 23). Secondly, while city centres tend to be cumulative in development, mixing architectural periods and styles without a unifying theme, malls appropriate themes to lend identity to non-places. Gottdiener writes: "As a specific destination, malls require some overarching means of identification . . . an image meant to be attractive to potential consumers" (Gottdiener, 2000: 275). Such images are increasingly found in the media, so that merchandising by media companies sells clothing and food, which in turn sell videos and other media products, or in ersatz history as in heritage malls.

Early heritage malls such as Faneuil Hall Market and Harbor Place, Baltimore were influenced by Disney (Boniface and Fowler, 1993: 147). Disney's "imagineering" reduces the world to a nicely packaged set of commodities, re-presenting the spectacle as a totality which the visitor is invited to discover as she or he travels a simulated globe – Mexico is only a few minutes away from China – while international pavilions offer kitsch versions of national cultures. Countries are thus reduced to signs of their pasts – Norway is Vikings and Japan Samurai – and authenticity re-programmed through technological enterprise. Michael Sorkin writes of Disneyland (founded in 1955) that a ". . . monumentalized commodity fetishism is reduced to the pith of a haiku" (Sorkin, 1992: 216), and argues that the system is validated by the visitor's choice of going there,

> One has gone nowhere in spite of the equivalent ease of going somewhere . . . has preferred the simulation to the reality . . . The urbanism of Disneyland is precisely the urbanism of universal equivalence. In this new city, the idea of distinct places is dispersed into a sea of universal placelessness as everyplace becomes destination and any destination can be anyplace (Sorkin, 1992: 216–217).

He concludes that "Disneyzone", as he terms it, is a hyper-city with billions of consumers but no residents, a world without crime, litter, and surliness (Sorkin, 1992: 231). One might add substance abuse and domestic violence, and that the visitors pay handsomely for the privilege, staying in Disney hotels and eating in Disney-themed food outlets as well as going on the rides and buying the souvenirs. The pattern is increasingly replicated in theme parks and malls, including local developments such as Universal City Walk in Los Angeles, a shopping development by Universal Studios.

Universal City has just 38 boutiques, restaurants, and amusement attractions. It is pedestrianised (beyond the parking garage), has palm trees, no graffiti, and draws up to 25,000 visitors/consumers a day. Andy Beckett sees a darker side to this "shopping citadel", linking it to concerns for security and surveillance. Quoting its designer, he notes that it is a *replacement* [his emphasis] for Los Angeles: "... a compact, clean alternative to the scattered, dirty city" insulated from "trouble-makers", where entry is free but parking and eating expensive, and the nearest bus stop fifteen minutes away. It cost twice as much as *Jurassic Park* to build and rents are twice the local average, so its outlets use the notion of speciality to cover costs – autographed basketballs selling at $399.95, for instance, and novelty two-foot slices of rubber toast at $69.95. To lend a civilised aspect there is a University of California annex selling courses in media studies (Beckett, 1994, in Pile *et al.*, 1999: 147). But just as culture is imported to the mall, so the mall colours the operations of cultural institutions whose shops and restaurants are increasingly integral to their marketing. Crawford concludes, citing the extension to the National Gallery of Art in Washington DC, that the only reason goods are no longer the most prominent entity of global consumption is that "... history, technology, and art ... have now become commodified" (Crawford, 1992: 30). Esther Leslie's view of Tate Modern as "a brand that markets art experience" (Leslie, 2001: 3, cited in Chapter 4) confirms this. And the site of dwelling, too, is now, for those who can afford choices, a commodity.

Celebration: housing as commodity

Celebration, Florida, is a new town developed by the Disney Company. Not surprisingly, aspects of the theme park pervade its design and operation. Celebration is promoted as an American small town with a low crime rate and ample public space. It has white picket fences and colonial-style facades. From a distance, it constitutes an amalgam of the factors which define urban living: proximity of all functions, heterogen-eity, and liberty. From within, the view may differ. Celebration epit-omises new urbanism in North America.

The context for Celebration is the globalisation of capital. This is not the only form of global networking: communications using e-mail and the internet, and resistance (as in demonstrations against bodies such as the World Trade Organisation) are also global today; but the global flow of capital is the dominant aspect of the post-industrial economy. Zygmunt Bauman (1998) sets out its human consequences, contrasting the increase in mobility enjoyed by the rich with an increase in controls on movement by the poor and migrant. He notes that trans-national companies can avoid local regulatory interventions by appeal to trans-national organisations reflecting their interests. It might be argued that capitalism is stronger than ever. And, as Bauman also observes, security is a prime concern. The outcome is a global spread of gated apartment complexes, not only in places where they might be expected such as Los Angeles, but in the non-affluent world as well. Jeremy Seabrook writes of such a complex in Delhi:

> The only sound in the still morning was of the sweeper's brush as she scooped up the fallen petals of the bougainvillaea. Servants moved with muffled footsteps on cold marble. At the gate, shrouded in a thick blanket, the *chowkidar* (watchman) sat with his gun... (Seabrook, 1996: 211).

Seabrook finds the scene frightening, signifying a fear on the part of the global affluent class which none of their security measures will appease. At the next social level, of middle managers, the owners of small businesses, and professionals such as lawyers and doctors, Seabrook finds a reflection of the gated complexes (whose occupants shop internationally) in more modest but still protected condominiums: "These are the people for whose purchasing power the malls and gallerias compete" (Seabrook, 1996: 212). Elsewhere he writes of another Delhi whose inhabitants glean what they can:

> After a night of torrential rain, the poor who sleep on the streets are drying out; clothes and bedrolls on railings and improvised washing lines between the trees... The conditions in the factories are reminiscent of Engels's descriptions of England in 1844. The units are dirty and cramped. Often there is no drinking water, and the temperature inside the factories is far higher than the 40°C heat outside... (Seabrook, 1993: 61–62).

The two sets of conditions illustrated by these verbal snapshots are complementary, and there is nothing new in this except the scale of variance. As Conrad Lodziak (2002: 141) notes, citing Elizabeth Dore (1992: 73), in 1890 the per capita wealth of Europe was twice that of

China or India, while in 1990 it was seventy times. But the scale of
difference is startling, too, within the affluent society, as Engels saw in
Manchester in 1844, concluding from his walks through the sites of
dire poverty that the impoverishment of industrial workers was (is)
a consequence, not a failure, of the system of production and its spatial
organisation. James Donald glosses: "Poverty is what makes the display
of wealth possible" (Donald, 1999: 35).

Perhaps what is also new, in the globalised world, is the extreme
separation of wealth from evidence or sight of poverty. Hence in cities
such as New York, homeless people are cleared from the streets. Peter
Marcuse writes of the independence of the wealthy from cities which
have become hugely profitable to them, noting that 75 per cent of New
York's chief executives lived outside the city in 1975, and that those
who do remain are insulated by walls and security systems. He continues:

> The new architecture of shopping malls, skywalks, and policed
> pedestrian malls is a striking physical mirror of the social separation.
> Downtown skywalks, for instance, both symbolically and physically,
> permit the men and women of business to walk over the heads of the
> poor and the menial (Marcuse, 2002: 95).

According to Freud, what is repressed returns, if in a mutated form. An
application of this to a whole society implies that, as was genuinely
feared in Victorian London, the poor and vagrant, mythicised as an
excluded underclass, will errupt in riot; this irrational but explicable fear
produces a fortification now of the urban environment – as in suburban
Los Angeles as represented by Mike Davis in *City of Quartz* (1990),
whose description of armed response signs on neatly manicured lawns is
frequently cited. Davis also describes the strategies used to deny homeless people access to city spaces, such as fountains which operate randomly in places where they might sleep, but he seems drawn into his
dystopian story, linking the city's trajectory to that of the disaster
movie (see Miles M., 2003; Miles, S., 2003); Edward Soja comments (2000:
300–303) that he ignores the self-organisation of marginalised groups,
though his emphasis on the encroachment of the privatised on public
space is, we suggest, accurate (see also Davis, 2000, cited in Chapter 4).

New urbanism arises in this cultural-economic climate. It is an
expression of privatisation, fusing urban planning and architectural design.
Its products include the construction of new towns, or gentrification of
city districts, as model (middle- and high-income) communities in an
era when genuine senses of community seem lost. If contemporary cities

are dangerous, new settlements which visually mimic the safe old days, protected by the latest surveillance while strictly regulating entry, are an escape. The new urbanists have learned from the dislike of standardisation and low density in suburban development (MacCannell, 1999: 107), and introduce a selective diversity of architectural type and style. Soja cites Seaside, Florida (a second-home resort designed by Andreas Duany and Elizabeth Plater-Zyberk) and the Playa Vista development in Los Angeles (a commercial and residential development on land once owned by Howard Hughes), both characterised by "a peculiar postmodern combination of historical urban nostalgia and present-day postsuburbia" (Soja, 2000: 248). The Prince of Wales favours what might (if slightly uncharitably) be called an English equivalent of new urbanism in his foray into planning and architecture in the new village of Poundbury, Dorset (see Barton and Kleiner, 2002: 78–79). Bettina Drew, a writer living in Connecticut, writes of Celebration as an extension of the urban theories of Jane Jacobs: "Championing walking, public transport, and the mixed use of buildings" and contrasts this with a "business-oriented vision" of sprawl (Drew, 1998: 191). Although having visited Celebration she has reservations about Disney's level of control, and points out that while Disney excludes other franchise chains in Celebration, it fills the malls with its own outlets. Drew tends to naturalise new urbanism, for instance quoting Duany and Plater-Zyberk: "Like the habitat of a species, the neighbourhood possesses a natural logic that can be described in physical terms" (in Calthorpe, 1993: xvii, cited in Drew, 1998: 191).

In 1925, in the paper in which he introduced his concentric ring diagram, E. W. Burgess also used a biological model to explain the tensions of transitional zones in urban expansion. His use of natural science as metaphor for a socio-economic process sets it outside history, thus outside human intervention. New urbanism, too, tends to rely on a notion of natural solutions to urban social problems, its artificial environments (as likely to spawn artificial behaviour as the arcade) implying a return to a primordial model of settlement. But the design of Celebration, which we take to epitomise new urbanism, is an eclectic mix of styles from heritage sites such as Savannah, Georgia and Charleston, South Carolina. It resembles a theme park by more subtle means, with live inmates. The selected pasts on which its architectural styles draw stand, like the fetish commodity, for a desire projected. Journalists Douglas Frantz and Catherine Collins, who lived in Celebration for a year, write: "Nowhere was that backward vision more evident than in the *Celebration Pattern Book*, which was assembled to serve as the design bible for the town" (Frantz and Collins, 1999: 64). They point out that pattern books such as Asher Benjamin's *The American Builder's Companion* represented a design consensus for builders, architects, planners, and homebuyers but died out in the post-war period, and that in Celebration the book does not represent a voluntary consensus but a regulation. And as to nature, they write: "Cathy, our gardner, was disappointed by the landscape plan's total disregard for native plantings and its insistence on lots of grass", adding that the particular type of grass specified is in Cathy's view "a weed" (Frantz and Collins, 1999: 66).

Control is the key to Celebration. Dean MacCannell (1999: 108–109) cites the Ahwahnee Principles agreed by a group of architects (including Duany and Plater-Zyberk), planners, lawyers, and community activists in 1991 at Ahwahnee Lodge in Yosemite National Park as the generally accepted basis of new urbanist planning and design. These liberal ideals include that towns should have discernible centres within walking distance of dwellings, that there should be a variety of rental and owner-occupier housing, small playgrounds, a public school, tree-lined streets, and so forth. This is a reformist vision, not entirely out of keeping with Cerdá's 1859 plan for the extension of Barcelona; and MacCannell accepts that Seaside is successful. Yet at Celebration the basic principles of new urbanism become a new totalitarianism: the town manager is not an elected official but a Disney executive; residents must sign up to a set of rules which specify details of appearance such as the colour of curtains (white or beige), and height and kinds of shrub to plant in gardens; pick-up trucks are banned from parking in the street, and only one garage sale a year is allowed per property. The list goes on. MacCannell quotes Robert M. Stern, a Disney planner: "It makes them feel their investment is safe. Regimentation can release you" (in MacCannell, 1999: 112). MacCannell comments: "It is not as though he told them, '*Arbeit Macht Frei*'. These are, after all, surface matters, not much more intrusive than the required architectural details..." (MacCannell, 1999: 112).

But in a postmodern world surfaces are what we have and, as MacCannell continues, the design of the houses references traditional types but is singular in constructing a panopticon-like visual tunnel through the middle, from the front door to the back yard (see Foucault, 1991). This is the case regardless of price category. Frantz and Collins write: "Most front doors would open into a small foyer, with a dining room on one side and a living room on the other. A wide center hall would lead to the heart of the house – a modern kitchen opening onto a large family room lined with windows overlooking the backyard..." (Frantz and Collins, 1999: 66). The interiors (designed by contractors) are seen by Stern (an architect) as "horrendous" (cited in MacCannell, 1999: 113). Drew gives the prices as ranging from $150,000 for cottage homes to $425,000 for detached estate homes with verandas (Drew, 1998: 176); and Frantz and Collins as up to $1 million (Frantz and Collins, 1999: 103). This suggests a middle-income population who might not see themselves as needing to be deprived of privacy. Was the design an oversight, or as regulated as the colours for house facades (white, or pastel shades of blue, yellow, pink, and buff for some styles, and yellows, beige, gray, blue, and green for others)? MacCannell's explanation is that the panoptic house meets a nostalgic need for centralised authority which – he could have said like God's eye – penetrates everywhere, and "is designed to replace the unconscious" (MacCannell, 1999: 113). This seems odd but makes sense as a metaphor, and one where form may condition human function in that the unconscious is the zone of repressed material – the messy stuff suburban life seeks to avoid – which may deliver it back unless abolished. MacCannell states,

> The panoptican dwelling eliminates the possibility of discovering anything that might disconfirm the hypothesis of deep spiritual harmony. The entry hall has become the entire house. When one enters this space just beyond the front door, one has a sense of expansiveness... The doors into the bedrooms are clearly visible just beyond the stage-balcony railing (MacCannell, 1999: 113–114).

He adds that this open-plan interior makes the space provided seem larger than it is but that this visual deceit is less important than the absence of a central enclave, a domestic interior, as it were, of privacy. He concludes "This is a new kind of domestic space, without shadows... it is a successful totalitarian attempt to remove habitability" (ibid.). Conflict is identified by Richard Sennett (1970) as the spectre which haunts white, North American suburbia. Suburbanites are unable to deal with it and therefore project its causes onto outsiders who intrude to threaten a mythicised social harmony. Celebration has a predominance of white, middle-income residents and predictably low crime rate, yet is not immune to disturbance within the community, including a case of domestic violence. While it has little in the way of intrusion to fear – all residents sign up to the rules, and houses are expensive – it is not immune, either, to conflict between the needs of its citizens and the authority (Disney) which presides over it. All sources we use comment on arguments between residents and Disney over the "one-room" public school (in fact several but where all ages are taught together), reminiscent

of the school room in the television series *Little House on the Prairie*
but which requires a high student–staff ratio to be viable (Frantz
and Collins, 1999: 124–146; MacCannell, 1999: 112). And Frantz and
Collins describe the incident of domestic violence (Frantz and Collins,
1999: 267–269). Perhaps living in Celebration is not as ideal as the hype
would have us believe.

Conclusion

The presiding motif of the arcades, the mall, the theme park, and the
suburban settlements of new urbanism is artificiality. New urbanism
can be seen as anti-urban, deleting the elements of diversity and
contestation which contribute to cosmopolitanism in favour of a highly
regulated and selective nostalgia for the white picket fence and the
safety of fictional communities. Drew writes that it is "haunting and sad"
that new urbanism appeared only after the end of the Cold War (which
she calls "the fall of the Soviet Union"), explaining this as a by-product
of a demonisation of community – like commun(itarian)ism – during
the Cold War. But a better explanation might be that once the old
enemy has ceased to have the ability to organise a global war, a new one
must be identified within the dominant society.

Such an enemy is found in the underclass, a generalised term for the
homeless, graffiti writers, migrants, and other socially excluded groups
whose marginalisation does not, in fact, make them a unitary class. The
underclass is seen as a threat identified with big cities in particular, and
while liberal opinion turns against the uniformity and dullness of suburbs,
new urbanism offers a panacea which deals both with fear of crime and
fear of uniformity. Just as mass-produced goods, like cars and furniture,
can be customised, so can houses and streetscapes, and new urbanism
offers a simulation of the diversity of older neighbourhoods within its
pattern books. Crucially for this chapter in a book on cities and
consumption, houses are thus commodified in the same way as goods
in the department stores and arcades. That is, they take on the
attributes of the fetish, as sites onto which desires can be projected. We
see this in all aspects of consumerism concerning "lifestyle" choices,
but its extension to housing seems relatively new, at least in the way
housing now takes on, in certain cases such as those described above,
the image of safety. We say this because, to put it more briefly than it
warrants, safety in the environment is probably as impossible to grasp
as more conventional objects of desire. This leaves us with a possibly

bleak picture. Gottdiener writes that themed environments offer consumers a spatial experience which is an attraction in itself, as well as any consumption which takes place: "People may come to the mall ... to shop, but they come there to see and be seen, much like people have done for centuries ..." (Gottdiener, 2000: 284), and concludes that future changes will reflect fashionable shifts in desires and induce new kinds of spaces. Yet the themes available, as the entertainment industry encroaches on all aspects of life, seem to us unreal. In the end, not only do we not live in a movie or a television soap, but we might prefer not to. On the other hand, we might also be lulled into looking for themes as a way to order our lives, or lend them a meaning they seem to have somehow lost. But the themes, we should recall, are manufactured by the producers to suit the fantasy of an ever-expanding capitalist economy.

CHAPTER 6

Consuming Chance: The Gambling City

In an increasingly commercial world, governments and policy makers have sought to find new ways of ensuring the future of cities on both an economic and cultural footing. Many cities have become awash in the symbolism of consumer culture which has been created by commercial interests as a means of promoting mass consumption and indeed, of putting those cities on the global map (see Hannigan, 1998). Gambling is particularly interesting in this regard insofar as it has clearly had a major impact on some of the most iconographic cities in the world. Las Vegas, which we will discuss in more detail shortly, is the most obvious example of a city defined on the surface by gambling, but underneath (and not very far underneath at that) by the apparently endless possibilities associated with consumption. Since the work of Venturi *et al.* (1972), many authors have seen Las Vegas, in particular, as somehow emblematic of broader changes in city life. In this chapter we want to consider what gambling in the city tells us about the way in which cities, for better or for worse, are changing and whether cities more generally can learn real lessons from the gambling industry. What is the relationship between consumption, gambling and the city? More pointedly, is consumption the servant or the master of the contemporary city life?

This chapter is partly concerned with the casino and its impact on city life, insofar as the casino represents what George Ritzer (1999) describes as a new means of consumption; in effect a cathedral of consumption: a place that has been designed artistically and scientifically to lure people in order to consume. From this point of view the casino does not permit us to consume, it is apparently structured to lead and even coerce us into consumption. It manipulates time and space. Casinos are usually and deliberately designed without clocks and windows so as to ensure the consumer has no idea what the time might be. Such spaces often incorporate awe-inspiring spaces, such as the Atrium at the Luxor, Las Vegas, which again serve to disorientate the visitor. The end-result according to Ritzer is a dream-like world in which time loses its significance. As Anderton and Chase (1997a) put it, "The aim behind the design of these casinos is, simply, to expose people to the maximum number of revenue-producing entities – opportunities to gamble – in as entertaining a way as possible." These are controlled spaces, what Goldberger (1996) describes as "urbanoid environments", private spaces cavorting as public ones. According to Goldberger the end result is a highly prescribed and contrived city, held together by consumerism, entertainment and popular culture. The casino is indeed the embodiment of consumer ideology. It presents the consumption of the imaginary (the imaginary in these circumstances often being the win) as an entirely natural state of affairs. In many casino resorts there is no alternative but to consume. But such resorts also highlight the vulnerability of this ideology. After all, you do not have to penetrate much beyond the surface to realise the emptiness of the dreams that such places have to offer. The gambling city constitutes a highly divisive model of city life, and in effect maintains its own kind of apartheid. While purporting to be an energetic and culturally vivid version of city life the "urbanoid environment" robs the city of its disorganised reality, whilst excluding those members of the population that do not fit in to its middle class vision of what city life should be all about.

In an era of globalisation, ever new sophisticated and arguably controlling ways of consuming are evolving. But this development goes hand in hand with the more political dimensions of the process. As McMillen (1996) notes, globalisation has created a paradoxical situation in which the power of core organisations is increasingly centralised and yet a chain of localised casino developments are emerging, scattered worldwide, that are increasingly connected with one another. It could even be suggested that in the guise of gambling, consumption is actively taking what we traditionally think of as the city apart. The casino industry, for example, is underpinned by its determination to bring in more outsiders or consumers into its environs than locals. Indeed, many casino resorts have traditionally been run on the principle that locals should actually be excluded from the casino environment. The gambling city is therefore a transient city: a city more about the provision of services than it is about the people it serves. In the early days of casino construction, as Eadington (2000) notes in his discussion of trends in casinos and tourism for the twenty-first century, the major clientele were, by definition, tourists attracted to resort areas or spas, which by their very nature were to be found away from major centres of population. This isolation reflected a pre-1960s world, which, according to Eadington, saw gambling as potentially dangerous and which only tolerated casinos if they were kept out of the urban eye.

Since this time, the urban perceptibility of gambling has increased dramatically in many parts of the world. In Australia, for example, commercial tourism interests have been a primary impetus behind casino developments as a means of promoting tourism growth and regional economic development. Moscow alone has 73 licensed casinos (Hannigan, 1998). Meanwhile, in the United States, the American people's disdain for personal and property taxation has lead politicians to see gambling as a potentially lucrative way of raising revenues for declining social services (Parker, 1995: 223). The fact is that American casinos have been commercially successful and the symbolic value of casinos to the image of cities as exciting and progressive cannot be underestimated. Hannigan (1998) for example, cites Inglenook in Southern California as a small city that benefited from a casino development which created 800 new jobs. This development also helped to elevate property values, whilst improving local schools and public services via an increased municipal operating budget. In other parts of the world such as Australia, the economic impact of gambling on the city has been mixed. It may well be the case, that the initially positive impact on the local economy is short-lived (McMillen, 1991). Many commentators cite Atlantic City as an example of how casinos do not always fulfil their economic potential. Since 1978 when casinos were first introduced to the city, 80 per cent of the city's restaurants were closed. Atlantic City's population is now 10 per cent less than it was when gambling was first established in the city. This is a city that might well be described as, "seedy, crime-ridden, and going nowhere" (Hannigan, 1998: 164). Perhaps the benefits of attracting investment via casinos and tourism outweigh the associated social costs of such developments.

It is worth remembering that economistic arguments and assumptions have, as McMillen (1991) points out, been instrumental in minimising careful analysis of the social and political effects of gambling in the city. Between the 1960s and the end of the twentieth century, moral attacks on gambling appear to have been superseded (despite the social problems associated with gambling, such as debt, family breakdown, and depression being as real as ever) by a vision of gambling as light-hearted entertainment: "What is new is the spread of a distinctly American attitude toward placing your bets: Gambling is neither sin nor profligacy. Instead, it's wholesome, out-of-the-closet entertainment to be pursued guilt-free in front of the kiddies" (Cooper, 1995: 24). The new onus on gambling as a form of harmless urban entertainment reflects a situation in which the very ambience of city life is being transformed, as we will go to illustrate with a detailed discussion of Las Vegas, below. You might even go as far as to argue that in those cities in which gambling has managed to establish itself as a core component in economic development as opposed to one aspect of a broader tourism strategy (McMillen, 1991: 159) the very essence of consumption has been transformed to the extent that those cities are "consumed" in a sense that other cities are not (see Chapter 9). Cities such as Las Vegas and Atlantic City are less physical places and are more places consumers construct in their imagination. But ironically the imagination is only allowed to operate within the boundaries that consumption dictates. It is apparently the removal of the immoral stigma associated with gambling that has made all this possible (Gottdiener, 1999).

A key dimension of the sociological impact of gambling consumption on the city is that of the community. As McMillen (1991: 166) suggests, "The economic and symbolic rewards gained from casinos are immediate and electorally very persuasive, while benefits of reforms to improve community impacts may be small and often slow to accrue." In this context, there is a particular concern that the very fabric of the local community is undermined simply because casinos construct their own mono-communities in the form of a one-stop consuming experience on tap. Consumers do not need to leave the casino because it provides them with everything the local community could have offered them and more. As such Parker (1995) discusses the displacement of the population caused by the gambling industry. The arrival of gambling in Atlantic City, for example, accelerated the decline of affordable housing and the local homeless problem also worsened as a result. Such displacement, as Parker (1995: 235) goes on to suggest, constitutes a graphic demonstration of the dissolution of community,

At one time, Atlantic City was a tightly knit, diverse community with many subcultures and ethnic enclaves (including a once vibrant Puerto Rico population, and Italian enclave and a well-established middle-class Jewish community). With the city's famous boardwalk and the ocean for entertainment, many residents viewed Atlantic City as a warm, welcoming place to live. By eliminating many affordable apartments, grocery stores, and movie theaters (all within walking distance of most homes), casino gambling wiped out long-term residents' quality of life.

The problem here is that gambling (and indeed consumption) can never be the messiah that the local people hope it will be. To this end Parker quotes Steve Wynn, the Las Vegas casino developer who argues that local residents and businesses always have unreasonably high expectations of casino developments and that in the longer term they always direct the venom of their disappointment at the gambling operators. The crucial thing for Wynn, and of particular relevance to this discussion, is his point that the gambling industry simply is not in the business of rebuilding housing or of revitalising communities. Gambling operators are in the business of making money and can only revitalise cities insofar as they pay workers wages, and taxes to the state. But this is not always the case; the development of native American Indian gambling operations in recent years has had a profound and positive effect on city life. For instance, the Cabazon Band of Mission Indians of California opened the Indio Bingo Palace and Casino in 1992. In doing so they also made significant long-term investments in infrastructure and economic diversification. They have invested earnings in housing programmes, and have also developed a generating plant that sells power to Consolidated Edison. Meanwhile, the Grand Casino Mille Lacs Project in Minnesota served to virtually eliminate a 45 per cent unemployment rate. Much of the casino's earnings have also been invested in long-term community projects such as a history museum intended to help maintain the tribe's heritage. Such developments are the exception that proves the rule, "it is no exaggeration to suggest that corporate gambling not only fails to develop communities but also produces many negative side-effects that are destructive to the process of upgrading a community's standard of living" (Parker, 1995: 246).

Gambling as ethnic cleansing?

The key question here then is this: how far does the impact of gambling upon city life actually benefit consumers? And if it does, *which* consumers actually benefit? In other words, there is a particular concern that the local population are, in effect, being priced out of their communities and that the developments that do happen in such cities are on the whole of benefit to those who can afford sky-high prices. Expensive properties may be being built but they are so expensive that the prices of nearby houses rise accordingly, as do taxes, leaving the local people in a particularly vulnerable position: a position worsened by the knowledge that they live in a city that is not designed for them in the first place.

Young (2000) goes as far as to describe the above as a process of "ethnic cleansing". From this point of view, gambling is not about creating wealth for the benefit of the local population. All it does is re-circulate money into the hands of those people who least need it. In Chapter 1 we suggested that a consuming city is a divided city. The opportunity to consume what the gambling city provides will inevitably create problems that will have a disproportionate impact on certain segments of the population as Gottdiener *et al.* (1999) note. Similarly, Parker (1995: 244) quotes J. Terrence Brunner, executive director of the Better Government Association in Chicago who states that

> The in-direct costs of casinos include regressive and local taxation, transient employment, and a decrease in economic diversity... Land-based casino gambling is most likely to harm those who are not already socially and economically marginalized and thus have little power.

It is certainly true to say that gambling cannot be expected to achieve the impossible. The gambling industry cannot transform the economic basis of city life single-handedly. It can only be hoped that casino developments complement existing tourism in attracting further visitors and thereby expanding the tourist market. As such, "Policy makers who hope to use casinos as major catalysts for tourism development need to be realistic in assessing the likelihood that casinos will have a major impact on their tourism product. If not they might end up sorely disappointed" (Eadington, 2000: 9). More profoundly perhaps, in those cities in which it has a high-profile presence, gambling in the city is fundamentally changing the way individuals relate to city life. Perhaps the problem with gambling in the city is that it makes the individual feel like they are at the epitome of city life. Gambling promotes an urban world which puts the individual at its core. It encourages the consumer to believe he or she is omnipotent and that at any given moment he or she is in control. But the whole point is that the gambling city vividly illustrates just how the city in general has spiralled out of control in the name of consumerism – precisely because the pleasures and the freedoms it offers the consumer are fundamentally illusory. Consumerism serves to camouflage the less palatable reality of poor wages, addiction, and social exclusion. The consumer is in fact controlled *by* the consuming city. In this sense the gambling city is an illusory city, and is no better demonstrated than in an extended discussion of Las Vegas which Rothman (2002: xx) describes as "socially sanctioned deviance. Its brand is just more comfortable to more Americans than it used to be."

Consuming Las Vegas

Tacky, ugly pop culture or a once-in-a-lifetime inspirational experience? Las Vegas is a city that divides its critics, and that division is consumer-driven. It is worth noting that there is a debate as to how far we can extrapolate from the Las Vegas example. Indeed, it might be argued that Las Vegas is, in many respects, unique and that as such can tell us very little about the broader picture. However, as many authors have began to argue, Las Vegas actually serves as a microcosm of contemporary city life *and* of city life in the future. Las Vegas represents city life magnified a thousand times and as such it provides an invaluable means of understanding how consumption has forever changed the nature of the urban landscape and how we consume it. Above all perhaps, Las Vegas is a city of self-promotion and hype. It did not emerge from nowhere by chance, but as a result of a raft of sophisticated marketing techniques. As Donnovan (2000) notes in this respect, image is as important as reality in determining the future prosperity of a city.

Las Vegas is the fastest growing metropolis in the USA. Its population has more than doubled since 1985 and it is the gambling experience that lies at the core of such massive growth (Cooper, 1995). The city welcomes over 36 million visitors per year and is home to 19 of the world's 20 largest hotels. In many ways Las Vegas is not simply a mere city; it is home to a whole host of cities each of which takes refuge within the walls of the larger-than-life casinos that give Las Vegas its unique character. The history of Las Vegas as a city is a complex one, but it is possible to identify some key moments. First, the building of the Hoover Dam, completed in 1935 which brought the city new workers and new roads to serve a fledgling city. Second, the legalisation of casino gambling in Nevada in 1938. The infamous mobster Benjamin Siegel was clever enough to realise the massive potential underlying Las Vegas and he subsequently opened the city's first super-casino, the *Flamingo*. The 1950s saw a massive building boom in Las Vegas – a boom that highlighted the key relationship between the casinos and the mob. In the years that followed, various entrepreneurs invested hundreds of millions of dollars in the city, and in the process the influence of the mob on city life was gradually decreased. After a period of stagnation, the mid-1970s saw a period of deregulation and therefore of considerable growth. And such growth extended beyond the resorts themselves. As Gottdiener *et al.* point out, the combination of cheap land and a rapidly growing population meant that the Las Vegas region went on to be a prime housing market. All of this was only possible as a result of the intervention of mobsters, businessmen, small-time entre-preneurs, and powerful politicians who were able to obtain billions of federal dollars for the region.

By the 1980s an entirely new Las Vegas was emerging. Entertainment became the name of the game, most vividly perhaps in the form of Steve Wynn's spectacular *Mirage* which opened the floodgates to a series of mega-resorts the kind of which the world had never previously seen. Las Vegas became what Gottdiener *et al.* describe as a national pleasure zone. In this context, hotels were no longer places to stay but attractions in their own right. The Las Vegas economy had succeeded in identifying new non-industrial strategies for future growth that would provide a model, the world over: Las Vegas became a city whose economy was based on attracting transient funds from outside the city limits (Rothman, 2002). And such a policy has undoubtedly succeeded: the resorts on the strip alone outpace the revenue of all the theme parks in America put together (Gottdiener *et al.*, 1999). Although it is fair to say that since the 1990s such developments have slowed down, and that the pursuit of the family consumer appears to have been watered down, there is no doubt, as Gottdiener (1999) suggests, that the guiding logic of Las Vegas and of course of its architecture is undiluted commercialism. As such, Hannigan (1998) estimates that between 1989 and 1999 Las Vegas welcomed $16 billions of investment in entertainment-related mega-projects.

Las Vegas is founded upon a desire to seduce the consumer. This is a point well expressed by Anderton and Chase (1997b: 8) who argue that "Las Vegas expresses, in exaggerated form, the state of the art of popular entertainment as well as the potential and failures of untram-melled private development and the subjugation of nature." But Las Vegas is changing. As Lubove (1996) points out, the enormous amounts of new visitors that Las Vegas has attracted are less and less likely to be gambling and more and more likely to be simply gawking at the sights that surround them. Las Vegas presents to the consumer what is a fan-tastical out-of-this-world experience, something that does not appear to be real, but which at the same time is packaged as being the most readily available and natural of experiences (see Rothman, 2002). In short, Las Vegas is the ideal city of consumption: a city devoted to consumption and a city devoted to the needs of the consumer. To this end Spanier

(1992) discusses five markets which are attracted to Las Vegas: (1) the tour and travel market on short 2–3 day visits; (2) the convention/ conference market; (3) the "free and independent traveller" market; (4) the higher roller market who are interested in high stakes gambling and account for about 300,000 consumers in the USA and (5) local business with a population approaching 1 million. It might be suggested that Las Vegas has become increasingly democratic insofar as the credit-card society has made virtually everything Las Vegas has to offer available to more and more consumers. Perhaps more than anything it is the architectural life of Las Vegas that asserts its democratic intent. How can this be a bad thing? It can only be considered as such, if we accept the idea that choice and the availability of choice is always a good thing. From this point of view as Venturi *et al.* (1972) suggested, Las Vegas is indeed founded on an "architecture of inclusion" and the end product of this is a vast multi-themed space for consumption. Las Vegas provides more free opportunities to consume than anywhere else in the world; though of course it is only prepared to do so, in the knowledge that there will, in the end, be a pay-off.

So what is it about Las Vegas that attracts such interest? Above all Las Vegas is the city of the commodified spectacle. As Gottdiener (1999: 92) argues, "Behind the glittering façade of 'archi-entertainment' and other Vegas-style 'hyper-real' spectacles lies the 'real' logic of commodity production. The self-styled 'entertainment capital of the world,' Las Vegas, embodies, in the most extreme form, the relentless pursuit of profit in the leisure sphere, first described in detail by the critical theorists ..." In this respect it is very important that we delve beneath the surface of Las Vegas in order to try and make sense of the sociological impact of consumption upon the city. The impact of consumption, may indeed be more profound than a more superficial analysis might imply.

Many authors have described Las Vegas as a city of signs. Spanier (1992) for example, argues that in Las Vegas the sign and the symbol is more important than the architecture (see Venturi *et al.*, 1972). Las Vegas is a new kind of city willing to embrace the world beyond the confines of social space. At one level, the city is dominated (or at least was in the 1970s) by an automobile-friendly landscape which required a commercial environment founded on "explicit and heightened symbolism" (Venturi *et al.*, 1972: 19). In this context, as Gottdiener (1999) also indicates, the symbol gradually overcame the architectural form and as an essential means of seducing the consumer. In one sense, you could even say that what Las Vegas promises is actually more important than what it actually produces. Las Vegas overwhelms you with its signs and its symbols; no more so on the Strip which,

> creates its own system of signification through metonymical contrasts and has become an immense, themed consumer space. The pastiche of inclusive architecture is quite remarkable and ranges from the symbols of ancient Egypt, through tropical fantasies, medieval apparitions, neoclassical, Roman, rococo, baroque, mock Tudor, Taj Mahal, Arabian Nights fantasies, and the fantasized Wild West or Barbary Coast of San Francisco. (Gottdiener, 1999: 281)

The amazing thing about Las Vegas is the way in which it appears to make the entire world immediately available to the consumer. In recent years, new resorts have included *Venice* and *Paris* which re-create the urban structure in a microcosmic form in order to accentuate the consuming experience. In the aftermath of the September 11th bombings, Rothman (2002) reports that people treated *New York* like it was the city itself. It became a shrine, a "stand-in" for the real thing, providing people with a direct focus for their emotions. In this respect, in the imaginations of many people at least, Las Vegas's version of New York became real.

Out of nothing, Las Vegas emerged as a city. This was a transition from the archetype of unreality to that of a real city which is undoubtedly underpinned by entertainment (Orbist and Koolhaas, 2001). Although gambling has always been the mainstay of Las Vegas (and continues to be so insofar as it constitutes about 60 per cent of revenues in a large hotel (Todd, 2001)) the growth of the city has very much been accompanied by the growth of the resort: the growth of Las Vegas as a city of entertainment (much of which is provided free as an inducement designed to encourage consumers to part with their hard earned cash on the gambling tables). Perhaps, nowadays, above all, Las Vegas is in the tourism business. It was only able to make a success of that business, however, due to broader social changes,

> The change to the individual-oriented culture of personal choice of the cusp of the new century created the context for the rise of leisure and the transformation of socially unacceptable "gambling" into the recreational "gambling". Las Vegas had perfected the service economy long before the rest of the nation encountered it. The rise of entertainment as a commodity increased the cachet of the city. (Rothman, 2002: xxiii)

The inauthentic city

In short, Las Vegas becomes whatever the consumer wants it to become. Las Vegas constitutes a world of escape, a world of unrelenting fantasy in which anything is possible. As Hess (1993) argues in Las Vegas "form follows fantasy". The themes of Las Vegas are constantly changing, but they need to do so in order to reflect the fantasies and desires of the public. Las Vegas is indeed a city of excess. A key question is this respect is this: is Las Vegas in some sense inauthentic? This is an issue addressed most directly by Ada Lousie Huxtable (1997) who debates the benefit of themed-environments and their impact on city life,

> Our cities, shattered by change, victimized by economics, are still the rich containers of our collective culture, the record of our continuity, the repository of the best we have produced. But themed parodies pass for places now, serving as the new planning and design models as real places with their full freight of art and memories are devalued and destroyed... Illusion... is the commodity used to fill the vacuum of imagination and ideas when commercial expediency builds to the bottom line.

But although Huxtable is damning about the synthetic nature of the architecture of fantasy, she actually commends Las Vegas where "real fake" has been developed into an art form. In her words, "The outrageously fake has developed its own indigenous style and lifestyle to become a real place" (Huxtable, 1997: 75). Las Vegas may be real, but in actuality it only serves to magnify the empty entertainment-filled world of the shopping mall, the theme park, and the rehashed manufactured and historically barren architecture of new urban housing.

Of course Las Vegas is inauthentic. That is precisely why consumers find what it has to offer so seducing. Todd (2001) points out that many critics disparage Las Vegas for the fact that it represents a sanitised experience: the consumer gets to visit the cities of the world all in easy reach of each other, but without having to encounter any of their less savoury elements. In this sense, the desire for authenticity amounts to little more than snobbery. Consumers are not visiting the resort hotels under the illusion that this is the real thing. Perhaps the consumers of the gambling city are the ultimate embodiment of Urry's (2002) post-tourist. They are enjoying the spectacle of Las Vegas for their own selves. Self-consciously aware of the commodification that surrounds them, they construct their own reality for their own playful ends. The experience is in fact an end in itself. From this point of view we can identify two key components of the Las Vegas experience: (1) the re-contextualisation of space and (2) the simultaneous individualisation of that space. In one sense consumers of Las Vegas are consuming something very different to what they would have done in the past. The vaguely corrupting and titillating world of 1970s Las Vegas has been replaced by an apparently wholesome family resort (Cooper, 1995) equally dependant upon seduction as its previous incarnation, but in a rather different guise. The role of the sign as discussed above is crucial in what is essentially a virtual environment. As Gottdiener (1999: 284) puts it, the new spaces of consumption are actively designed as extensions of the commodity/culture milieu in the way in which they incorporate magazines, advertising, movies, computer cyberspace, and the like in order to construct what in effect is a hyper-real world of consumption: "Themed environments work not only because they are connected to the universe of commodities and are spaces of consumption but also because they offer consumers a spatial experience that is an attraction by itself, that is, they promote the consumption of space."

The above is most vividly illustrated in the form of the changing ecology of the Strip, Las Vegas' main street and home to most of the major resort hotels. The experience of consumption is no longer simply about consumers spending their money on gambling, but it is also about changing definitions of public space. In this light, as Ritzer (1999) suggested above, the casino is designed to confuse; to rid the consumer of practical concerns and to envelope him or her in the sights, sounds and activities of an entirely new world (Hess, 1993). Although as I will go on to suggest, in other respects Las Vegas is about the individualisation of experience, the Strip is very much about the reinvention of the strip as pedestrian public space which people stroll up and down in order to catch the volcano at the *Mirage*, the pirate show with 30 actors performing on moving ships in Buccaneer's Bay at *Treasure Island* or even the changing skies and fountains that regularly come to life at the Forum Shops, *Caesars Palace*. Anderton and Chase (1997b) argue that such attractions are not merely intended to entertain, but to disorient, and, of course, entrap the visitor who is subsequently lured into the casino itself. Similarly the $70 million Freemont Street experience: a giant, computer-generated light and show that arches over the core of Las Vegas, attracts thousands of consumers who crane their necks in order to catch the latest spectacular and, most importantly, free show. But in a sense the renewed element of this form of urban consumption is little more than a means to an end. Once these people have got to Freemont Street and once they have viewed the short light show they are once again fair game to the casinos, and in this case to casinos that they would probably never have visited otherwise. This apparently constitutes a more advanced form of consumption, which is all about delaying gratification and seducing the consumer into a frame of mind in which consumption becomes an entirely natural (and therefore an ideological) act. The irony here, as far as the consumption of city space is concerned is that such attractions create (literally in the case of Freemont Street) an overarching identity, whilst stripping individual buildings of their own specificity. The Las Vegas streets might well be said to be adopting the spectacular at the expense of character which is arguably being lost. The new Las Vegas goes on unabated whereas the old Las Vegas is being recycled regardless of its historical value (Gottdiener *et al.*, 1999). So while Las Vegas, a city with less history than most others, actively rids itself of the history it does have, it does so in such a way as to make the individual's experience of that city feel unique. The marketeer's dream, a mass produced product which the individual can engage with on an individual basis.

So what does all this mean for the consumer's experience of Las Vegas? Does Las Vegas tell us anything profound about the future, and indeed, the present of consumption? First and foremost it is important to recognise that the above process works because Las Vegas has a unique way of making the individual feel as though they are at the epicentre of the city's life. In the above context, Rothman (2002: xiii) describes Las Vegas as an illustration of the broader "orgy of the unruly combination of experience, self and commodity" that has come to characterise American culture. In this culture people no longer crave goods, but rather experience as a means of affirming themselves. As Rothman (2002: xiii) goes on to argue,

> Postmodern, postindustrial capitalism is about consuming experience, not goods, about creating insatiable desire that must be fulfilled in front of an approving audience. Las Vegas is geared to meet this challenge, to provide the audience, to deliver more than anywhere else and hold out the possibility of still more. The ability to quench desire brings people; the chance to dream of more brings them back again and again.

From this point of view Las Vegas represents the rationalisation of pleasure as a socially useful resource. It allows the consumer to be who or what he or she wants to be and it provides the experiences that are consumed as a means of being accepted. In effect, Rothman (2002) argues that Las Vegas provides the consumer with a script, that he or she goes on to write, produce and do with as he or she sees fit. Las Vegas is consumer ideology writ large. In so-called "nobrow culture" entertainment and the self have become pivotal especially so in Las Vegas which tells you as a consumer that as long as you can pay for it, you can have or do anything that you desire.

Accidental space?

Las Vegas may well tell the consumer that anything is possible, but that does not necessarily reflect the reality. It is very easy to get carried away with an image of Las Vegas as a sort of consumerist nirvana. But all is not as it may seem. In many respects Las Vegas is a transient city. But how is city life for those people who live in the city permanently? Spanier (1992) has suggested that what is missing from Las Vegas is any genuine sense of public values or community. The rapid growth of Las Vegas and its resort hotels has attracted hundreds of thousands of new residents who have put an almost irrepressible tension on local roads, schools, water supplies, sewage and even air quality, none of which can cope with the demands made of them. An estimated 60,000–80,000 new residents arrive in the Las Vegas every year to the extent that living in Las Vegas is, "like living on a constantly changing and moving stage" (Gottdiener et al., 1999: 196). It has been suggested that Las Vegas is a city at saturation point; A city of world class casinos and world class traffic jams (Cooper, 1995). In this respect, the reality simply does not reflect the rhetoric. As Anderton and Chase (1997b: 7) put it, the brazen exhibitionism of the Strip and the power of its imagery serve to mask the human and experiential aspects of living in Las Vegas, the city, "The real Las Vegas has jumped from 220,000 to 1 million inhabitants in 20 years, and it is generating culture at the same time as it is trying to keep pace with the traffic, pollution, homelessness, and other urban ills that such rapid success brings." From this point of view, Las Vegas is what Boyer (1993) would describe as a "city of illusion", in which promotional spaces are eagerly developed regardless of their social implications (see Hannigan, 1998). Indeed, the world presented to the consumer through Las Vegas actively conceals the real logic of commodity production and the social relations of production that underpin it. Large numbers of homeless people come to Las Vegas seeking a city paved with gold: low unemployment rates and rapid levels of job creation.

What they find in reality is as Gottdiener *et al.* (1999) point out, a city in which about a third of new positions pay between no more than \$6 and \$8 an hour.

Las Vegas does of course offer many residents a very good standard of living and quality of life, and some commentators argue that Las Vegas should be commended for providing solid middle-class incomes to unqualified workers (Rothman, 2002), but there is also evidence of environmental and social problems (Gottdiener *et al.*, 1999). From this point of view the entry-level work is often not enough to sustain family life and many family problems are exacerbated as a result. As Gottdiener *et al.* point out, Las Vegas continues to have the highest divorce rate in the USA while it also performs badly in terms of teenage pregnancies, child-abuse rates and, pointedly, the provision of child-care. The low wages are a negative consequence of reliance on the gambling industry, while rapid population growth has lead to overcrowding in schools, the class segregation of housing, poverty – none of which are helped by air, water and land pollution and uncontrollable social debt which reflects a city that is changing faster than its infrastructure can handle. Not only are a large percentage of the population unable to access the casino due to their lack of resources, but they are often effectively forced out of the urban spaces which they formerly occupied (Hannigan, 1998). In this respect, perhaps consumption is indeed having a detrimental impact upon city life. Traffic may well be the most visible illustration of the difficulties that Las Vegas finds itself having to deal with. A city designed around the car has been taken over by it. Precisely the same thing could be said about the impact of consumption upon Las Vegas.

For most residents casino gambling is little more than an inconvenience and a local is more likely to identify with a local community than with the city as a whole. Many casino and bank employees wear badges that indicate their first names and their city of origin. In this respect Las Vegas is not a real city at all, but rather an accidental space in which people from diverse backgrounds happen to live. Anderton and Chase (1997b) describe the Las Vegas beyond the strip as being shockingly ordinary and prosaic: mile upon mile of wholly predictable residential neighbourhoods and garrisoned townhouse communities; the latter providing a telling indication of the urban paranoia that characterises Las Vegas: the city that never sleeps because its residents are too scared to do so. In dealing with this issue, Gottdiener *et al.* describe a process of normalisation in which a city begins to take on the essential characteristics and institutions associated with more developed cities.

Las Vegas's development as an urban centre is as much about a struggle for daily living as it is about tourism and gambling. It is essential in the future as Gottdiener *et al.* go on to indicate that the poorest areas of the city and not just the walled enclaves receive the benefits of such a transition. It is equally important that Las Vegas recognises its over-dependence upon tourism and legislates for this accordingly. For Gottdiener *et al.* the fragile nature of local civic cultures and fragmented political structures (the city is organised under the jurisdiction of five separate areas) represent a key priority. Las Vegas is a large city, experiencing a diverse range of growing pains none of which can be solved overnight. And ironically, the city of signs, the city of rapid development is likely to become increasingly reliant upon broader national trends, simply because it is so dependent upon the precarious ups and downs of the tourism industry. Gottdiener *et al.* (1999) quote a study conducted by the Las Vegas Convention and Visitors Authority which indicates that shopping and dining have actually replaced gambling as the city's primary attractions. The Forum Shops, is indeed America's most profitable shopping centre. But whether or not consumption can provide a stable enough economic foundation to ensure Las Vegas's long-term economic future has to be a matter of considerable doubt. The city of neon has been replaced by the city of spectacle, but the spectacular may not constitute a sustainable foundation for community life in the city.

Conclusion

Perhaps at the moment the only sense of community to be found in Las Vegas is that located within the gaming halls. Consumers of gambling feel a sense of camaraderie with their fellow gamblers. The casinos make you and your fellow consumers feel important with simple (manipulative) gestures such as the provision of free drinks, and the illusion of freedom around the card table in an environment in which everyone is perceived to be equal. Each casino resort may in some respects constitute a city in its own right. Indeed, Las Vegas self-consciously rearranges the specialised neighbourhoods of a traditional city, as Hess (1993) notes with shopping, business and residential districts all being provided, at least in what he calls their "leisure-time equivalent". And meanwhile, the "real" Las Vegas struggles for any sense of its own identity. Located in the middle of a desert, Las Vegas might well be said to be drowning amidst a hedonism to which everybody is welcome to partake, unless you actually live there. There are signs, however, as Gottdiener *et al.* (1999) suggest, of improvement such as the development of better planned suburban areas which are providing local people with more of sense than of self, notably through libraries, community activities, and recreational sites. The Neighbourhood Department represents one such initiative aimed at promoting poorer local neighbourhoods on an equal footing to that of upscale residents. But such measures may constitute little more than a drop in the ocean.

Las Vegas is a city at the forefront of the processes we describe throughout this book. You could even go one step further to suggest that Las Vegas is more determined by the opportunity to consume than virtually any other city in the world. It has extended the realm of urban consumption into the unreal. Rothman (2002) suggests that one of the keys to understanding Las Vegas lies in an understanding of the way in which it appears to transcend public and private space. It provides the consumer with private space that appears to be public and which appears to be secure. It allows you, the consumer, the joy of winning however occasionally, and however small the monetary reward, and yet helps you feel that you belong alongside the thousands of aspirants that surround you. The urban spaces of Las Vegas work, as Gottdiener (2000: 285) suggests, precisely because "they are connected to the universe of commodities and are spaces of consumption but also because they offer consumers a spatial experience that is an attraction by itself, that is, they promote the consumption of space". They promote the consumption of non-specific space.

In many respects, the history of Las Vegas has been a success story and although in many ways, Las Vegas is indeed unique, in some ways it did manage to become a real city, albeit constructed upon somewhat artificial foundations. Las Vegas was,

> the first city of the consumption of entertainment, and to be the first at anything in a fluid culture guarantees significance. Las Vegas offers an economic model to which cities, states, and regions look to create their own economic panacea – even as they hold their nose. Its consistent re-invention, once scorned as flimsy and fraudulent, shaped its transformation from peripheral to paradigmatic and has become a much-envied trait. Las Vegas has become normal; even more important, it points to the twenty-first century. (Rothman, 2002: xxvii)

As far as Rothman is concerned, Las Vegas became a paradigm of the post-industrial economy; and its version of a new economy, based on the consumption of gambling, has indeed been transferred to cities including New Orleans, Missouri, and Detroit. For Gottdiener *et al.* (1999: 218) "Las Vegas may also be seen as a unique combination of the exotic and the mundane that increasingly typifies the postmodern urban environment in the nation as a whole." But whether or not the consumption of gambling and all the other opportunities to consume in Las Vegas have actually fulfilled the promise of local, civic and economic regeneration is highly debatable. In many ways Las Vegas remains a city divided and a city divided *by* consumption. The everyday experience of the city and its mundane suburban reality will always live in the shadow of the Strip. The Strip will always accentuate the nature of that division and the role of consumption as the most visible of tools of social exclusion. If Las Vegas is the paradigm of the post-industrial city then perhaps the post-industrial city is a slightly more complex beast than was at first imagined. Perhaps the post-industrial city is not something that we should aspire to at all.

Las Vegas is a city of extremes and it also provides a vivid illustration of the ups and downs of the consuming city which offers plenty, but can only ultimately disappoint. Las Vegas could be said to constitute the risk society writ large. It offers a world of individualised adventure and risk, while simultaneously subjecting consumers to a process of control. In the risk society the individual appears to be less constrained by social structures and yet ironically more constrained by his or her private whims and fears (Beck, 1992). Las Vegas is the risk society resort par excellence insofar as it offers individual freedom, but offsets or undermines such freedom with an institutional dependency. The consumer of Las Vegas feels better, feels that he or she is the centre of the experience the city offers, when in actuality he or she is subject to a process of standardisation just like everybody else. The risks that consumers experience in Las Vegas could therefore be described as "riskless risks": Las Vegas appropriates and disembowels the cultures it presents and then markets them as safe sanitised versions of the real thing. The impact of consumption on city life is, ironically, to make that life ever more predictable and secure (Hannigan, 1998). Las Vegas does not provide the freedom to consume; but rather the freedom to be mastered by consumption. And that is no sort of a freedom at all. As far as the consuming city is concerned then, gambling represents one example of a broader pattern in which gamblers no longer consume mere commodities, but the means of consumption itself (see Ritzer, 1999).

Many critics of the sociology of consumption have trouble coming to terms with how it is that something can be consumed without it physically being "used up". Las Vegas illustrates how it is that consuming cities can offer the consumer something more than a mere commodity: a sense of escape, a sense of individuality, a rush of blood to the head; an intangible yet deeply meaningful experience in which consumption is less about "using up" and more about fantasy and desire and in which the city is less about its physical manifestation and more about its place in the imagination. Anderton and Chase (1997b) describe Las Vegas as a "vast stageset" based upon the principles of pragmatism and private enterprise. Indeed, the real danger as Venturi indicates in an interview with Orbist and Koolhaas (2001) is that Las Vegas becomes an "exotic theater" rather than an actual place. Or as Dear (2000) puts it, Las Vegas hotels are the film sets and the sound stages upon which ordinary people can act out extraordinary lives. There are two Las Vegases – the real one in which people live and the one that has a place in the consumer's imagination. Las Vegas represents the extremes the city can reach should it continue to pursue the consumerist ideal (which it will of course inevitably do). Consumption in cities like Las Vegas is about quick fixes and as such this is a city better consumed on a 3-day trip than for life. Perhaps the most fitting description of the gambling city is best borrowed from the work of Horkheimer and Adorno. The gambling city is indeed a city that,

> perpetually cheats its consumers of what it perpetually promises. The promisory note which, with its plots and staging, it draws on pleasure is endlessly prolonged; the promise, which is actually all the spectacle consists of, is illusory: all it actually confirms is that the real point will never be reached, that the diner must be satisfied with the menu. (Horkheimer and Adorno, 1973: 139)

If the prediction that Las Vegas represents the city of the future proves to be correct, then there are genuine grounds for concern that planners, urbanists, geographers, and the like urgently need to consider. Las Vegas may be full to the brim of consumers of culture, but those consumers are not, ultimately, creative players in control of this process. They can only be creative players *within* the process. The consuming experience we associate with Las Vegas may ultimately be a sterile one. Hannigan (1998: 197) asks the crucial question here: "Will the entertainment economy, then, make twenty-first century cities more liveable or will it further accelerate the fragmentation and loss of community which have been the recent hallmarks of urban history?" The chances are that even if gambling does bring economic renewal into a city, those people who could most benefit from such investment are least likely to ever see it. Pre-packaged corporate entertainment may not, after all, be the messiah the city is looking for. Even if the gambling city or indeed the city of the spectacle manages to fulfil its economic remit, there will surely and inevitably be a price to pay. And that price is a city that is entertaining but one that simultaneously laughs in the face of social division and exclusion. A city that pretends that everything is okay. As Hess (1993: 23) puts it "In no place at all, someplace could be created. That is Las Vegas' genius." Win or lose, gamblers are more than happy to conspire in their own downfall because, what the hell, at least they feel good about themselves in the process.

CHAPTER 7

Reinventing the Consuming City

Cities take many forms. In recent years it could even be argued that an entirely new kind of city has emerged: a de-territorialised "urban" space that challenges our very sense of what we mean when we talk about "the city". In the last chapter, we discussed the emergence of Las Vegas as what in a sense is an artificial city: a city apparently constructed for the consumer rather than for its inhabitants. But Las Vegas only takes us so far in demonstrating the omnipresence of consumer cultures and its impact on how we relate to place and space. In recent years, an equally fascinating trend has been the emergence of locations which adopt particular characteristics that we might associate with cities, but which, in the conventional sense, cannot really be described as cities at all. The point here as Urry (1995) points out is that the visual consumption of both space and time has been both speeded up and abstracted from the logic of industrial production, to the extent that the city has been reconstructed as a centre for post-modern consumption:

> These dreamscapes pose significant problems for people's identity which has historically been founded on place, or where people come from or have moved to. Yet postmodern landscapes are all about place, such as Main St. in EuroDisney, world fairs or Covent Garden in London. But these are simulated places which are there for consumption. They are barely places that people any longer come from, or live in, or which provide much of a sense of social identity...
> (Urry, 1995: 21)

In this chapter we will discuss aspects of the de-spatialisation of urban space before discussing the cruise ship as an example of de-territorialised urbanism. As such, we will suggest that although cities are funding new forms of expression, that expression tells us as much about what consumption cannot give us as much as what it can.

Various authors have pointed how space and place define the world of the consumer. One of the most important authors in this respect is Sharon Zukin whose work is discussed in more detail in Chapter 3. Zukin refers to the "postmodern urban landscape". In this context, Zukin sees fantasy architecture as the literal stage set for consumption. As such, resorts such as Walt Disney's World constitute a dreamscape, a landscape of post-modernity which presents the consumer with a shared commercialised fantasy based upon the juxtaposition of real and fictional landscapes, "While the façades on Disney's Main Street abstract an image of security from North America's historical vernacular, the paste-board stage prop of his Magic Kingdom evokes a continuity between childhood fantasies and new construction. This is the landscape for the eye of the child in the mind of an adult" (Zukin, 1991: 233). Zukin goes on to discuss the existence of a Disney realism, a utopian re-imagining of the past. It is almost as if real cities no longer satisfy; they do not fulfil the requirements of a population with limited attention spans. This suggestion is very much reflected in the thoughts of Walt Disney in 1966 during which time he was planning, a technological community of the future, the Experimental Prototype Community of Tomorrow (EPCOT) which did not actually come to fruition until the 1980s:

> a city that caters to the people as a service function. It will be a planned, controlled community, a showcase for American industry and research, schools, cultural and educational opportunities. In EPCOT there will be no landowners and therefore no voting control. No slum areas because we will not let them develop. People will rent houses instead of buying them, and at modest rentals. There will be no retirees. Everyone must be employed. (Zukin, 1991: 234)

For legal reasons this model new town could never be built and ultimately the apparently utopian place that Disney had in mind for EPCOT became nothing more than a hi-tech tourist resort. Disney in short was not able to create a new model community or city, but rather what Zukin calls a "substitute for social reality": a symbolic reality which artificially creates economic value where it did not exist before; an imaginary city created not for consumers by consumers but by economic power reasserted through the dominance of a market culture. Consumers use the spaces which they consume to help us create socio-spatial identities. That is the urban power of consumption. Most interestingly from an urban perspective, consumption weds people or consumers to places that are not really places at all. And it does so because the utopian visions we have for our cities are simply not practicable. We envisage a consuming city; but the reality we end up with is a pale vestige in which consumption does not enhance reality, but seeks instead to replace it.

In his book *The Romantic Ethic and the Spirit of Modern Consumerism*, Colin Campbell highlights the imaginary nature of consumption. He argues that the development of modern hedonism is characterised by a shift in primary concern from sensations to emotions, "for it is only through the medium of the latter that powerful and prolonged stimulation can be combined with any significant degree of autonomous control, something which arises directly from the fact that an emotion links mental images with physical stimuli" (p. 69). In contemporary society then, individuals deploy their imaginations in order to construct mental images which they consume for the intrinsic pleasure such images provide. Consumption is not as such materialistic in nature, rather Campbell (1987) identifies a shift towards an increasingly symbolic role for consumption in a world where consumption is equated with desirous daydreaming. Campbell (1987) therefore argues that

> the idea that contemporary consumers have an insatiable desire to acquire objects represents a serious misunderstanding of the mechanism which impels people to want goods. The basic motivation is the desire to experience in reality the pleasurable dramas which they have already enjoyed in the imagination, and each "new" product is seen as offering a possibility of realizing this ambition. (p. 90)

Representations of the city

In an analysis of city as an arena in which consumption takes place, it does not take too much of a leap of the imagination to suggest that if representations of products have a key role in feeding our imaginative pleasure, the same can be said of representations of city life. If our conception of city life is drip-fed to us through consumption, then we as consumers are constantly open to aids which will help us construct our daydreams. As such, cinematic portrayals of city life can be said, for instance, to constitute far more than a mere reflection of city life. The city is constructed not only in a physical sense but also in an imaginary one. The cinema represents a key way in which we establish meanings for the city in which we live.

Many authors have argued that cinemas had an important role to play, notably in the early twentieth century, in shaping the experience of city life and that as such film actively feeds into the way in which we conceive of and interact with the city, "they provided, as it were, a mediating pedagogy between the reality of the metropolis and its imaginary place in mental life" (Donald, 1999: 63). The parallels with the work of Benjamin and Simmel and their work on the city here are more than coincidental. It is very important to recognise, as does Simmel, that the changing nature of city life over time, notably in Europe during the nineteenth century, had a profound impact not only on the city itself, but also on the "mental life" of city inhabitants. Meanwhile, Benjamin in the year 1970 notes that film corresponded to changes in the way in which human beings perceive the city. Particularly important for Benjamin in this respect is the flâneur who strolled through the nineteenth-century city constructing a personalised aesthetic definition of urban space (see Chapter 4).

As far as Simmel was concerned, the city emerged as an arena of over-stimulation which in turn undermined enduring structures of perception. This is an issue taken up in the work of Clarke (1997) who identifies a crisis at the turn of the century in which human beings were increasingly distracted and during which the cinema was increasingly able to feed into this distraction. As such, Donald uses the example of Rudolph Valentino's "The son of the sheik" in which a commodified version of sexuality was presented to American women. Cinema therefore offered consumers "an alternative horizon of experience, which they could in turn, feed into their experience of city life" (Donald, 1999: 65). The cinema created a new form of public space: a space in which the inherent changes of modernity could be both represented and fiercely debated. This suggestion might be difficult to comprehend at a time when television has clearly surpassed cinema in such respects, but in many ways it was the urban origin of the cinema that made it such a powerful medium:

> One thing cinema – or at least film has continued to do since the nineteen twenties has been to teach its audiences across the globe ways of seeing and so imagining the modern city, whether or not they live in one. The imagined landscape of the city has become, inescapably a cinematic landscape. But the city in cinema does not operate just as a backdrop. Nor is the representation of the city really the use. To use Lefebvre's term film presents urban space as itself representational, as simultaneously sensory and symbolic. It thus

provides the real-imagined space of the city as haunted. It establishes distraction as an ontological norm. (Donald, 1999: 68)

The way in which films use architecture is therefore self-consciously loaded with meaning. For instance, portrayals of fantasy cities are usually not real in any sense at all, but construct an imaginary sense of the city that feeds into our perception of the real city. *Metropolis*, for instance, the seminal screen city, was a city built from matted models but its impact upon how we perceive of the development of city life is undoubtedly profound. Similarly, Bass (1997) argues that cinematic representations of Rome actively alter the reality of Rome insofar as it constructs an avalanche of simulations that become reality, Rome is more than anything else becoming a city of films, directors, and representations. The cinema represents a very powerful medium that can actively construct not only our perception of cities, but also of consumption's role in that city. In *28 Days Later*, for instance, Director Danny Boyle portrays London as a city decimated by a man-made virus which turns people into angry zombie-like creatures. The early frames of the film depict a city deserted, but a city whose heart has apparently been ripped out by consumerist excess. The landscape may be barren and deserted but advertising hoardings continue to tower above the urban landscape, apparently reinforcing to the viewer the inherent emptiness of the consuming city.

Touring space

This brief discussion of the relationship between the cinema and the city raises a critical question as to the paradoxical nature of the city which appears to be at one and the same time inherently mundane and yet phantasmagoric. The suggestion underpinning this chapter is that it is consumption that creates this paradox. By its very nature city life is routine. It has to be that way to make it manageable on a day-to-day basis. Consumption feeds the consumer's imaginative needs whilst camouflaging the less stimulating and more calculated nature of everyday city life. In effect consumers of the city consume a vision of that city that may be more about their imaginations than it does about the city itself. In many respects then, as Donald (1999) suggests, the city is not a place at all, but a historically specific "mode of seeing". The point here is that consumption predefines the parameters within which consumers develop such modes of seeing. As such, Robert David Sack

(1992) has suggested that the everyday landscape of consumption intentionally alters aspects of reality. In effect, everything in the consumer society is created as a common space of consumption. Tourism (which we discuss in more detail in Chapter 4) is particularly interesting in this regard insofar as, "Creating tourist places embeds the tensions of commodities into the landscape" (Sack, 1992: 157). As far as Sack is concerned then, landscapes of consumption ultimately consume their own contexts. Tourism will not only degrade the natural environment but the cultural context as well. As such, tourism homogenises space which hosts highly contrived versions of indigenous culture. Whether the tourist likes it or not, and he or she apparently often does, consumption landscapes are inauthentic landscapes. By their very nature from this point of view the places tourists visit must be as familiar as possible and yet retain a modicum of specificity to be attractive. This then, constitutes, Baudrillard's (1988) age of simulation, a hyper-real world in which the only reality is the consumer's reality,

> But not everything in the consumer's world is smooth, even on the surface. The threads which it interweaves threaten to unravel. This is a world without constraints and without responsibility. It makes each of us the arbiter of what is important and how much to consume. How do we choose one thing over another when they are no clear obligations and responsibilities and when there is no necessity? How do we form social relations and define ourselves when we have no particular objects or tasks? The unrestricted freedoms of the consumer's world could also create a weightless and disorienting world. (Sack, 1992: 199)

In many respects, as Urry points out in the second edition of his *The Tourist Gaze* (2002) we live in a mobile world in which not only tourists travel, but so do objects, cultures and images. In this respect you could even argue that the sense of identity we associate with the place in which we live or indeed from which we come is less significant than it was in the past. An illustration of this development, as Urry points out, is the relationship between international mega-events and the identity of individual cities. Such cities benefit from the symbolic nature of these interventions as much as they do from the economic renumeration. The Olympics, the World Cup, and Expo are therefore discussed by Urry as examples of events that can reinvent the identity of cities on a global scale. From this point of view, broad conceptions of territory are less central to the definition of a place. Of more significance are specific

places, landscapes and symbols and not least consumption opportunities. In this light Urry describes the increasingly nomadic nature of
contemporary social life. To this end he quotes Makimoto and Manners
(1997: 2) who argue that such geographically independent people will
be "free to live where they want and travel as much as they want". The
degree of freedom here is clearly exaggerated and has to be tempered
with a grounded understanding of the sorts of resource issues that inevitably frame consumer's abilities to travel. Indeed, the experience of the
nomadic consumer tells us as much about the failings or exclusionary
nature of the consuming society as it does about its successes.

The cruising city

As Sacks points out above, landscapes of consumption will ultimately
consume their own contexts. In other words, landscapes of consumption
are by their very essence unnatural; they are only real inasmuch
as consumers experience them. They constitute what is in effect, an
inauthentic reality. This point raises the possibility that cities can potentially, at least, transcend space. They need not be fettered by the pre-existing
use of space, as the recent emergence of Las Vegas discussed in Chapter 6
partially illustrates. In this sense, many cities can be described as being
imaginary; as transcending space and place. In fact, we do not really
have a word that adequately reflects the impact or the nature of the
"simulated" city. Urban environments have indeed become deterritorialised and perhaps the best illustration of this process is that of the
moving city or the city at sea. The cruise ship is relatively free from
political regulation; it is unconnected to any territorial location other
than that outlined in its itinerary and amounts to a floating theme park –
a city that is more important a destination than the ports in which it
docks (see Wood, 2000). In what remains of this chapter, we will put
forward the suggestion that the cruise ship represents a whole new kind
of city: what is in effect a placeless city. In short, in its determination to
find new markets through the commodification of city life, consumer
capitalism has reached the stage where it can now actively transcend place
in the form of a mobile city, a city without place, but *with* consumption.

The nomadic nature of tourism, and indeed of the consumer society
more generally, is expressed particularly vividly in the rapid growth in
recent years of cruising. Cruise ships provide the ultimate experience
for the nomad. To consume a cruise is to consume a variety of different
cultures and experiences on tap. The cruise ship represents the ultimate

floating location for the flâneur, but not necessarily in a subversive sense. It provides a relatively confined space which is actively designed both to encourage passengers to stroll through observing one another whilst taking advantage of apparently endless opportunities to consume. At port-side the opportunity to observe unfamiliar (and yet familiar) cultures is extended.

As Wood (2000) points out, however, sociological and anthropological analyses of cruise tourism are virtually non-existent. A positive step in this direction is provided by Cartwright and Baird (1999) who discuss Urry's notion of the "tourist gaze". Tourists have preconceptions about any trip they are about to go on. Anticipation is indeed, often the greatest pleasure of a holiday. According to Urry, tourists think that they go on holiday to experience something new, and the familiar is only worth their gaze if it is reconstituted in an unfamiliar context. Cartwright and Baird argue that an understanding of the cruise industry is enlightening at least in the respect that cruising fulfils the requirements of the tourist gaze. It presents the consumer with the familiar in an unfamiliar guise. A cruise-line passenger can cruise the world's seas, whilst simultaneously living in an environment that is reassuringly familiar. But in order to fulfil the consumer's requirements, those experiences must not be *too* alien. "The need for a sufficient comfort zone and enough of the unfamiliar to satisfy the gaze gives a major challenge to those promoting tourism products. There is a need to provide new horizons within the safe familiarity of home" (Cartwright and Baird, 1999: 15).

The growth of the cruising industry was particularly marked during the 1990s. Between 1988 and 1998, the number of cruise ships increased from 97 to 129 and the number of berths almost doubled from 68,474 to 127,943 (Cartwright and Baird, 1999). The global threat of terrorism in the wake of September 11 has forced the industry to re-assess a situation in which share prices have dropped rapidly, and in which American passengers, in particular, are less prepared to fly than they were in the past. However, there are signs of recovery in this regard, and The World Cruise Market Update (Travel and Tourism Analyst, 2002) suggests there are reasonable grounds for cautious optimism. Although estimates as to the drop in custom through 2002 range from about 7–15 per cent, the American Association of Travel Agents actually went on record to say that cruising was the sector least affected by September 11, and indeed was likely to be the first to recover.

But regardless of the current economic situation, there is no doubt that cruise ships provide a highly concentrated form of floating consumption. They are indeed mobile vessels designed to provide 24-hour access to consumption; consumption that is not curtailed by the boring predictability of space and place. Above and beyond the opportunity to tap into a variety of cultures before returning to the security of the ship, passengers need not leave the ship at all. Cruise ships pride themselves on their 24-hour service, the almost constant provision of food and entertainment, the diverse range of cabins and public rooms to suit every imaginable taste and their total devotion to the constant relaxation of the passengers. Of course, passengers also constitute what is very much a captive market. Although entertainment and food is (on the whole) usually included in the cost of a cruise (which incidentally, cost-wise are generally at the high end of the holiday market), there are many additional opportunities for passengers to put their hands in their pockets. Passengers are encouraged to dwell over the vast range of tour excursions offered by most cruise companies, before and during the voyage. Beverages are an additional cost on most cruises. Indeed, many such companies ask their passengers to pay for a glass of champagne provided by roving waiters as their ship departs from its starting point. Other extras such as beauty treatments, photographic services, the casino, and even art auctions also allow the relaxed holidaying passenger to treat himself or herself. Meanwhile, modern cruise ships all have their own shopping facilities and many offer one-off sales of jewellery or perhaps watches at special prices which they are able to offer due to bulk-buying. A cruise ship is a moving cathedral of consumption as much as it is a traveller's refuge. This is a point picked up upon by Ritzer (1999) who describes the cruise ship as a new means of consumption, which offers the tourist everything they might need under one roof: altering the experience of shopping by making it far more efficient in nature. The cruise ship is indeed a selling machine. For Ritzer, cruise ships are what you might call "total institutions". They conform to Goffman's (1961) notion of a place of residence that encloses people off from wider society and provides them with a highly administered life:

> Passengers are not nearly as constrained as members of the crew, to say nothing of inmates of prisons or mental institutions, but there is nonetheless significant constraint on them. They cannot leave the ship while at sea, they can only do what is available to them on board, and they can only consume when and what the ship offers. (Ritzer, 1999: 92–93)

Much like the casino resorts we discussed in Chapter 6, cruise ships are vast stage sets within which consumers carry out their fantasies. But the fantasies in which passengers partake arguably promote a vision of the passive consumer. Attending a show on a cruise ship, for instance, is not likely to promote creativity on the part of the passenger. The ship has to provide for a mass market and will regularly repeat shows. Individuality is not an ingredient that is suited to such an environment. This very much reflects, Chaney's (1993) related argument as Ritzer notes, that today we live in the society of the spectacle, as opposed to the spectacular society of the past. In other words, spectacle used to be an integral part of our culture (in the form of local carnivals and country fairs, for example). And although such events still go on, we now prefer to seek out our drama and consume it passively. Many spectacles are created for us, simply in order to create profit and to enable consumer capitalism to tick over accordingly. One example of this is evident in the massive investment of television companies in sport, and in particular, football. Although, in England at least crowds remain relatively high, a whole new industry of football consumption has emerged in the home and in the public house, where it simply is not necessary for the consumer to get involved in the spectacle in any direct fashion, beyond buying the latest Manchester United shirt. Similarly, the spectacle of the cruise show can from this point of view be seen to be inherently passive. Contemporary consumers do not participate in the spectacle, but merely observe it.

Perhaps the most fundamental recent development in cruise ship design is in their sheer size. Robert Wood, for instance, points out that Royal Caribbean's *Grand Princess* is taller than Niagara Falls and almost a fifth of a mile long. Many such ships fit into a new category of "post-Panama" ships too big to go through the Panama Canal. As Ritzer points out, the dimensions of many new cruise ships are simply mind-boggling. Many house large theatres, fitness centres, climbing walls and even ice rinks. The danger for Ritzer is that the people on such ships are more impressed by the on-board spectacle and architecture than they are by the vistas that surround them. Is there a danger that the sea and the views it provides become nothing more than incidental? There does indeed appear to be a trend towards the ship itself becoming the main attraction rather than the destination ports. In many respects, cruise ships are in competition with land-based resorts such as Las Vegas and as such market themselves as resort destinations. Wood (2000) goes as far as to suggest that "destinational cruising" where the port is the core focus of the trip is actually now considered to be little more than a niche market in the industry. The onus on ships is indeed on the consumer to look inwards. The architecture of such ships is often built in an inward-looking fashion, to the degree that the sea is optional, but consumption is not. It could be argued in many respects that the cruise ships, and especially the larger cruise ships, constitute placeless cities; a placelessness juxtaposed with the pseudo-reality of the tourist centres consumers visit along the way. There is considerable debate amongst sociologists of tourism as to the degree of authenticity of tourist sites. Meethan (2001) for instance, notes that there is an inherent conflict between the developmental nature of modernity and the traditional cultures that modernity, by its very nature, supplants. Commodification plays a key role here insofar as it arguably decontextualises traditional ways of life. However, as Meethan goes on to note, the whole debate surrounding authenticity is in danger of descending into an elitism that patronisingly claims to be able to defend traditional cultures that may not need defending in the first place.

Cruise ships actually take this debate one step further insofar as local cultures are often almost entirely excluded from the tourists' experience. The time in which tourists have to consume local cultures is sometimes as little as half a day and is therefore inevitably abridged or censored. Of even more interest in this respect is the fact that many cruise companies own their own "fantasy islands" which are therefore available exclusively to passengers and employees. As Wood (2000) points out, six of the eight major cruise operators own islands in the Caribbean which they market as the authentic Caribbean experience, somehow better than the real thing and yet in a way not real at all. Royal Caribbean, for example, owns two "islands", "Coco Bay" and "Labadee". The latter is not in fact an island at all (despite company literature suggesting otherwise), but a part of Haiti surrounded by a ten-foot-high wall and patrolled by armed guards, "Freed of spontaneous contact and experiences, these carefully-planned and artificially-created environments are said to take cruise passengers back to the real, authentic Caribbean-one that existed 30 years ago but no longer exists except in reconstructed form on these fantasy islands" (Wood, 2000: 362). All is well and good for the tourist, but this state of affairs may have a significant knock-on effect for the local economy of a port that would otherwise have been on a ship's itinerary. In other words, the floating city may provide a consuming paradise, but that paradise is not without its negative implications. The cruising experience is not designed to encourage the consumer to critically consider the hidden power dimensions that lie behind the production process; in fact it actively conceals the divisive nature of the production/consumption relationship (Marx, 1990).

The city-like character of cruise ships is especially marked when you consider the production-side of the equation. In another sense, cruise ships are placeless global cities. As Wood (2000) indicates the success of the cruise sector is at least partly the result of the adoption of flags of convenience. Cruise ships do not usually carry the flag of their home country (only one major cruise ship, the SS Independence flies the US flag and a has an American crew) because if they were to do so they would have to deal with more rigorous labour laws, taxes, and maritime regulations. In this sense cruise ships are legal havens. The flags of convenience they adopt free them from labour laws whatsoever. As Wood points out, when it was realised, for example, that Panamanian law guarantees one day off a week, the cruise ship industry successfully lobbied for an exemption. If ships pay less wages, less taxes and are able to make more demands on their work-force they will, in turn, make more profit, but as a result they will also create a hierarchical structure not entirely different to the social division found in all cities. The needs of the passengers are of course dealt with on demand. Meanwhile the traditional hierarchy of a ship consisting of the captain, officers, technicians and seamen is super-imposed onto that of a resort with separate hierarchies associated with the kitchen, the dinning room, housekeeping, entertainment and so on: a large ship may have over 1000 working passengers in over 160 occupational roles. Ships are usually ethnically diverse, but are organised in clear horizontal and vertical lines of ethnic stratification. Indeed, "It is hard to conceive of a more compact and diverse 'ethnoscape' than that of a cruiseship, nor one more directly linked to . . . global mediascapes, technoscapes, financescapes and ideoscapes" (Wood, 2000: 353). From this point of view, such ethnic diversity might suggest that large cruise ships constitute the ultimate placeless, global city. According to Wood, companies such as Carnival and Royal Caribbean typically have crews from 40 or more countries in a single ship. While the passengers' experience of the floating city is usually short-lived, many of the crew are long-term residents. The ship is their home and their workplace rolled into one. Crew members do, of course, have their own segregated areas. They are in effect excluded, from parts of the city, at least at the residential level. Cruise ships are segregated in the same way that cities are segregated, much like richer areas of cities that often exclude "undesirables", in the form of gated communities for example. The ability to consume in these environments is of course biased in favour of the passengers, whilst below deck crew members are both susceptible to institutional racism and paid far less than their "colleagues" who work deck-side.

A cynic might suggest that the link between cruise ships and city life is a little on the tenuous side. After all, cruise ships are in a sense placeless entities. However, when you consider the way in which the cruise ship industry is developing, the similarities between city life and that of the cruise ship comes into sharper focus. In this respect, we might suggest that current conceptions of the city are too limiting, simply because we are unable to comprehend the degree to which consumption can change the nature of city life. Consumption is so omnipresent and so powerful that it can create entirely new social forms that challenge the traditional labels that we depend upon. From this point of view, cruise ships are the cities of the future. In order to illustrate my point I want to consider the new generation of cruise ships. *The Voyager of the Seas*, with room for 3114 passengers, was formerly the world's biggest cruise ship and includes a rock climbing wall, skating rinks, an internet lounge, and video arcade amongst its amenities. *The Voyager of the Seas* is 1020-feet long and 158-feet wide and as the "Popular Mechanics" web-site points out the inside cabins overlook a promenade wide enough for three lanes of traffic, shops, restaurants, and a casino, ensuring that the ship rather than the ship's destination is the main attraction (http://popularmechanics.com/science/transportation/2001/5/heavy_cruiser/index2.phtml). This is a ship that even houses science laboratories.

At the moment there appears to be a constant flow of massive new cruise ships. In January of 2004, 2600 passengers paid $48,000 for the privilege of setting sail on the 150,000-ton Cunard vessel *Queen Mary II*'s maiden voyage. Perhaps even more impressive is the rather modestly named *The World*, which cost £384 millions to construct and which, crucially, markets itself as the world's first and only "residence at sea". A 43,000 ton, 200-metre-long passenger ship, it is the first of a new generation of "floating condominiums" with apartments as opposed to cabins ranging in price from $2 millions to more than £7 millions (*Sydney Morning Herald*). Broadly speaking, the plan is and was to provide a "designer ship" for wealthy retirees which perpetually circumnavigates the globe. Interestingly, the project has undergone a variety of financial setbacks and construction delays, and as such, was scaled back from its originally intended 85,000 ton due to financing difficulties (the original projected outlay was $700 millions) and concerns about it being unable to enter the smaller attractive ports it was promising its potential clients due to its sheer size. Each of the 110 private apartments have 50-year leases. Interestingly, given my discussion about the above, residents are not permitted to claim *The World* as their primary residence, therefore offsetting criticisms that it is acting as a tax haven. One of the benefits of this particular cruise ship is that residents have the power to customise their own itineraries. They must also show a net worth of $5 million before being welcomed aboard. As general manager Anthony Stevens puts it when describing shorter term guests who can rent apartments for $14,700 a week or suites starting at $5595 a person, "We aim for those who want enrichment, not Las Vegas-style shows." Bleecker and Bleecker (2002) describe the ship as an "upscale community". Meanwhile, Freddy Dellis, ResidenSea President and CEO, who Bleecker and Bleecker (2002) interviews, argues, "[*World*] is not a cruise ship. So it is not regimented. You don't have a captain's welcome party, where everybody dresses up. You don't have a captain's farewell party ... You really live in a resort community and you do as you please" (3). There are nonetheless more than enough opportunities to consume. Residents can take in special world events built into the ship's itinerary such as the Olympics, the British Open, or the Monte Carlo Grand Prix (Shriver, 2002); stay in ports for an average of 2 and a half days (as opposed to one night on a conventional cruise ship); buy a $10,000 watch or a £360 jar of caviar-extract face cream. As one resident, Karyn Planett puts it, "My only concern is that we'll be seen only as a ship of millionaires and nothing but that. It's more a ship of adventurers and pioneers. I don't think we'll go around the world shopping" (p. 5). Need she say more?

Perhaps the most intriguing project of this kind, and still in develop-ment, is the *Freedom Ship*, a massive project that will cost an estimated $11 billion. The ship has its own web-site intended to attract funds (www.freedomship.com/overview.html). The ship, 4500-feet long and 750-feet wide, markets itself as a floating city four times longer than any current cruise ship, and one in which consumption is at the core. "The design concept includes a mobile modern city featuring luxurious living, an extensive duty-free international shopping mall, and a full 1.7 million square feet set aside for various companies to showcase their products" (1). Indeed, two of *Freedom Ship*'s three primary objectives have consumption at their core.

The Freedom Ship Project's Primary Objectives (www.freedomship.com/overview.html):

- Provide a unique, travelling residential community, combining the amenities of a modern city with those of the finest resorts, in an attractive, stimulating, and secure environment.
- Create a vigorous commercial community whose privately owned and operated on board enterprises will sell their products and services worldwide.

- Establish the world's largest duty-free retail shopping mall and bring it to markets around the world with a steady and substantial stream of resident and visiting customers.

The above web page makes every effort to dissociate itself from the traditional concept of a cruise ship. It even states in black and white that it is not a cruise ship at all, but a permanent city that circles the globe twice every year. As an article in the *Herald Tribune* (2002) put it, this is a city on the sea with all the attributes of a small but highly sophisticated city with its own railway system and park areas. In actual fact, the original idea for the project was to create a new city on the 50-square-mile uninhabited island of East Caicos, south of the Bahamas, what Norman L. Nixon the main figure behind the development described as a "modern Hong Kong". However, for political reasons the idea never got off the ground, hence the decision to pursue the vision for a floating city: a city large enough to be home to 50–60,000 residents, 15,000 employees and 20,000 day guests accommodated by 17,000 homes and 4000 businesses. *Freedom Ship* aspires to have its own mini-airport, serving private and commercial aircraft, and in addition to residential, retail and wholesale space it will apparently boast a library, top class schools, banks, hotels, restaurants, offices, warehouses, and light manufacture and assembly enterprises. The deterritorialised nature of the *Freedom Ship* underlies its rationale: the project aims to include a top-class hospital costing $200 million and to call upon world-wide medical procedures and unfettered by the controls of specific countries. This is apparently, a veritable "Community on the Sea" which can support its own local economy:

> The primary focus of the project is to create a community that offers unique life-style opportunities. *Freedom Ship* would be the world's first mobile community. It would provide an international, cosmo-politan, full-spectrum, residential, commercial, and resort city that circles the globe once every two years. It would offer a wide array of novel opportunities for business ownership, travel, and daily living. The ship is as large as it is, simply because that is the minimum size required to make the community economically self-sustaining and a desirable and attractive place to live. (http://www.freedomship.com/common_misperceptions.html)

As its name indicates the whole project is a capitalistic dream (and indeed whether or not the dream comes to fruition remains to be seen) underpinned by the freest and the most mobile of free markets. It is founded on the notion that this will be the freest capitalistic society on earth – A society based on personal freedom and free enterprise, that nonetheless comes with its very own patrolling 24-hour security force; A city, in effect, founded on the myth of consumerism. Those responsible for this project would argue that this ship is less elitist than it might sound. The sheer size of the *Freedom Ship* represents, apparently, an effort to make this floating city as affordable for as large an amount of people as possible. The intention, at least on paper, is not to establish another floating and walled city for the upper classes. *The Freedom Ship* plans two hundred times as many units as *The World* and a wider range of options. As the *Herald Tribune* article suggests, residences would range from a $153,000 "motel room" to a 5100 square feet unit with extensive water views for $9,137,000. Meanwhile, additional commercial fees would range from $220,000 to $2.3 millions. *The Freedom Ship* represents what would be an amazing engineering feat, and also what is ultimately an equally amazing commercial one. It may not be as elitist as other similar projects, but that does not mean it is not elitist. We are talking degrees of elitism here.

Ultimately, all the projects I have discussed constitute floating refuges for the consuming classes. In researching these mega-projects none of the literature we have read focuses on the flip-side of the coin. What about those people providing the labour-power that may or may not make these projects work, as well as those "consumers" who do not have the necessary resources to take part in what are inevitably exclusionary projects. The question then is what do these cruise ships say about the way in which our notion of the city is apparently changing? Perhaps above all, they illustrate the power dimensions inherent in the freedom to consume. These ships might well be described as elite cities that free consumers from the ravages of the real world. They represent a belief that consumption can create a city free of undesirables and free of the less palatable aspects of city life, such as homelessness, drug use, prostitution and at a more mundane level straightforward working classness. In this respect, consumption has been sanctified as a source of new hope; hope engendered through the freedoms of the market.

Conclusion

It is not unusual for commentators to identify the emergence of new kinds of cities that challenge how we conceive of urban life. For instance,

Light (1999) considers the suggestion that urban environments are increasingly commodified and that the authenticity of cities is in decline, not least due to the apparent breakdown of informal public life and community. In this respect, Light's work is worth considering in some detail. The suggestion here is that public space appears at least in some sense to have been replaced by "simulations". The concern here for Light is that such spaces market themselves as revitalising public life when they are in fact wholly exclusionary in nature. From this point of view such simulations, of which you might argue the mega-cruise ship is a prime example, signal not only a loss of authenticity but also a loss of reality. Light goes on to suggest that this process of commodification is not recent, but reflects a long-term process evident as far back as the nineteenth century in the form of the Parisian department stores, for example (see Chapter 5). Light describes Paris at this time as "an object to be visually consumed and collected" (115). The commodification of public space is not therefore a recent phenomenon and moreover, as Light points out, there is a strong argument to suggest that consumers use such space far more critically and creatively than might be assumed. Similarly, Light critiques those commentators who have condemned the inauthenticity of contemporary architecture. This too is nothing recent or unique argues Light: nineteenth century railway stations were equally derivative and as such suggest something of a romanticisation which is less a reflection of reality and more a reflection of a particular class position.

Light goes on to link city space to cyberspace, arguing that the profound impact of various media in the home has arguably had a role to play in the decline of public space in the city. This is a point made equally effective by Mitchell (1995) who argues that traditional conceptions of space have been undermined by the world-wide computer network which radically redefines how we perceive notions of place, community, and urbanity. Nowadays, communities no longer need a single location, but can just as easily be located in cyberspace:

> This will be a city unrooted to any definite spot on the surface of the earth, shaped by connectivity and bandwidth constraints rather than by accessibility and land values, largely asynchronous in its operations, and inhabited by disembodied and fragmented subjects who exist as collections of aliases and agents. Its places will be constructed virtually by software instead of physically from stone and timbers, and they will be connected by logical linkages rather than doors, passageways and streets. (p. 24)

From this point of view city design is as much about writing effective computer code as it is about configuring public space. The new media has apparently had a negative impact upon cities and Light goes as far as to suggest that cities are actually becoming dematerialised in people's minds. She thus quotes Sorkin (1992) who argues that recent years have seen the emergence of a wholly new kind of city without a place attached to it" (p. xi) or in other words, entirely divorced from local geographies. What is going on here both in terms of cityspace and cyberspace is the breakdown of reality as we used to know it, "It is not only cities that are disappearing, but 'reality' – an idea which stands in for authenticity, community, public space and an idealised non-commercial realm" (Light, 122). This point is equally well made by Soja (1998) who argues that "As our ability to tell the difference between what is real and what is imagined is weakened, another kind of reality – a hyperreality – flourishes and increasingly flows into everyday life...reality is no longer what it used to be" (239–240). From this point of view, consumption is arguably ridding us of a sense of reality. Although cities are of course constantly being reinvented perhaps we have reached a stage in which that reinvention has gone so far that we need to re-evaluate what we mean when we actually refer to the "city". In order to do so, it is necessary to take a step back. In Chapter 1 we referred to a tendency to exaggerate the impact of consumption on the city, and in particular to venerate the emergence of the post-industrial city. As such, it is necessary to be cautious in discussing the so-called reinvention of city life. It may well be true that the city form is exploring new kinds of expression. But it is important to remember that the city has always been a foci for social and economic change. Even more importantly, we should avoid any temptation to generalise about how consumers use city space. To this end, Soja (2000: 324–325) quotes Iain Chambers (1990) who points out, quite rightly, that

> The city exists as a series of doubles; it has official and hidden cultures, it is a real place and a site of imagination. Its elaborate network of streets, housing, public buildings, transport systems, parks and shops is paralleled by a complex of attitudes, habits, customs, expectancies, and hopes that reside in us as urban subjects. We discover that urban "reality" is not single but multiple, that inside the city there is always another city.

Consumption may well have always played an important role in determining the character and form of city life. What is more important is the fact that ultimately these forms of expression, so visibly illustrated in the context of the floating city simply serve to extend the divisive nature of consumption. The imaginary city is only real to the select few able to afford it. The consuming city is imaginary precisely because it is *not* democratic and can never be democratic. Similarly, Disney World might offer a whole new kind of escapist urbanism. In the imagination of millions this provides a dream-like urbanity, but it is only actually available to the smallest minority of consumers. This, unfortunately is the reality of the consuming city. Whatever form it takes, imaginary or otherwise, the consuming city will always apparently divide more than it can provide.

CHAPTER 8

Alternative Consumption

So far we have examined urban consumption in the late twentieth century, and aspects of consumerism in today's globalised economy. In this chapter we look forward to speculate that a post-consumerist society is at least a possibility, if as yet remote. Consumerism, we admit, will not suddenly cease to be a dominating force in the lives of most people in the affluent world – their lifestyles are too captivating for that to happen – but despite that we think it worth asking what evidence there is for a sense of criticality on the part of consumers today, and what signs there are of emerging forms of consumption which could, if linked to a differentiation of human need from the wants manufactured by the market under consumerism, form the basis of a post-consumer economy and society. We accept that such signs are highly localised, and that many initiatives for alternative consumption are set in non-urban contexts – outside the centres of majority population. But, given the remoteness of revolutionary change, we see these signs as the currently available indicators of a possibility of *incremental* change towards a post-consumerist society.

The question is presented in the context of mounting evidence of climate change, species loss on an unprecedented scale, widespread environmental damage, and a realisation that consumerism on its present scale, globally exported, assumes an exploitative view of the planet. None of this is sustainable. This is not to say a post-consumerist society is necessarily an environmentalist society, but it is to say that consumerism is part of an economic system which drives environmental destructiveness. There are, in any case, several kinds of environmentalism, as adopted by governments and trans-national companies, by agencies, by individual commentators, and by campaigning groups (Pepper, 1996). These environmentalisms include a notion of sustainability which seeks merely to modify the present system in order to maintain it in a less damaging form; radical philosophies such as social ecology

(Bookchin, 1980, 1990; Light, 1998) and deep ecology (Naess, 1989), and less formalised proposals for social transformation on the part of thinkers such as Ivan Illich (1981) and Herbert Marcuse (1969) who first raised environmental issues as socio-economic issues in the late 1960s; and the direct action taken by an increasing number of individuals and groups, for instance in animal rights campaigns and anti-road protests (McKay, 1996; Wall, 1999). While there is a vast gap between, say, road protest and state policies on sustainability, and the causes of road protest are more complex than a concern for either local landscapes and wildlife habitats or global pollution, that such campaigns have engaged people from a wide social spectrum and in large numbers, and that green issues have risen (if cynically) on government agendas, indicates a possibility of change. Taken singly, each element is slight, while the power of trans-national companies to pillage the planet's wealth seems inexorable; yet each voice raised against environmental destruction is an intervention which shifts the matrix.

The difficulty with incremental change is that it may be either too small a rupture of the dominant system to be effective, or subsumed within the dominant system so that it is no longer a rupture of it. Green consumption – the consumption of environmentally non- or less-damaging goods and services – is prone to the latter, as industries niche-market goods which, while less damaging to the environment than others, remain integral to an economy based on a fantasy of permanent increase in profits for producers, fuelled by the sale of dreams. For example, motor vehicles which have low fuel consumption are greener than those which guzzle gas, but still use large quantities of materials and energy in manufacture, and contribute (if less) to pollution. A more radical strategy would be a switch from private to public transport, but that requires a policy to provide the quality of public transport which would persuade motorists to make the switch. It would be detrimental to the profits of the motor and oil industries, both of which are powerful global lobbies, and such a proposal inevitably leads to controversy and perhaps a stronger realisation of the links between governments and trans-national companies – campaigning groups often being adversaries of both. Sandy Irvine, in *The Ecologist*, makes a similar point about the cosmetic industry (a branch of the petro-chemical industry as the list of ingredients on a shampoo bottle will confirm). Arguing that "Human fulfilment is still defined largely in terms of the purchase of commodities," he contrasts a conventional with a seemingly progressive high-street store to say that while one is more socially and environmentally enlightened "both want you to fill out your bathrooms with deodorants, perfumes and all the other paraphernalia of conspicuous consumption" (Irvine, 1989: 88). Driving a low-fuel car, or buying a cosmetic product which is not tested on animals are steps in the direction of a more sustainable and humane society, but both mask the need for a far more radical revision of wants – for an alternative economy, not just a green-tinted economy.

The concept of an alternative economy we propose includes greener forms of consumption, but also a change in the basis of economic organisation, moving away from the global towards the local. There are several difficulties which we do not pretend to be able to address adequately: first, radical change may require regulation in order to be accomplished, while in a climate of globalised de-regulation such intervention will not happen. Secondly, a change instituted by regulation – from above – may not change the power relations in a society. Thirdly, local initiatives are not only dwarfed by global consumerism but also prone to either self-marginalisation, or a gradual adoption of the methods they began by refusing. Discussion below of organic vegetable box delivery schemes, and a local cooperative bottling and distributing Dartmoor water, illustrate some of the problems, while both indicate a viable post-consumerist society. A key question in all this, however, is the extent to which there is, or not, an active or critical aspect to contemporary consumption. Whatever the problems of regulation, if consumers themselves take responsibility for the consequences of their consumption, then real change seems nearer. Consumers, though, do not constitute a unitary or coherent social group, and, as the sociology of consumption shows, the evidence for consumer intervention on ethical grounds is inconclusive. We preface examination of that, and then of cases of possible alternatives to consumerism, with a brief discussion of the differentiation of needs from wants which underpins any move to a more sustainable economy.

Wants and needs

The difference between wants (a new car, new fashions, or the latest mobile phone) and the needs of human survival (food, water, clothing, shelter) is obvious, but the difference between what is a reasonable or unreasonable level of expectation, conditioned either by global consumerism and a global mass media industry or by awareness of the planet's finite resources, is a matter for argument. When consumption not only reflects wealth but is aspirational, what is needed becomes psychological, and a material analysis becomes inadequate. At the same time, restaurant reviews in Sunday broadsheet newspapers in the UK commonly give prices for a meal for two which equate to the entire weekly income of a non-employed parent and child. In more dramatic contrast are the average incomes of citizens in rich and poor countries, a gap which cannot be explained by failures to produce on the part of states in the non-affluent world which are coerced by trans-national trade agreements and crippled by debt repayments. But if poverty is not the fault of the poor, it is no accident either: Conrad Lodziak sees the increasing impoverishment of non-affluent countries as a product of the system of global capitalism, prefacing his argument with the statement that "... capitalism has a long history of destroying human life" (Lodziak, 2002: 142). Similarly, geographer Aram Eisenschitz argues that "The history of capitalism demonstrates its scant regard for human life" (Eisenschitz, 1997: 153) in an essay on urban socio-economic exclusion in the United Kingdom in the 1980s and 1990s. The free market, it seems, is highly rewarding for those who control flows of capital, production, and distribution, but costly for those consuming and producing at the disadvantaged end.

Lodziak sees factors such as built-in obsolescence and mythicised consumer choice as designed to expand home markets and increase profits. Meanwhile, hitherto self-reliant societies outside the affluent world, with appropriate means of governance and culturally based divisions of space, are frequently plundered for raw materials and low-cost labour. Most colonised societies are now independent states but their political elites adopt the affluent world's model of development – Lodziak argues that the import of technologies, the planning of colonial-style cities, and the reproduction of social divisions result in massive borrowing from the world financial system, while the erasure of cultural boundaries produces wars that are "highly lucrative for the producers and suppliers of armaments" (Lodziak, 2002: 142). Lodziak may over-state his case, but we see his drift, as it were, as appropriate. He writes, for instance, that third-world economies are forced by debt repayment to move from local agricultures to intensive agri-business in order to gain hard currencies, and that this aids increasing control on the part of trans-national companies over their affairs, in a *system* of deprivation. Though Lodziak does not say so, the manufacture of genetically modified food confirms this when countries such as India and Brazil become test-ing grounds for a technology designed to ensure seed monopolies for trans-national companies at the expense of local producers who would otherwise be able to meet local food needs (Shiva, 2000). Lodziak continues that "...more underdevelopment is available with the help of loans made necessary by the impoverishment imposed by earlier 'development' itself", which is illustrated by Susan George (1991), who quotes a Peruvian joke in which an official says "You'll have to tighten your belt" and a citizen replies "I can't. I ate it yesterday" (Lodziak, 2002: 143).

George herself argues that the problem is not a lack of food but the means of distribution and the strings attached to aid: "Food aid is a means for developing markets, for helping agribusiness, for gaining a stranglehold on the policy decisions of needy governments and for promoting US foreign policy and military goals" (George, [1976] 1991: 212). In the markets of sub-Saharan cities such as Bamako, Ouagadougou, or Kumasi it is not unusual to see sacks of rice or grain marked with the name of a donor country and sold at prices (because the supply is initially free) which undercut local farmers, whose cultivation ceases to be viable. Meanwhile, new buildings are constructed in concrete, steel, and other imported materials, and the largest aid deals underwrite the commissioning of Western companies to build roads, airports, cement factories, dams, and power plants. Dirty industry which would fall foul of regulation in the affluent world is dumped where arrangements are more open to short-term money or political incentives. The country in question gets "developed" (a term which assumes it had no previous social organisation or culture) and the quality of life of its people is worsened and cheapened.

We can see from the above that development is a construct, and that, just as anthropologists since the nineteenth century have rejected the notion of a single trajectory of human cultural development, so it gives more respect to human difference to speak of multiple ideas of development than of one – such as that hawked by global capital. The argument is not confined to the development of the non-affluent world, but applies equally to the construction of marginalised groups within the affluent world. It is not only pollution but also social exclusion which the system produces, not as an oversight or failure but by design.

There is much radical thinking on the potential for self-empowerment of groups in the non-affluent world, and on the benefits of local knowledge (Peet and Watts, 1996). We suggest it is appropriate to map some of that thinking onto the affluent world today. But while protestors direct their anger against the perpetrators of environmental destruction, and anti-capitalism becomes a cause as vibrant as protest against the US war in Vietnam in the late 1960s, less is said about what kind of alternative economy might replace capitalism. This is a limitation, too, in Lodziak's critique,

> The brazen genocidal policies of the most powerful agents of capital are complemented by...their cavalier approach to finite resources, renewable resources and pollution. For some time now ecologists have warned that producing for high levels of consumption in the advanced capitalist societies and the consequences of affluent consumption are destroying the ecological balance of the planet. (Lodziak, 2002: 145–146)

But what to do? Lodziak sees self-imposed consumption reductions on the part of individuals as restrained by the absence of a system in which such reductions are experienced as beneficial, and emphasises the larger potential for institutional changes, as in eliminating add-on service industries. He calls for a reassertion of human autonomy through a separation of survival from wages, brought about by provision of a basic subsistence allowance for all. But while that would be interesting, he does not say how the state which frees its citizens from toil will come to power. And, though it makes sense to say that individuals less concerned to compete against each other would be less mired in consumerism as a means to identity formation, payment of a social income will not necessarily break the mould of consumption. Besides, the call for individual autonomy seems at odds with his privileging of institutional change, by which he seems to mean change through state and corporate agency. This leads us to look at what concepts and counter-concepts are available which might inform a change in the institution (in the sense of a social normalisation of a specific state of affairs) of consumption itself.

The colonial concept of development and the new concept of sustainability are fused in the often cited definition of sustainable development of the Bruntland Report (World Commission on Environment and Development, 1987): "Development that meets the needs of the present without compromising the ability of future generations to meet their own needs" (in Elliott, 1999: 7). Other definitions include maintaining a rate of growth without depleting non-renewable assets; and a stability in the net productivity of bio-mass over time. But such definitions are open to interpretation, and to date have not produced significant change in the face of either global deprivation or climate change. It may be that development as we know it *is* the problem, and continues to reproduce inequalities regardless of (or because of) the introduction of new technologies. The Brandt report of 1979, for instance, urged "intensified agricultural development" as an answer to world hunger (Brandt, 1980: 271), from which sentiment a so-called green revolution has destroyed locally productive farming and the social organisation it supported in many poor countries. A more radical concept is required which encompasses social and cultural as well as economic aspects. An example is the idea of conviviality advanced by Ivan Illich as a counter-concept for productivity. Illich writes in *Tools for Conviviality* that "The increasing demand for products has come to define society's process. I will suggest how this present trend can be reversed and how modern science and technology can be used to endow human activity with unprecedented effectiveness" (Illich, [1973] 1990: 11). This reflects a progressive model of history in which scientific development opens the doors to utopia – ending the economic problem of scarcity by finding new ways to produce enough to meet demand – but what is interesting is how Illich defines productivity's antithesis, conviviality, as "... autonomous and creative intercourse among persons, and the intercourse of persons with their environment; and this in contrast with the conditioned response of persons to the demands made upon them by others, and by a man-made environment" (ibid.). This is utopian, perhaps, but conviviality is a social relation of inter-dependence which interprets autonomy not as atomism but as mutual aid. It replaces an ends-directed system of production for profit by a means-centred system likely to generate appropriate technologies and economies based in genuine need. The given is a refusal of consumerism. He goes on:

> I propose the vision of a convivial society. A convivial society would be the result of social arrangements that guarantee for each member the most ample and free access to the tools of the community and limit this freedom only in favour of another member's equal freedom. (Illich, 1990: 12)

This is underpinned by a joyful sobriety and voluntary austerity. The vision may seem fanciful, yet corresponds to recent trends to voluntary reductions in work and income level for a better quality of life, and the growth of alternative communities such as new-age communes (Miller, 2002) and eco-villages (Barton and Kleiner, 2000).

In North America, distinct from Europe, withdrawal from metropolitan society to a new-age commune or eco-village may reflect an aspect of the society's mythicisation of itself in its history. Michael Ignatief writes of a new sense of republicanism in the late eighteenth century – which informed the founders of what is now called the United States – related to Western perceptions of the indigenous peoples of North America as uncorrupted by "subjection to the craving for more", exhibiting "autarkic virtue and happiness" while the colonisers took a (Roman) republican ideal to stand "as the last best hope of finding a polity which, in subjecting men [sic] to a collective regime of autarkic self-restraint, would free them from enslavement to the spiral of material progress" (Ignatief, 1984: 108). The dialectic may still operate in Illich's conviviality. At the same time we should recall that Illich, like Marcuse, was a key thinker in the late 1960s when the Woodstock generation seemed to embody a new society based on sharing, loving, and mutual respect, some of whose members attempted to construct an anarchistic society of free, recycled and second-hand goods available according to need – in September 1967, a free store operated by a collective of new-age Diggers opened at 264 East 10th Street, New York (Doyle, 2002: 87).

The concept of conviviality stresses the need to see the Emperor Consumption as having no clothes (which is viable only when the clothes are no longer desired), and emphasises socio-cultural as well as economic factors. In some ways, conviviality is like solidarity (see Crow, 2002) with a more forward-looking programme of social, cultural and economic change; but it also needs to be practical, and Victor Papanek's *Design for the Real World* [1984] (1991) and *The Green Imperative* (1995) show how appropriate technology and design, often using recycled materials, can meet needs for food distribution, dwelling, mobility, and communication. Papanek states: "Design must be the bridge between human needs, culture and ecology" (1995: 29). In practical terms, the solutions exist or can be invented (the detail being outside the scope of this book but published widely, from Papanek onwards – see Vale and Vale (1991) for instance, on green architecture), but what sometimes seems insurmountable is the difficulty that people need to be persuaded in mass to switch from consumerism as identity formation to consumption according to need. It may be that, for easy targets such as tobacco, fossil fuels, and the chemical-ridden products of intensive agriculture, withdrawal would be seen by a significant minority at least in an affluent society as aligned to a more desirable lifestyle. Environmental campaigns and supermarket advertising for organic food may both support this, but progressive consumption, as it might be termed, which moves from less to more healthy food and other items also costs more. It tends to be the preserve, or status marker, of the middle classes – while the poor eat junk food because it is convenient and allows them to partake in the dominant society – and is thus prone to reproduce the relation between consumption and desire which is the foundation of consumerism.

Consumption and resistance

In the late 1960s, it seemed radical social change might happen. When Herbert Marcuse lectured at the Free University, Berlin, for instance, revolution seemed imminent. In fact, in 1968 it failed, though the student protest in Europe and north America was a factor in ending the US occupation of Vietnam. Even before this became evident, however, Marcuse (1970: 69–82) was unable to answer the question as to how radical social change would happen, falling back on a notion that a drive (in a psychoanalytic sense) for freedom is as if naturally produced in a society of contradiction (Marcuse, 1969). The difficulty was in part that, under the influence of German Idealism, critical social thought tended to locate the new society in a future time. Recently, the cultural turn in geography (Soja, 1989, 1998; Massey, 1994), influenced by Henri Lefebvre, has redirected attention to space, and to a postmodern under-standing of diverse spatial practices which construct space and give it multi-valent meanings. This allows a shift of the problem of radical change from tomorrow to elsewhere, a trick of words perhaps but one which allows the new society to be seen in the present, in what Lefebvre thought of as moments of liberation within the routines of everyday life (see Shields, 1999: 96–103). For radical planner Patsy Healey, the concept of everyday life offers an alternative to conventional urban planning's separation of areas of service delivery such as health, education, and employment: "An everyday life perspective focuses instead on the multiplicity of roles people play and the services they use as they accomplish each day" (Healey, 1998: 59). Widening Lefebvre's insight to, say, the ingenuity and in certain ways the stability of informal settlements (Turner, 1976; Hamdi, 1991; Fernandes and Varley, 1998), activities such as house-building outside the main economy can be seen as sites of liberating social development, despite the dire circumstances in which such acts take place in non-affluent countries.

Jo Beall (1997), writing on urban development in non-affluent countries, sees three phases in a methodology of social development: an analysis of the situation; a process of change which may be spontaneous (as in squatter settlements) or planned (as in the work of agencies), and may entail interventions such as rent strikes or occupations of land; and evaluation which moves beyond good (iterative and reflective) practice to a sense of a best practice which can be adapted for (never merely replicated in) initiatives in other situations. She adds that "Nothing is more silencing and disempowering than invisibility", and argues that working with difference requires recognition of power differentials between individuals and groups (Beall, 1997: 13–14). This puts on professionals who work with communities a responsibility to facilitate self-empowerment. The point, however, is that if there are instances in which the meeting of needs is freed from the power of social exclusion, it may be that the meeting of other needs can be freed from the stranglehold of market forces.

This brings us to a key question for this book, which is the extent to which consumers in an affluent society are able to, or have already, become knowing manipulators of the market system, or can resist it. The arguments revolve around at least two key issues: changing attitudes to the environment (or natural world) and increasing concern for – or alarm at – rates of species depletion and environmental degradation which many observers link to economic expansion under capitalism; and changing understandings of identity and the processes through which it is (re-)formed, which tend to involve consumption – and could involve alternative consumption trends. Macnaghten and Urry (1998) offer evidence that consumers' attitudes towards goods which have an environmental aspect, such as food and fuel, have indeed changed since the 1980s. They contextualise this through the growth of environmental campaigns and increased participation in the work of organisations such as Greenpeace. Major oil spills and the like have galvanised the opinions of diverse publics into hitherto unpredicted actions. They write: "No longer did NGOs play the role of activists . . . Now the rest of the world appeared to share their agenda and was looking to NGOs for the next move" (p. 60). They cite data such as the rise in Greenpeace membership (50,000 in 1985 to 320,000 in 1989); and note the popularity of books such as *The Green Consumer Guide* (Elkington and Hailes, 1988). They go on: "Throughout 1989, green consumerism became one of the most fashionable concepts in public life" (p. 60). Whether it remains so today is, of course, another question. What is also in question is the power of consumerism to shape the economies it feeds, or simply be moulded by producers. Mica Nava (1992) argues that "consumerism can be argued to exercise control through the incitement and proliferation of increasingly detailed and comprehensive discourses". She sees this in part as a reclamation by citizens of the bodies society, in a Foucauldian analysis, disciplines. Youth fashion might illustrate her case well. She continues: "Yet because of the diffuse nature of this control, because it operates from such a multiplicity of points...it is also vulnerable" (p. 165). She adds that consumerism offers resistant options at the same time as it imposes on consumers.

So, can shoppers manipulate markets? There is some research which claims they can (Hearn and Roseneil, 1999). This literature is a reaction to a previous inclination to see consumers as hapless dupes of the system, and is parallel to a strand of cultural studies since the 1980s (the generation after Williams, Hall, and Hoggart) in which consumer sovereignty is asserted in the context of identity formation (Lee, 1993; Oh and Arditi, 2000; Lodziak, 2002: 11–29).

Martyn Lee, for instance, writes of new modes of consumption as offering freedom through juxtapositions – an eclecticism of consumption – which rupture consumerism's previous codes:

> What all this amounts to is essentially the emergence of a new form of cultural politics. This can be differentiated from the sort of cultural politics of an earlier stage of capital by the fact that it does not seek its self-valorisation by locking into a set of meanings and cultural values that are framed under a broad hegemonic umbrella...but by asserting itself simply through its own radical difference and sense of otherness. (Lee, 1993: 173)

The do-it-yourself fashion of ripped and cut jeans comes to mind, but the market is adept at absorbing each new stage of departure from its conventions, and the autonomy predicated is not guaranteed to progress any agenda beyond that of a fetishised identity. Some more recent claims for consumer resistance within consumption may be harder to uphold. One study proposes that junk mail offers the consumer a chance to domesticate, as the authors put it, the process of identity-construction which, they say, junk mail and consumer surveys provide (Reynolds and Alferoff, 1999). From their field work the authors cite tactics such as throwing junk mail in the bin, taking the free gifts but not responding, giving false information on questionnaires, and using catalogues to feed fantasies of dressing up. They recognise there are limits to this nice idea and that many consumers see junk mail as having a surveillance function. But could we not say simply: it is a nuisance; and a waste of paper, usually from non-renewable resources? Using the pre-paid envelopes to return the stuff is hardly resistance to consumerism, even if it satisfies a need for spite. Resistance, surely, requires more public and visible action such as a boycott of unethical companies, picketing of outlets, adaptation of advertising (on billboards or in cyberspace), or at least returning wasteful plastic packaging to the supermarket every week in front of the local press. Daniel Miller concludes, however, from an ethnographic study of shopping in north London that although middle-class consumers refer to boycotts of certain goods or manufacturers, they usually do so nostalgically (Miller, 2001: 118–119). He writes that "...the evidence from my work and from others is that pure 'Red' shopping based on the selection of goods primarily in consideration of benefiting others is extremely rare" (Miller, 2001: 119). From observation of 50 shopping trips in north London, he noted only one case of taking material back for recycling, and two of explicitly ethical purchasing (124), despite a sympathy for ethical shopping expressed by several of the shoppers. Oh and Arditi (2000) focus in a broader (non-ethically framed) way on the idea of active shoppers (from Featherstone, 1991; Shields, 1992; Ritzer, 1999), if seeing some claims as exaggerated. Taking a middle-road approach, they remark on the evacuation of use-value from commodities, their emptiness of meaning (citing Lury, 1996), and a dominance of marketing strategies: "Consumption-led approaches...suggest that it is above all the shopper who invests goods with meaning" (Oh and Arditi, 2000: 72). They continue that "...contemporary subjectivities pursue their own desires, although these may be the product of varied influences" (ibid.). Among these is gender, from which perspective Nava sees women's consumption as modernising society, and a way out of domestic confinement (Nava and O'Shea, 1997, in Oh and Arditi, 2000: 73; see also Nava, 1992). Yet, as Oh and Arditi say, even if shopping ruptures previous gender constraints, "...this break does not necessarily imply an emancipation, or liberation, or even an empowerment of women" (Oh and Arditi, 2000: 74). A different view is cited from Miller (1998), in which the purpose of shopping is to support social relations, so that "...the meaning of commodities is imbued with the significance that objects acquire as a function of this practice [of shopping as a devotional rite]" (Oh and Arditi, 2000: 78). Buying the groceries or clothes for children, or a summer vacation for the family, might, then, be a polysemic act, if particularised within specific situations and social relations.

From this, Oh and Arditi move to Baudrillard and the permanent availability of goods without seasonal restriction which makes every day a feast of plenty, and take the advent of internet shopping as adding a further layer to this as well as clarifying the problems raised. In fields such as books and popular music, e-sales may seriously challenge traditional outlets, and ordering food on-line is a growing practice, while all e-sales are available twenty-four hours a day, all week and all year. The result is a sensation of hyper-abundance, a new form beyond Benjamin's phantasmagoria, in which "...the regime of needs and desires is...literally disembodied", but no less seductive as new techniques of promotion such as manufacturing affinities by listing what others have purchased replace the material-bound practices of the department store (Oh and Arditi, 2000: 84–85). This new experience is not, of course, universally available – in 1996, 63.7 per cent of internet hosts were in the US but only 0.008 per cent in India (Elliott, 1999: 27).

Alternative consumption

Oh and Arditi conclude that a view of shoppers as active participants offers a more gender-sensitive, if fuzzier, understanding of consumption. But it does not show, we argue, how the operation of global consumerism which depletes the planet's non-renewable resources of energy and material can be challenged. If, as Marx claims, the point is to change the world, not just explain it in various ways, then more needs to be known about alternatives *to* consumption and consumerism in an affluent society, and how they may arise, not alternative readings of its manners and minutiae.

Stacey Warren makes a valuable point, from Gramsci, that ruling elites are not unified, their hegemony produced through alliances, while the ruled are similarly fragmented in aims: "Hegemonic plays for leadership result in mobile combinations of culture, as dominant groups incorporate opposing ideas and interests in an effort to win over the subordinate groups" (Warren, 1993: 176). Warren's argument is that, while Marxist critiques of mass culture tend to disdain it, popular culture can be what it says – used by diverse publics. Adorno refuses the term popular culture (1991: 85–92) in favour of that of "culture industry" to describe the production of cultural goods such as music for a mass public; and states the content of such genres as manipulative and deceiving, using standard formulae to oil the wheels of capitalism (Lodziak, 2002: 161–165). But the widespread pirating of popular music and availability of inexpensive equipment for sound mixing and broadcasting has spawned new cultural intermediaries who, while probably not producing anything Adorno would like, make a gap in the market-led system which, given Warren's point above, could widen as the music industry apes the styles of producers in the informal economy. The system absorbs

departures from it (Lukes, 1993) but may find itself in the process led
into terrains it ceases to control. Warren observes, however, that few
would take popular culture as social struggle.

How can this insight be applied to other areas of consumption? If, as
Vandana Shiva argues, "The rebellion on the streets and the rebellion
within the negotiations [at the World Trade Organization meeting in
Seattle in 1999] has started a new democracy movement..." (Shiva,
1999), what can shoppers do? And, equally (since shopping is a form of
relation between producers and consumers), what can local producers
do outside the global free-trade market? To take the second question
first, producers can make direct relations to consumers through farmers'
markets, farm shops, and organic vegetable box delivery schemes
sourced from identified local producers. These, like self-built housing,
cut out most centres of profit-making after the producer and thereby
begin to constitute an alternative economy – not green consumerism
but a different system of meeting needs for consumption. They also
tend to reduce the energy used in transporting goods by drawing on
local suppliers. As well are the local economy trading schemes (LETS)
which take money out of the relation by linking the producers of goods
and services to each other through an extended form of barter (also
largely outside the tax system). Those who participate in such networks
are still, no doubt, affected by the pressures to consume which are
present in the wider society, but such pressures are possibly countered
by a counter-consumerist culture among alternative networks, allowing
at least a partial reappraisal of need and a closer link to localised (and
humanised) sources of supply.

The economy constructed through such mechanisms is more likely,
then, to be socially useful – less wasteful and more flexible, strengthening
voluntary bonds between people while enabling a reasonable quality of
life at a cost below that of a consumerist lifestyle. This may affect
employment and raw material use patterns as people work less, or for
less, and produce/consume less as they depart from the principle of
productivity. If a second-hand economy comes increasingly into play
then a reduction in the size of the production economy will result,
using less energy and raw materials. A second-hand economy, too,
can have its devotees – as shown by the crowds who flock to car boot
and garage sales (Gregson and Crewe, 2003: 54–62). Retro retailing, as
with clothes from the 1960s, is part of the means to assert a visible identity for certain groups in the affluent society. It happens not, probably,
for environmental reasons but as freedom from large-scale producers
who dominate the new clothes market to dictate styles and the season's

colours. But it still re-utilises previously produced, not new goods. This has environmental benefits, even if a by-product, and demonstrates an interesting link between issues of resource depletion and self-determination.

Stephen Bodington, Mike George and John Michaelson state that "... in developing the socially useful economy, we are primarily concerned with extending the ability of people to control their own lives and to be involved in decisions concerning production of goods and services to meet their specific needs" (Bodington *et al.*, 1986: 143). They add that the state should encourage this, perhaps naively given the tendency of states to manage economies for capital in a de-regulated market. The absence of encouragement from above, however, is not a disincentive for action at grassroots level, for the making of what Illich calls tools for conviviality, of which farmers' markets may be an example. Thinking of Gramsci's model of alliances, parts of the apparatus of the dominant society may be drawn towards such schemes if they contribute, for instance, to a city planning agenda of revitalisation for downtown districts previously threatened by out-of-town malls. While such planning agendas are public-sector originated, developers, too, have an interest in urban revitalisation, from which money can be made. The heritage malls of cities such as Boston and Seattle may be followed by more everyday markets in which producers (growers, craftspeople, cheese-makers, and so forth) sell directly to consumers. A report on public markets in North American cities states:

> Public markets are needed today because they can effectively address some of the vexing problems of our cities: the need to reinvigorate urban shopping districts and make inviting and safe public spaces; the need to support small-scale economic activity and confront the problems of street vending; the need to provide fresh, high-quality produce to inner-city residents; and the need to protect open space and preserve farming around cities. (Spitzer and Baum, 1995: 16)

This is a liberal view, seeing un-regulated (itinerant) street vending as a problem (see Crawford, 1999), yet it is a progressive view, too, which seeks to regain the vitality of markets while reducing a city's footprint by bringing its food supply nearer to consumers. The report continues that the number of farmers' markets is likely to grow due to consumer demand and an under-representation of supermarkets in inner-city areas. Markets will thus contribute to urban regeneration, and so weaken – because most of the money goes to a local economy – the hold of global systems of for-profit distribution. In a few cases now, farmers' markets are offered space outside a supermarket as a means to encourage customers to the site through an increase in the critical mass of goods available.

In the UK, there is a National Association of Farmers' Markets (NAFM) which promotes them and provides certification based on criteria for producer-sellers. Local authorities have encouraged such markets, sometimes in context of Local Agenda 21 initiatives (from the UN Conference on Environment and Development in Rio de Janeiro in 1992. Central government, too, supports farmers' markets through Rural Enterprise Schemes (RES) and Processing and Marketing Grants (PMG), while another government organ, the Countryside Agency, has drawn attention to the needs for further support for producers and, interestingly, expansion of the direct sale market by influencing consumer choices in favour of locally produced food, in part through greater awareness of the environmental benefits of direct producer-seller relations. Thinking of Gramsci again, hegemonic power is fractured; though it is difficult to measure the comparative extent to which the growth of farmers' markets and similar schemes is driven by regulation or by redirected consumer desires. Either way, farmers' markets account for a tiny percentage of food sales, and the global picture is one of resilient consumerism. As Sarah Buie writes, "... the market principle destroys the market place", and supermarkets give "aesthetic form to the forces at work in the market principle and mass production" (Buie, 1996: 229–230).

Organic vegetable box schemes have grown alongside farmers' markets in the UK, parallel to a rise in organic consumption through supermarkets – food you can trust in contrast to the Frankenstein foods of genetic modification. Supermarket organic ranges are not limited to fruit and vegetables, and include bread, biscuits, milk, juices, breakfast cereals, pasta, rice, pulses, eggs, soup, meat, fish, tea, coffee, honey, and many other foods, most of which are available as extras in box schemes. A difference between supermarket and box organic consumption is that supermarkets buy more from abroad, while boxes are mainly (not exclusively) filled from local production. A recent press report says that in 2001, 79 per cent of UK households made at least one organic purchase (*Guardian*, 15 October 2002). Given Miller's observations above, this is either a new development, a product of a combination of press coverage of food scares and advertising for organic foods as supermarkets see a new competitive edge in going green, or the figures (perhaps based on resistant consumers who lie to market researchers!) are misleading. But if there is a general rise in organic consumption it will decrease pollution, animal cruelty, and energy use, and increase bio-diversity – organic dairy farms, the organic milk suppliers cooperative (OMSCO), have five times more wild plants than non-organic farms (www.omsco.co.uk).

According to the Soil Association, organic box schemes contributed around £30 million to the UK rural economy in 2001, and there are now around 300 such schemes operating in the UK following the first at Northwood farm in Devon in 1991 (www.aboutorganics.co.uk). In some of the early schemes, in the US as well as UK, consumers subscribed on an annual basis to a specific farm, pre-purchasing a part of its production. Such schemes were very local, and customers sometimes volunteered to help with harvesting. Now, as organic distribution moves to a larger scale to meet growing demand, it begins in some cases to adopt market principles, offering a range of box types supplied by groups of producers, using imported items to add colour and year-round variety, and expanding catchment areas beyond the local. The largest scheme in the UK is probably Riverford Organic in Devon, selling over 5000 boxes per week to rural and urban customers in Cornwall, Devon, Dorset, Somerset, Gloucestershire, Hampshire, and cities including Exeter, Bristol, Bath, and Oxford (www.riverford.co.uk; see also www.sunnyfields.co.uk). The scheme began in 1992 when farmer Guy Watson was in negotiation with a supermarket over supplying them with lettuces and cabbages, and realised how much pressure big purchasers assumed they could exert over local suppliers like him. Watson writes of a supermarket executive "What made him an ogre was an impersonal organisation driven by the pressure to satisfy shareholders. That pressure is focused on the buyers who hold the futures of supplying businesses in their hands and ruthlessly exploit their godlike power in a most ungodly way" (Riverford, 2003). Riverford offers five box types, the proportion of UK-grown items ranging from 20 to 100 per cent, with an average of 74 per cent, in a randomly picked three-week period in January 2003. Together, the farm, farm shop, dairy, and box scheme employ up to 120 people in peak harvesting season. But is this still alternative consumption or does it slide towards green consumerism? Riverford's extensive catchment area might reflect supermarket techniques of distribution while competing with more local producers in areas to which it delivers several hours' drive from its base near Buckfastleigh in Devon.

But setting that aside, what is the attraction for consumers? Is it just tasty food, or is alternative consumption conducive to alternative ways of living? Jörg Dürrschmidt (1999), writing on an organic box scheme in Bristol, sets it in the context of globalisation and a release of individuals in postmodernity from traditional patterns of employment and dwelling into a global risk society (see Beck, 1992). In this new society, individuals construct their own milieux, but do so in conditions of insecurity which fosters a rediscovery of the notion of locality while subject to multiple identity choices. Dürrschmidt sees organic box schemes as expressions of "...more a form of self-actualization in a complex global society, than a form of local resistance against globalisation" (Dürrschmidt, 1999: 136), a finding not incompatible with Miller's (above). Among the influences Dürrschmidt analyses are anxiety about food, and a recovery of individual control over a basic area of consumption, though this, as he says, does not make a green lifestyle. Dürrschmidt observes of one respondent to his survey: "...it is fair to say that respondents' engagement in local organic food box schemes is a symbol of an alternative lifestyle, rather than an element of an actual lifestyle itself" (Dürrschmidt, 1999: 143). But he sees the scheme as a loose alternative support network between people, and glimpse of a self-created society. A glimpse is not much, but it may be that organic box schemes give individuals a practical way to attach themselves to an alternative direction for society, which equally provides for their food needs in a satisfying way and, crucially for some rural areas, retains the money in a local economy. A majority of the customers may be city and town dwellers, but the footprint of organic production, even on Riverford's scale, is far less than that of agri-business, and it may be that the steady growth of such schemes influences supermarkets to increase their organic provision. As we said at the beginning of this chapter, change is not revolutionary but incremental.

Change is also geographically specific, despite globalisation. We suggest, refusing a universalising approach, that the evidence of local cases can illuminate processes of change – processes which are taking place today in a wide variety of situations. In investigating the micro-scale case of Dartmoor Direct, we find it is not that a window opens on the macro-scale economy, but that the diversity of micro-scale cases is an alternative to the creeping uniformity of the macro-scale. For that reason, we look now at such a case, of water delivery in Devon. We include this in a book on cities and consumption in part because many of the consumers of Dartmoor water live in the cities of Plymouth and Exeter; but also because the models developed in rural economies can inform the operations of alternative suppliers in urban neighbourhoods which tend, loosely, to take on a village-scale distinct from that of the city as a whole. The consumption of bottled water is, too, an example of consumption specific to an affluent society whose members can afford (or have been persuaded by information on levels of chemical contamination) to avoid drinking water from the tap.

Dartmoor Direct

Dartmoor Direct is a cooperative venture supplying bottled water (and in some cases organic vegetables and associated items) to households, hotels, and restaurants in south Devon. It delivers around 2500 litres of water each week to households and three retail outlets, in Totnes, its most developed distribution area. Deliveries are made also to Plymouth, Ivybridge, South Brent, Buckfastleigh, Ashburton, Newton Abbot, Kingsteignton, Teignmouth, Dawlish, and Exeter but not outside Devon. While Exeter is the most affluent centre of population in the region it has been the most difficult market to penetrate.

The source of Dartmoor water is one of five underground rivers on the moor, to which the cooperative has sunk a bore hole. Although the characteristic rock of Dartmoor is granite, which is impervious, rain accumulates in a damp, peaty landscape, forming small pools which drain slowly into the underground rivers. Using an electric pump, water is extracted, filtered, and bottled in 5-litre plastic cans for domestic use and in glass bottles for hotels and restaurants. Both plastic and glass containers are collected from customers to be re-used. This is not only a contribution to minimising waste but also a contribution to the financial viability of the cooperative. When first established in 1995, 60 per cent of turnover was accounted for by packaging, while, with the recycling of containers, it takes only 20–25 per cent now (interview with Roger Mitchell, founder of Dartmoor Direct, 26 February 2003 – from which all quotations below are taken).

Water is an item of basic need, arguably the most basic in terms of survival, though there is clearly a difference between bottled and tap water. Both support life, but in many areas tap water is not drawn directly from a source but recycled through one or more areas of population. In Exeter, for instance, water from the Exe Valley goes first to Tiverton, and then (after it has gone through the sewage system) is re-processed for the city. It is drinkable, though there have been incidents in several areas of the UK, including Devon and Cornwall, of pollution in drinking supplies. Mitchell sees the market for bottled water as growing in response to such scares and a more generalised suspicion of authorities which means that whatever pronouncements are made by government agencies as to food or water safety are often distrusted. The handling of the 2001 foot-and-mouth outbreak exacerbated this, parts of Devon being devastated by it. Moreover, the outbreak raised public awareness of farming, and especially of livestock dealing, practices which are given to the rapid spread of diseases. Mitchell observes, too, that "tap water smells of chlorine, and contains aluminium sulphate and sodium fluoride – a by-product of the aluminum industry which they try to sell to water companies although it is not absorbed by the human metabolism like calcium fluoride". He also claims that some well-known bottled waters sold in supermarkets have a higher nitrate content than UK tap water. So, if a motive for consuming non-tap water is to avoid a supply perceived as tainted, and this drives a market for bottled water in general much of which is supplied by supermarkets, it also assists Dartmoor Direct in building up its market.

But the key aspect of Dartmoor Direct, which Mitchell describes as a niche market, is that it supplies *local* water. This, given the healthy associations of Dartmoor as a relatively uncultivated area of land known for walking and wild weather, is seen by consumers as a better guarantee of quality than official regulation, or the promotional material of large companies. Being local, however, is equally being environmentally beneficial by reducing transport and thus energy consumption (bearing in mind that tap water goes in pipes but bottled water goes in lorries or vans). Mitchell sees the reasons people buy Dartmoor water (which costs the same as the cheaper brands of supermarket still water, so is competitive) as related equally to health and ethics, with customers in Totnes seeing support for a local cooperative as part of the alternative lifestyle for which the town is known. Without having undertaken any surveys, we suggest Dürrschmidt's findings from Bristol (cited above) would be likely to be found in Devon as well, though the depth of commitment to an alternative lifestyle and economy would probably be greater in Totnes. This is speculative, but Dartmoor Direct's small team deliver in person and are in a position to take doorstep feedback. It was, indeed, in context of such a commitment to an ethical, local economy that Dartmoor Direct was set up in 1995, initially with about 20 members (now reduced to five) and lofty ambitions. Its aims were to promote locally produced, healthy food and drink; to operate a home-delivery service; and to act as distributor within its customer area for a range of local producers.

Home-delivery is particularly useful in rural areas where retail outlets are few or far away, and public transport poor. Local distribution has another kind of use, in making small businesses, such as small-scale farms, more competitive with larger suppliers. Several members left the cooperative fairly quickly. A core team has remained to develop the water business, with a small element of vegetable box delivery in some areas using only local suppliers. A recent innovation, in response to the difficulty experienced by some elderly or infirm customers in opening

and using a 5-litre can, is the introduction of an earthenware crock
which cools the water naturally and has a 19-litre can which the
supplier replaces as necessary. As the business grows, Mitchell sees the
surplus income generated as being returned to the local economy at
a time when small enterprises are increasingly vulnerable to the exploitative strategies of supermarkets. Speaking of the original plan for Dartmoor
Direct, he says:

> Most of it is a shattered dream, but it's a question of whether the
> timing is right. More and more people are questioning what is going
> on and although there is a long way to go before it reaches the
> majority – you see large, well-known companies suddenly vanish –
> over the next ten to fifteen years more people will be attracted to
> opting out of the system. It's a bit like politics: participating in some-
> thing like this [Dartmoor Direct] means putting a lot of energy into it
> but in the final analysis it doesn't matter who is in the government
> or County Hall ... (conversation, 26 February 2003)

The reason it does not matter is because at the local level, in terms of
a specific commodity and its distribution, change can take place outside
regional, national, or trans-national policies which favour mega-scale
production over micro-level consumption. Mitchell adds that alternative
consumption becomes more popular as national and international
politics seem less concerned with the lives of ordinary citizens. He sees
the current state of the business as a plateau, reached after eight years and
taking the energy available from its members, while he does not rule out
future expansion if this is driven by consumer demand. That expansion,
however, will be in keeping with the aims (and self-defined limits) of
the business – to support local producers and supply local consumers
with a healthy product. The ethical aim is implicit, but no less present
for that and the venture as a whole stands as a case of what may become
a significant departure from the dominant, consumerist economy.

Conclusion

Of course a critic might suggest that the sort of schemes we have discussed
here are in fact the preserve of the middle classes. But as a means of
ending this chapter we would like to offer a few reasons why very local
schemes such as this genuinely matter – reasons which could apply to
numerous other local, ethical enterprises and alternative economies.

Firstly, there is a direct impact on local and global economies, shifting the balance from the latter to the former and creating local employment and demand for locally produced goods. Local distribution also minimises transport and hence fuel use and pollution. The extent may be tiny, unlikely to be noticed by a supermarket or an internationally known bottled water company, but it is a shift nonetheless. It could be argued that big shifts consist of lots of little shifts, but perhaps more important is the demonstration that an alternative is possible. This demonstrative aspect is the second reason such ventures matter, and likely, we argue, to be central to any widespread change in societal attitudes to consumption. It is hard for people to imagine something which does not yet exist, even if they have a vague desire for a world which is better. When there is a practical example of how things might be other than the way the dominant society dictates, however, the glimpse offered can be grasped. It may be transfered, too, into other fields of change. When the system seems so big, its trajectory appears inevitable; any gap in its surface is helpful. Each crack shows that power leaks, and each crevice can be widened in a gradual but cumulative process of change. A third reason is that by making more direct relations between producers and consumers it re-establishes a social aspect to consumption, of a kind impossible in large-scale distribution. It may be that check-out operators in supermarkets are trained to say hallo to each consumer, but they do so in a standardised way which takes meaning out of the exercise, while the informal institution of a singles night in the supermarket's aisles – while indicative of a form of sociation specific to metropolitan cities – hardly constitutes a sense of community. That sense, of course, is elusive and frequently romanticised. Yet there is evidence that being a consumer of a locally produced ethical product does lend a feeling of membership of a milieu, and to an alternative tendency within but potentially superseding the wider society. Perhaps buying local water, vegetables, fruit, and so forth is, like taking the bottles and cans to a recycling point, one of few actions available to consumers who wish to depart from mainstream consumerism and the waste it generates.

Finally, it may look as though our antithesis to consumerism is a withdrawal to the countryside. As it happens both authors live in cities (not the same one) and are concerned primarily with urban societies and cultures. Globally as well as in Devon, most people now live in cities, and it is interventions in urban economies which will determine any major change in the pattern of consumption. But we justify this look to rural production on the obvious ground that most of the consumers of organic box schemes and the like are urban dwellers. The growth of such schemes should not, however, mask the need for city environments, too, to become greener, as in producing within a city more of what its inhabitants eat, as well as the more usual concern for reducing energy consumption.

In cities, some people still cultivate allotments, while others eat organic, buy what they can from charity shops or second-hand, recycle waste, buy green energy, and contribute in the ways available to them to what constitutes an alternative to consumer society. Their reasons are diverse and patterns of consumption remain reflective of class, but awareness of climate change, the activities of trans-national agri-business, and suspicion of official information contribute to a climate of consciousness in which – at some point – more radical alternatives may emerge. Will this be a post-consumer society in which consumerism is replaced by – not green consumerism – but a new model of consumption in which needs replace wants as the determining factor? If it is, it will also, we argue, rest on an alternative economy, in part post-money, in part post-globalised, which reflects ecological awareness in social organisation. The question remains however: how malleable is capitalism. Are such developments possible without them being subsumed within the system?

CHAPTER 9

Conclusion: The "Consumed" City

This book is concerned with the apparently omnipresent influence of consumption upon city life. More accurately, it has endeavoured to outline the ways in which consumption appears to play an increasingly pivotal role on how people live in cities. We have described a process of social, cultural and economic change and in doing so we have come to the conclusion that the consuming city is, in effect, *the consumed city*. The consumed city is the city as defined by and through consumption, a product of the "...uncontrolled, rampant emergence of a post-industrial consumer economy gone mad – pouring into cities in every part of the world, growing at an enormous rate, and consuming limited, precious resources (Safdie, 1997: 91). But the impact of consumption on the city is as imaginary as it is real. There has been a fundamental shift in the balance of power between the consumer and the producer of the contemporary city. The producer of the contemporary city: the financial speculator, the urban planner, the council official, the urban architect, and the like appear to have so much faith in consumption as the future of the city that consumption has taken on an exaggerated form: the symbolic value of consumption does not simply express itself through specific goods or services but through a mythologised vision of the city of our dreams. In other words, society has invested a degree of belief in consumption; consumption is so well-entrenched in the way we look at the world, that it cannot possibly fulfil the ambitions we have for it. We are consumed by *the idea* of consumption so that our cities are indeed *consumed*.

Consumption is assumed to be the saviour of the contemporary city. In fact it may be little more than the ideological manifestation of consumerism. What exactly do we mean when we say the city is consumed? Well, the evidence presented in this book suggests that the city is consumed on a number of levels. Perhaps most significantly the experience of city life has become increasingly individualised. In many respects the city has become something of a post-Fordist space where, on the surface at least, the needs and the desires of the consumer appear to be at its core. The city is presented to the consumer as a cultural democracy: a space where anything is possible and where anybody can aspire to anything. The contemporary city legitimises the consumer society. By doing so it makes a statement to the effect that consumerism constitutes a natural state of affairs. It would, of course, be disingenuous to suggest that the impact of consumption upon the city has been and continues to be entirely negative. This is far from the case. However, the city and those people responsible for the future of the city appear to have become infatuated by the obvious economic potential of consumer choice.

The point here is that consumer choice is not available to all consumers of city life at all times. In fact, the consuming city is not constructed to fulfil the needs of the consumer. Raymund Ryan (2001) asks who is it that is responsible for the state of the modern city: the architect or the businessman? His answer is unequivocal: the businessman. The business-man builds the city (usually) for himself. In the city, just like anywhere else, the rich get richer and the poor get poorer. More than that, markets require scarcity in order to function effectively (Harvey, 2003: 18–19), "[The markets] ... destroy our cities with their speculations, reanimate them with their donations to the opera and the ballet while their chief executives strut the global stage and accumulate massive wealth at the expense of millions." The consuming city does not generally prioritise the needs of its occupants. Only the high-spending, short-term inhabitants are the vital users of the city today (Ryan, 2001). The city is consumed in the sense that there is barely enough room in it for the people who actually live there.

The economic benefits of the consuming city come at a price. Consumer culture does not encourage heterogeneity but homogeneity: "The more cities become the same – same shops, same restaurants, same art galleries – the more they paradoxically yearn for some particular identity" (Ryan, 2001: 30). But the implications of the consuming city are manifested in a far deeper fashion than simply in the way the city looks. In her book, *Landscapes of Power*, Sharon Zukin discusses the complexity of the contemporary city which she points out exhibits two different kinds of spatial structure. The city represents both a localisation of global and economic social forces and a location in a world capitalist order. This may be the case, but as Zukin points out, urban space also structures people's "perceptions, interactions, and sense of well-being or despair, belonging or alienation" (p. 268). But the danger is that the former has taken priority at the expense of the latter; that the city as an economic entity holds far more weight than the city as a social entity. That in effect, the city has been consumed by consumption and as a result has lost track of its broader social role. Such a process is possible precisely because consumption appears on the surface to be democratic and can be sold as such to the consumers of the city, when in reality it is in many respects divisive and the opportunities and freedoms it brings are inevitably only partial in nature. Zukin is concerned that the reorganisation of space in terms of consumption is limited by the unpredictable nature of investment and the degree of support for such initiatives both amongst the elite and the population in general. She is absolutely correct to suggest that such a process encourages more pervasive corporate control over the visual imagination, our point is that it does so under the mask of democracy and freedom:

> When the landscape shifts entirely to a service economy oriented towards consumption, even the social imagination – the ability to envision alternatives – is corrupted. Nonetheless the terms of the debate have shifted. Critics can no longer call upon the working class to save society. That class is too differentiated and too involved in consumption to respond to the old industrial vision of reform. (Zukin, 1991: 275)

Society has in effect developed in such a fashion as to ensure that the future of the city is inevitably a future of consumption in which there is no choice other than the choice to consume if, of course, you have the resources to do so. In discussing the American experience, Zukin goes on to suggest that the social role of the city has been gradually wiped away to the extent that there exists an underlying assumption that economic benefits will automatically bring social ones. The problem is that it is in the interests of big business to promote consumerist solutions without recourse to the fact that the vast majority of initiatives they introduce to the city will only be available to those with cash to spend and cultural capital to invest, because consumer initiatives are primarily financial initiatives and it is simply not their concern (although it is often their remit) to consider which social groups might be excluded by such initiatives.

What appears to have happened here is that the idea of the city has been altered by consumption, but this too has practical implications for our actual experience of the city. In discussing the work of Lewis Mumford

(1938), Heinz Paetzold (1997) draws attention to the following definition of the city:

> The city in its complete sense, then, is a geographic plexus, an economic organisation, an institutional process, a theatre of social action, and an aesthetic symbol of collective unity. On the one hand it is a physical frame for the common place domestic and economic activities: on the other, it is a consciously dramatic setting for the more significant actions and the more sublimated urges of a human culture. The city fosters art and is art, the city creates the theatre and is theatre. It is in the city, the city as theatre, that man's more purposive activities are formulated and worked out, through conflicting and co-operating personalities, events groups, into more significant culminations. (Mumford, 1938: 300–401)

The problem is that consumption has colonised city space to such an extent that the theatre of the city can only apparently operate within the guidelines set by consumerism. The more "sublimated" urges of human nature can apparently only be expressed *through* consumption. Something is only significant or purposive if it abides by the rules that consumerism lays down. And those rules are laid by the richest inhabitants of cities:

> We live in a society in which the inalienable rights to private property and the profit rate trump any other conception of inalienable rights you can think of. This is so because our society is dominated by the accumulation of capital through market exchange. That social process depends upon a juridical construction of individual rights ... These rights encompass private property in one's own body (to freely sell labour power, to be treated with dignity and respect and to be free from bodily coercions) coupled with freedoms of thought, of expression and of speech. These derivative rights are appealing. Many of us rely heavily on them. But we do so much as beggars live off the crumbs from the rich man's table ... To live under capitalism is to accept or submit to that bundle of rights necessary for endless capital accumulation. (Harvey, 2003: 18–19)

This book is primarily concerned with the impact of consumption on the urban way of life. But to understand such an impact it is essential to contextualise our discussion in relation to *sites* of production. To this end, Häußermann (1997) points out that large cities are no longer the centre of a growing labour force and that a growth in the number of jobs in the service sector has failed to compensate for losses in manufacturing. The growth of the urban economy and the growth of jobs do not go hand in hand. Häußermann goes as far as to suggest that the urban way of living is in a state of crisis. The city, from this point of view has become a place of danger, hostility, marginalisation, homelessness, and exclusion from wealth, notably for members of ethnic minorities in the slums of American cities (Häußermann, 1997: 144). The end product of all this is indeed a divided city, a city where "The social group that has been pushed out is being neither exploited nor suppressed: it is simply being ignored and left behind" (Dubet and Lapeyronnie, 1994: 84).

But the important thing to remember, as Häußermann suggests, is that this division is especially visible where economic growth is most in evidence. Economic advances in recent years have been characterised by a continuum where many middle class occupations are thriving whereas the other end of the spectrum is characterised by unstable and low-paid jobs and it is in the big cities that these divisions are most marked (Häußermann, 1997). It is Häußermann's contention that in the light of such development the theories of authors such as Simmel, Wirth, and Park are no longer sustainable in the sense that the assumption of economic growth and integration upon which they were based can no longer be taken for granted,

> When differences become opposites, disadvantages lead to exclusion; when the prospects of being integrated into the system are being questioned, then integration through separation lacks a material foundation. Under these circumstances, indifference and a blasé attitude are no longer a form of accepting the stranger, but rather real cynicism, which then becomes part of a structural violence against the marginalised. (Häußermann, 1997: 145)

It is in context that Harloe and Fainstein (1992) identify the emergence of a "new service class", but even this development has been accompanied by a situation in which although many low-skilled and low-paid jobs are available, the opportunities for upward occupational mobility are few and far between, "we can identify a close link between economic change and intensified poverty and rising standards of living for relatively limited sections of the population and a more ambiguous combination of costs and benefits for any more" (p. 243). As a result of economic restructuring (including the decline of manufacturing and the growth of specialised consumer services serving the needs of high-status high-income workers), many of the world's cities are experiencing new or intensified old social divisions. But as Fainstein and Harloe argue, it is too much of a simplification to argue that this is a division between those at the top of the social scale and those at the bottom, between the haves and the have-nots. Most interestingly they argue that in terms of power, the upper classes and the upper echelons of the middle classes have expanded whilst those groups below including clerical, technical and sales workers actually have even less power than they would have had in the past. Meanwhile the working classes, in Britain at least, continue to suffer, notably as a result of a weakened Trade Union movement and a gradual removal of state benefits. It is the contention of this book that in the ten years since Fainstein and Harloe's analysis such divisions have been exacerbated by the consuming city which offers a solution to such problems in theory, but which in reality extends the degree of social inequality. Davis, for instance points out how 50,000 people, largely of poor Chinese, Mexican or black origin, were forced out of the newly developed downtown area of Los Angeles (a city of "over-consumption"), to make way for developments such as the new Lakers baseball stadium intended to revitalise the city centre (Davis, 2002). And the divisive nature of the consuming city extends well beyond the city boundaries. Of particular concern is the fact that these cities dump the negative aspects of such over-consumption, such as pollution and waste, on to their poor neighbours. From this point of view the contemporary city is unmanageable, not least in a climate in which American cities at least are currently as characterised by fear as they are by the search for profit (see Davis, 2002).

So-called post-modern urban development and planning has unashamedly targeted the affluent segment of the divided society. Such developments have tended to include new working environments for the financial and business service sectors, large shopping developments, bright new housing with intensive security, and restaurants, hotels, and private leisure complexes (Blackman, 1997). From this point of view whereas modernisation was about social coherence and social responsibility, the post-modern era is synonymous with a lack of social conscience precisely because the opportunity is rightly or wrongly per-ceived to be democratic and empowering despite considerable evidence to the contrary. In this context, Paddison (1997) is at pains to emphasise the political dimension to these issues (a point raised in Chapter 1 in relation to city planning in Plymouth). Paddison discusses scepti-cism regarding the trickle-down affect of capital spending on the construction of major cultural, tourist and convention facilities, as well as specialist shopping facilities. But the point is that such developments not only potentially serve the elites, but they do so whilst offering an unattainable promised land to the rest of us. Glasgow's year as European City of Culture in 1990 is particularly pertinent in this respect. Such initiatives can undoubtedly have a genuine impact on the nature of social exclusion, but such an impact cannot be assumed, it can only come about as part of a sustained and focused strategy to ensure consumption benefits to the people who *need* to benefit. As Harvey (2003: 19) puts it, "Free markets are not necessarily fair. 'There is,' as the old saying goes, 'nothing more unequal than the equal treatment of unequals.' The rich grow richer and the poor get poorer through the egalitarianism of exchange."

In the above light, Paddison raises a public concern that the City of Culture initiative betrayed the working class roots of the city whilst modernising parts of the city centre at the expense of run-down parts of the city periphery. He nonetheless acknowledges the fact that stricter financial controls have served to promote the needs of the socially excluded, as has the territorial restructuring of local government. But it is still questionable whether the marketisation of the public services seeped in the rhetoric of consumerism can actually provide *inclusive* freedoms. The irony is that, "denied full access to private commodity consumption, the disadvantaged rely more on public services to close the 'consumption gap'...markets are by definition discriminatory" (Paddison, 1997: 325). So too is the consuming city.

All this brings us back to a more general point: what is the value of consumption and how much does the consuming city actually give the consumer? The answer to such questions can never be straightforward. Consumerism can, of course, be attacked for actively thwarting individual freedoms through conformity and commercial manipulation. On the other hand it serves a variety of broader social and personal purposes. What is certain is that, managing consumerism is a challenge, for it is all too easy to be managed by it (Stearns, 2001: 142). Perhaps we should be wary of the extreme position of authors such as Lodziak (1995, 2002) who argue that consumerism constitutes a dominant ideology insofar as the basis of capitalistic economic structure is hidden from the consciousness of agents of production and that consumerism ensures that people are unaware of the real motivations of powerful elites. We might well accept Lodziak's contention that there is a fundamental link between the cultural and the economic, and we would say that the link is manifested most graphically in the form of the city. *Consuming Cities* is critical of consumerism and its impact upon the city, but we are

not arguing here that consumption is inherently bad, as Lodziak appears
to suggest. Consumption may be ideological and it is socially divisive,
but there is surely still room, at least to some degree, for consumers to
endow aspects of the consuming city with their own meanings. In this
respect, our position is that although consumers are to an extent active,
their activity is only possible within the boundaries laid down for them
by consumerism. The meanings which consumers invest in consumption
are diverse, but they are not in any genuine sense free. For that reason
consumption disempowers the consumer in the sense that the arena in
which he or she seeks that power is unavoidably constrained. Hence the
need to investigate alternatives to consumerism.

Perhaps the major way in which consumers are constrained is through
class. Pierre Bourdieu argues that classes express and assert themselves
through consumption or through cultural capital which they convert to
social power. However, many authors have suggested that Bourdieu's
(1984) analysis neglects social groups with limited power resources
(Swartz, 1997; Evans, 2002). In other words, regardless of the availability
of consumption, we still do not live in an equal society and the availability
to consume does not mean the same thing to people who live in different
social echelons. The freedoms to be had from consumption are perhaps
less straightforward than Bourdieu implies.

The consuming city is aimed at a mythicised consumer and one that
represents a minority. This is the "perfect consumer" described by
Featherstone (1987); the recipient of the enterprise culture (Burrows,
1991; Keat and Abercrombie, 1991) the cultural intermediary (O'Connor
and Wynne, 1996) who is the exception that proves the rule and who
simply reinforces romantic notions of what the city *could* be like.
Bonner and du Gay (1992) argue that this new petite bourgeoisie has
a strong sense of its own ability to educate others in what is and is not
appropriate to consume. The problem is that the new petite bourgeoisie,
for want of a better label, are precisely those people who propagate the
position that the consuming city can provide a never-ending path of
opportunity. The cultural elite promote the idea that consumption in
the city is good, and simplify its complex nature because it is clearly
in their best interests to do so. In this sense it is not the "masses" who
are controlled by consumption at all, but the middle classes who are
deluded by their ability to affect a future over which they have very
limited control. In this respect there are two sides to the consuming city
coin. On one side, there is the imaginary city where consumption
brings nothing but opportunity; on the other there is the city where
consumption will inevitably reinforce existing social divisions. The reality

lies somewhere in between. But the question remains how far that reality can be sustained and where might the consuming city take us as consumers in the future? Harvey (2003) argues that the right to the city is not simply about the right to access what property developers and state planners define, but it is about the right to make a difference. The consuming city may be imaginary. It may not have given us what we desire or need. Is now the time to re-imagine and re-evaluate the city *without* consumption at its core?

Can we, then, imagine a post-consumerist city? To do so would be speculation and might admit romanticised views of both pasts and futures which are as ideological in their way as present consumerism. At the same time, to imagine a future city could allow a latent or dormant hope to take shape in specific ways, working through what it might mean to move beyond consumerism. The difficulty then is that such an exercise tends to be academic, literally so in that it is the kind of speculation in which teachers, researchers, and students in universities can engage in reasonably informed ways, calling on the evidence of social research as well as arguments in critical social and cultural theory. But such debate is less open to professionals outside University departments such as local authority planners, is largely unwelcome for private-sector property developers, and is closed more or less to citizens. Where consumption touches political agendas is in single-issue campaigns on roads, animal rights, and genetically modified foods. A policy for public transport in place of private cars and road haulage would, for instance, have a significant impact on the oil industry, as would a ban on factory farming on agri-business, and a ban on genetically modified crops on the efforts of trans-national companies to achieve monopolies of seed production and guarantee continuing consumption of chemical fertilisers and pest controls.

So, consumerism is an unquestioned way of life for the affluent world, and is identified with cities which continue to be magnets of inward migration (not only in the affluent world – the fastest rates of growth are in Asia, Africa, and Latin America). Crucially in terms of the relation between consumerism as an inherently wasteful way of life and global conditions such as climate change, species depletion, and environmental destruction, consumerism is exported to the non-affluent world as a means to ensure future market growth for the affluent world's industries and financial system. At root, the fantasy of an ever-expanding economy which took shape in the fifteenth and sixteenth centuries, and took form in a material way with the exploitation of the New World, remains the guiding principle of global capitalism. Ecologists would argue it is a principle which, because it disregards the inter-connectedness of all elements in a bio-system (such as the planet), will fail. Socialists might argue that the system is in any case divisive and unjust. What is more difficult is to see how consumers might see through consumerism, and simply stop buying the countless things they are persuaded to want but do not need.

In this context, contemporary China is an interesting case, not least because, as a developed country (with a culture older than modern Europe's, in which paper money and gunpowder were invented) and as the largest population mass of the globe, it is poised between a pre-consumerist world (in which Western consumerism attained the status of a forbidden fruit) and accommodation of consumerism within a still highly ordering political system. While in the West, governments increasingly become subservient to the market, providing conditions of de-regulation in which trans-national companies in effect become the dominant force in society, in China the market is being introduced selectively. In part it is housed off-shore in Hong Kong while in part it also re-shapes the city of Shanghai, one of the fastest growing cities in the world.

In her essay "Mediating Time: The 'Rice Bowl of Youth' in Fin de Siècle China", Zhang Zhen sees Shanghai's vast building programme, designated as re-cosmopolitanisation, as dominating the city's east side, the Pudong Special Economic Zone (established following Deng Xiaoping's *nanxun*, or southern trip, in 1993). The city is "...one of the hottest spots of urbanization and global enterprise in the country, with rice paddies turned almost overnight into asphalt roads and commercial and resi-dential compounds" (Zhen, 2001: 134). There are skyscrapers, a concrete communications tower, a metro, and an international airport. Zhen continues:

> What is underway here is an immense project of spatializing time and arresting the future. Expressways, railways, bridges, airfields, elevators, assembly lines, infrastructure pipes, and tunnels rapidly being built or installed to speed up circulation of people and things. A perusal of *Shanghai Pictorial* and of pictorials from other major cities reveals an obsession with aerial panoramas of modern structures...these bold strokes of development are spatial-temporal *passages* (à la Benjamin) that link past and future but also inadvertently foreground the vast unevenness, or nonsynchronous simultaneity, between the old and the new, the rural and the urban, the inland and the coastal geoeconomical topographies. (ibid.)

Among the signs of the new economy in China is the use, banned in the Maoist period, of the title Miss (*xiaojie*) – as in Miss Public Relations, Miss Shopping Guide, and Miss Real Estate – indicative of the use of young women to promote new forms of consumption. Similarly, Zhen reports that new forms of periodicals have appeared to promote the consumption of fashions through an appeal to sensuality and social mobility alien to the culture of the previous regime. Zhen writes: "Such representations correspond to ongoing changes in social space and encourage identification and mimetic desire," adding that the production of beauty calendars encourages young women to be aware of the sexual appeal of their bodies, *and* to seek new careers in media production and entertainment. Western-style consumerism is not, however, uncontested. Zhen notes critical writing within China, as in the magazine *Chinese Woman*, where one item which contrasts the worldviews of a young woman, Xiaoli, who works in a foreign-owned hotel and has two Italian handbags, and that of her mother "who teaches political economy, picks pennies off the street, and conserves in a designated drawer plastic string for future reuse" (Zhen, 2000: 140). After a prolonged readers' debate, the magazine's editors closed the story by seeing Xiaoli give up ambitions to be a singer or a beautician and become a law student. This fits a situation in which state policy aims at "...completing the transition from a production-oriented socialism to a consumption-oriented postsocialism without yielding the power of the communist party, which is itself no longer the old vanguard of the revolutionary era" (Zhen, 2000: 151) while individuals are confronted with a growing culture of consumption based on youth and femininity. In ordinary life, as it were, such commodities (as they become) can be produced only for a while: "...those who consume youth are men...whereas women produce their youth as a special kind of commodity, one that expires quickly" (Zhen, 2000: 152). There is nothing new in this kind of commodification except its export to a society in which newness lends added value to the baubles, but there may be some hope in the criticism to which consumerism, while accepted, is subjected in a popular magazine.

The situation in China contrasts with Martyn Lee's view of contemporary (1990s) consumption in the UK. Looking at the magazine *The Face*, Lee begins from Bourdieu's (1984) critique of the consumption practices of a new, young bourgeoisie whose capital is mainly cultural. Seeing a primacy of form over function, Bourdieu advances a notion of pure taste unaffected by such mediating influences as collective memory; and Lee sees the adoption of de-contextualised cultural forms in a lifestyle of consumption as an evacuation of meaning:

Effectively dehistoricised, not yet written upon and therefore extremely malleable in the symbolic meanings which it may potentially assume, the object chosen as the receptacle for the storage of cultural values is in effect little other than a purely arbitrary token of a new form of cultural currency. The significance of this token is to be found, not in its nominal sign-values ... but rather in the fact that it has become the bearer of values which have emerged solely from its own radical symbolic *re-evaluation*. More accurately perhaps, it is the mode of consumption ... which becomes the social sign of storage of cultural value. (Lee, 1993: 172)

The new eclecticism masquerades as cultural freedom, yet the predominance of display – the desire to be seen as living this supposedly free life – imposes a subjugation of cultural forms to the new taste. Lee cites *The Face* as a vehicle for this form of roaming cultural currency expressed in advertising formats and features alike. The styles in question may be located in urban streets, but they remain tied to consumption and – though Lee does not make the point as such – to global capital. What he does say is that the economy of intellectual effort such magazines (which are primarily visual) require from their readers paradoxically produces an impression of "a readership who possess a knowledge that appears to surpass the most advanced forms of learning and reading" (Lee, 1993: 173–174), as could be said, too, of certain kinds of television programme – Lee cites *Twin Peaks* – which contravene given ways of making a narrative.

Returning to Shanghai, it is questionable whether Chinese society or the natural environment of China can support a wholesale lurch to consumerism, which in any case is not what is happening even if the rapid growth of Shanghai might give the impression it is. The critical, popular positions expressed in Chinese magazines, however, are not consumed by Western migrants seeking to exploit China's growth economy. A guidebook to Shanghai for US ex-patriots, *Living in Shanghai* (Dawson and Dawson, 1998), states that shopping is the most popular leisure-time activity there for locals and foreigners alike. Guidebooks, like picture postcards, are useful because they give an uncritical representation of the dominant culture, not the mediated view of the cultural critic or academic who might ask how many social groups are included in the term "locals". The Dawsons, untroubled by such distinctions, write:

A great variety of imported food items and familiar Western brand names can now be found in Shanghai's grocery stores ... The problem

lies in not being able to do a Western-style "one-stop" shopping trip
once a week. Grocery stores are scattered throughout the city, and
no single place ever carries everything on one's list. It is usual for
shoppers to have to make rotation trips to various stores that carry
particular items...This of course requires much extra time and
planning. It helps to have a separate storage freezer at home for
stocking up and cutting down on numerous trips...(Dawson and
Dawson, 1998: 46)

The authors, who are owners of a relocation agency for U.S. businesses
and their executives, add that although supplies are sometimes irregular,
an increasing range of Western goods is available in Shanghai. This is
taken as a self-evidently good thing. The book's cover shows a street
scene in which a Coca-Cola sign is the most prominent feature together
with some Chinese writing, a mother and children, and a sunny blue
sky. The Dawsons list outlets from supermarkets to department stores,
water suppliers to ice cream and candy shops, and for electronic goods,
carpets, bedding, and numerous other categories. In other sections they
list country clubs, restaurants, and pet care firms, as well as nunneries.
There are 35 department stores, but as yet only three mega-marts, for
one of which a membership card is required for admission. Going to
several shops to buy different things is seen as a problem, to which
a weekly one-stop shopping trip (as in a mega-mart) is contrasted as
more desirable for busy people, while eliminating the social or conver-
sational aspect of shopping in smaller establishments. The passage cited
above illustrates much that is taken for granted in the affluent society
of the West, and the guidebook reads like the junk mail sent out by
credit card companies. The guidebook includes, for example, an advert
for a country club's 27-hole golf course, fringed by a green and sylvan
slope resembling, maybe, Connecticut. It claims, too, that the lifestyle
offered by its villas (designed by a firm from California) is unique; these
offer "...a perfect blend of Chinese Courtyard style with western lifestyle and interior design...sure to become Shanghai's benchmark in
suburban living" (Dawson and Dawson, 1998: 90), and look, from the
artist's impression, as if they could be in Celebration (see Chapter 5);
their inhabitants, as pioneers of a new economic colonialism, will find
the Shanghai Centre just like any other part of the global, high-rise city.
It contains 472 luxury apartments, 25,000 square metres of grade "A"
office space, and a tri-level retail plaza (Dawson and Dawson, 1998: 41).
At the back of the book is an order form for customised copies of the
guide, with gold-stamped covers if required.

In some places, it seems, the idea of a post-consumer society has yet to be even an irritant. But if Shanghai's current development illustrates a future for consumerism exported to places it has yet to saturate, in the affluent countries from which it is exported there is a growing disaffection. Is it, then, possible to reconfigure our conceptualisation of the city for a post-consumerist world? At the outset of such speculation a distinction between consumerism and consumption is helpful. It is not that all consumption will cease – it obviously will not – but that consumers may develop increasingly critical and active relations to it, while some governments may decide not to abandon regulation for a free market which costs their electors dearly. At one level, the dialectic of consumerism and post-consumerism will be played out by states and the trans-national companies who drive its technologies, its mass cultural products, and its mythicisation of choice. At another, glimpses of a post-consumerist society can be gained in moves to differential forms of consumption, such as the choice (even if it is restricted mainly to the middle classes) of organic foods rather than the junk of agri-business. Local schemes connecting producers and consumers, as discussed in Chapter 8, have their limitations and contradictions, but reduce the footprint of a city.

But, in the end, that footprint must be reduced by more than the difference made by a few green cabbages. In terms of food, there is scope for at least part of a city's consumption to be grown not in a nearby countryside but within the city itself in gardens, greenhouses, and allotments. In terms of clothing and furniture, there is considerable scope, outside the fashion magazines, for recycling through second-hand and charity shops. In terms of shelter, there is scope for self-build schemes, urban eco-villages, and other departures from the commodification of housing (as well as the use of energy-efficient and non-poisoning materials) which align new modes of housing production with more cooperative modes of living (Barton (ed.), 2002). Besides that is the option to plan cities in such a way as to mix living, working, and socialising in proximity, reducing transport, and to increase housing densities so as to reduce land use. To examine such possibilities would be the scope of another book – here we must leave the ideas floating even if this opens us to a charge of dreaming – but what we can, perhaps, say in conclusion is: first, that within the limits of necessary consumption (food, clothing, shelter, and so forth) there is the technical possibility to reduce the destructiveness of consumption, in part through regulation but in part, too, through initiatives on the part of consumers; and secondly, that this will work only in context of a re-evaluation of wants in favour of needs. This does not mean a new Puritanism, but, more searching than a culture of denial which is prone to aestheticisation, it does mean accepting at first a shrinking and then a steady-state economy, and with it major changes in patterns of employment and – in effect – the end of capitalism as we know it, not to suddenly disappear but to transmute incrementally into a new, less destructive form.

The question as to how such a quiet and self-organised revolution might come about is difficult, and again would form the material for another book. As clichéd as it may sound it seems there is a case for research which asks whether new patterns of consumption are aligned with, or lead to, new patterns of political allegiance. Dürrschmidt (1999) cites responses from consumers in an alternative sector who state a feeling of belonging to a milieu (which could be contrasted with Lee's remarks on the fluidity of social relations in a consumerist society cited above), and a sense of solidarity might be a prerequisite of radical change driven not by regulation but by groups within society. Not much, however, can be deduced from one such study, and the field of alternatives to consumerism (rather than alternative positions of complicity, resistance, or indifference within it) is as yet largely unculti-vated. Studies which investigate specific responses to local conditions within a global context, rather than in the acrobatics of a literature which sees resistance to capitalism in, say, reactions to junk mail, offer, potentially at least the prospect of radical change. What follows is a question that lies at the very heart of the various disciplines that have informed this book: has the time come for a more self-consciously critical agenda that puts the needs of the future rather than the needs of the present at its heart? If not, perhaps we can feast while the city implodes, and see counter-culture in chewing gum, until voices other than those of affluence intervene to silence us.

References

Adorno, T. W. (1939) "Fragmente über Wagner", *Zeitschrift für Sozialforschung*, vol. 8, 1–2.

Adorno, T. W. (1991) in J. M. Bernstein (ed.) *The Culture Industry: Selected Essays on Mass Culture* (London: Routledge).

Alfino, M., Caputo, J. S. and Wynyard, R. (eds) (1998) *McDonalidization Revisited: Critical Essays on Consumer Culture* (Westport (CT): Praeger).

Anderton, F. and Chase, J. (1997a) *Las Vegas: A Guide to Recent Architecture* (Cologne: Könemann).

Anderton, F. and Chase, J. (1997b) *Las Vegas: The Success of Excess* (Köln: Könemann).

Barber, S. (1995) *Fragments of the European City* (London: Reaktion).

Barton, H. and Kleiner, D. (2000) "Innovative eco-neighbourhood projects", pp. 66–85, in H. Barton (ed.) *Sustainable Communities* (London: Earthscan).

Barton, H. and Kleiner, D. (2002) "Innovative Eco-Neighbourhoods", pp. 66–85 in H. Barton (ed.) *Sustainable Communities: The Potential for Eco-Neighbourhoods* (London: Earthscan).

Bass, D. (1997) "Insiders and outsiders: latent urban thinking in movies of modern Rome", pp. 84–99 in F. Perez and M. Thomas (eds) *Cinema & Architecture* (London: BFI Publishing).

Baudelaire, C. [1855] "Critical Method – on the Modern Idea of Progress as Applied to the Fine Arts", pp. 458–459 in C. Harrison, P. Wood and J. Gaiger (1998) *Art in Theory 1815–1900: An Anthology of Changing Ideas* (Oxford: Blackwell).

Baudrillard, J. (1988) "Simulcra and simulations", pp. 166–184 in M. Poster (ed.) *Jean Baudrillard: Selected Writings* (Cambridge: Polity).

Baudrillard, J. (1998) *Consumer Society: Myths and Structures* (London: Sage).

Bauman, Z. (1998) *Globalization: The Human Consequences* (Cambridge: Polity).

Beall, J. (1997) *A City for All: Valuing Difference and Working with Diversity* (London: Zed Books).

Beck, U. (1992) *Risk Society: Towards a New Modernity* (London: Sage).

Beckett, A. (1994) "Take a walk on the safe side", *The Independent on Sunday*, 27 February, 10–12.

Bell, D. (1976) *The Cultural Contradictions of Capitalism* (London: Heinemann).

Benjamin, W. [1973] (1997) *Charles Baudelaire* (London: Verso).

Benjamin, W. (1999) *The Arcades Project*, trans. H. Eiland and K. McLaughlin (Cambridge (Mass): Harvard).

Benson, J. (1994) *The Rise of Consumer Society in Britain 1880–1980* (London: Longman).

Berger, J. (1972) *Ways of Seeing* (Harmondsworth: Penguin).

Berman, M. (1983) *All that is Solid Melts into Air* (London: Verso).

Bermingham, A. (1995) "Introduction: the consumption of culture; image, object, text", pp. 1–20 in A. Bermingham and J. Brewer (eds) *The Consumption of Culture 1600–1800: Image, Object, Text* (London: Routledge).

Betsky, A. (2000) "All the world's a store: the spaces of shopping", pp. 108–144 in J. Pavitt (ed.) *Brand.new* (London: V & A).

Bianchini, F. (1993) "Culture, conflict and cities: issues and prospects for the 1990s", pp. 199–213 in F. Bianchini and M. Parkinson (eds) *Cultural Policy and Urban Regeneration: The West European Experience* (Manchester: Manchester University Press).

Bianchini, F. (1999) "The Relationship between Cultural Resources and Tourism Policies for Cities and Regions", pp. 78–90 in Dodd and van Hemel (1999) *Planning Cultural Tourism in Europe: A Presentation of Theories and Cases* (Amsterdam: Boekman Stichting).

Bianchini, F., Fisher, M., Montgomery, J. and Worpole, K. (1988) *City Centres, City Cultures* (Manchester: Centre for Local Economic Strategies).

Bird, J. (1993) "Dystopia on the Thames", pp. 120–135 in J. Bird, B. Curtis, T. Putnam, G. Robertson and L. Tickner (eds) *Mapping the Futures: Local Cultures, Global Change* (London: Routledge).

Blackman, T. (1997) "Urban Planning in the United Kingdom", pp. 128–149 in M. Pacione (ed.) *Britain's Cities: Geographies of Division in Urban Britain* (London: Routledge).

Bleecker, A. and Bleecker, S. (2002) *World view: on the world of ResidenSea, you're free to give the globe a spin* March 17, www.sun-sentinel.com/travel/features/sfl-livecruzmar17,0,2726413.story?coll=sfla-travel-headlines-other.

Bloch, E. [1959] (1986) *The Principle of Hope* (Cambridge (Mass): MIT).

Bocock, R. (1993) *Consumption* (London: Routledge).

Bodington, S., George, M. and Michaelson, J. (1986) *Developing the Socially Useful Economy* (Basingstoke: Macmillan).

Boniface, P. and Fowler, P. J. (1993) *Heritage Tourism in the Global Village* (London: Routledge).

Bonner, F. and duGay, P. (1992) "Thirtysomething and contemporary consumer culture: distinctiveness and distinction", pp. 166–183 in R. Burrows and C. Marsh (eds) *Consumption and Class: Divisions and Change* (Basingstoke: Macmillan).

Bookchin, M. (1980) *Toward an Ecological Society* (Montreal: Back Rose).

Bookchin, M. (1990) *Remaking Societ: Oathways to a Green Society* (Boston: South End Press).

Boudaille, G. (1964) *Gauguin* (London: Thames & Hudson).

Bourdieu, P. (1979) *Distinction: A Social Critique of the Judgement of Taste* (London: Routledge, Kegan and Paul).

Bourdieu, P. (1984) *Distinction: A Social Critique of the Judgement of Taste* (London: Routledge).

Bourdieu, P. (1993) *The Field of Cultural Production* (Cambridge: Polity).

Bowlby, R. (1993) *Shopping with Freud* (London: Routledge).

Bowlby, R. (2000) "Supermarket futures", p. 152 in J. Pavitt (ed.) *Brand.new* (London: V & A).

Boyer, C. (1992) "Cities for Sale: merchandising history at south street Seaport", in M. Sorkin (ed.) *Variations on a Theme Park* (New York: Noonday Press).

Boyer, C. (2001) "Twice-told stories: the double erasure of Times", pp. 30–52 in I. Borden, J. Rendell, J. Kerr and A. Pivaro (eds) (2001) *The Unknown City: Contesting Architecture and Social Space* (Cambridge (Mass): MIT).

Boyer, M. C. (1993) "The city of illusion: New York's public spaces" in P. Knox (ed.) *The Restless Urban Landscape* (Englewood Cliffs: NJ: Prentice-Hall).

Brake, M. and Harrop, K. (1994) "Selling the industrial town: identity, image and illusion", pp. 93–114 in J. R. Gold and S. V. Ward (eds) *Place Promotion: The Use of Publicity and Marketing to Sell Towns and Regions* (Chichester: John Wiley).

Bramson, L. (1961) *The Political Context of Sociology* (Princeton: Princeton University Press).

Brandt, W. (1980) *North-South: A Programme for Survival – The Report of the Independent Commission on International Development Issues under the Chairmanship of Willy Brandt* (London: Pan Books).

Braudel, H. (1974) *Capitalism and Material Life 1400–1800* (New York: Harper & Row).

Buck-Morss, S. (1989) *The Dialectics of Seeing* (Cambridge (Mass): MIT Press).

Buie, S. (1996) "Market as Mandala: the erotic space of Commerce", *Organization*, 3, 2, 225–232.

Burrows, R. (ed.) (1991) *Deciphering the Enterprise Culture* (London: Routledge).

Byrne, D. (1997) "Chaotic places or complex places? Cities in a post-industrial era", pp. 50–72 in S. Westwood and J. Williams (eds) (1997) *Imagining Cities: Scripts, Signs, Memory* (London: Routledge).

Byrne, D. (2001) *Understanding the Urban* (Basingstoke: Palgrave).

Calthorpe, P. (ed.) (1993) *The Next American Metropolis: Ecology, Community and the American Dream* (New York: Princeton Architectural Press).

Campbell, C. (1987) *The Romantic Ethic and the Spirit of Modern Consumerism* (Oxford: Blackwell).

Campbell, C. (1995) in D. Miller (ed.) *Acknowledging Consumption* (London: Routledge).

Carrier, J. (1995) *Gifts and Commodities: Exchange and Western Capitalism since 1700* (London: Routledge).

Cartwright, R. and Baird, C. (1999) *The Development and Growth of the Cruise Industry* (Oxford: Butterworth-Heinemann).

Castells, M. (1977) *The Urban Question: A Marxist Approach* (London: Edward Arnold).

Chalkley, B. and Goodridge, J. (1991) "The 1943 plan for Plymouth: war-time vision and post-war realities", pp. 62–81 in B. Chalkley, D. Dunkerely and P. Gripaios (eds) *Plymouth: Martime City in Transition* (Newton Abbot: David and Charles).

Chambers, I. (1990) *Popular Culture: The Metropolitan Experience* (London: Metropolis).

Chaney, D. (1983) "The department store as a cultural form", *Theory, Culture and Society* 1, 3, 22–31.

Chaney, D. (1993) *Fictions of Collective Life* (London: Routledge).

Cilliers, P. (1998) *Complexity and Postmodernism: Understanding Complex Systems* (London: Routledge).

City of Plymouth Planning Department (1986) *Tomorrow's Plymouth* (Plymouth: Plymouth Planning Department).

Clammer, J. (1997) *Contemporary Urban Japan: A Sociology of Consumption* (Oxford: Blackwell).

Clarke, D. (1996) *Consumption and the City, Modern and Postmodern*, School of Geography, University of Leeds Unpublished Working paper 96/10.

Clarke, D. B. (1997) "Introduction: previewing the cinematic city", pp. 1–18 in D. B. Clarke (ed.) *The Cinematic City* (London: Routledge).

Cochrane, G. (2000) "Creating Tate Modern: 1996–2000", pp. 7–8 in I. Cole and N. Stanley N. (eds) *Beyond the Museum: Art, Institutions, People* (Oxford: Museum of Modern Art).

Cook, I. (1994) "New fruits and vanity: symbolic production in the global food economy", in A. Bonanno, L. Busch, W. H. Friedland, L. Gouveig and E. Mingiovie (eds) *From Columbus to Congra: The Globalization of Agriculture and Food* (Kansas: University Press of Kansas).

Coombes, A. (1994) *Reinventing Africa: Museums, Material Culture and Popular Imagination* (New Haven: Yale).

Cooper, M. (1995) No more sin city, *Worldbusiness*, 4, 22–28.

Corrigan, P. (1997) *The Sociology of Consumption* (London: Sage).

Crawford, M. (1992) "The World in A shopping Mall", pp. 3–30 in M. Sorkin (ed.) (1992) *Variations on a Theme Park* (New York: Noonday Press).

Crawford, M. (1999) "Blurring the Boundaries: Public Space and Private Life", pp. 22–35 in J. Chase, M. Crawford and J. Kaliski (eds) *Everyday Urbanism* (New York: Monacelli Press).

Creswell, T. (1997) "Imagining the Nomad", pp. 360–382 in Bento and Stohmayer (eds) *Space and Social Theory: Interpreting Modernity and Post-Modernity* (London: Sage).

Cross, G. (1993) *Time and Money: The Making of Consumer Culture* (London: Routledge).

Crosswick, G. and Jauman, S. (eds) (1999) *Cathedrals of Consumption: The European Department Store, 1850–1939* (Aldershot: Ashgate).

Crow, G. (2002) *Social Solidarities: Theories, Identities and Social Change* (Buckingham: Open University Press).

Curtis, B. and Pajaczkowska, C. (1994) "Getting there: travel, time, and narrative", pp. 119–125 in G. Robertson, M. Mash, L. Tickner, J. Bird, B. Curtis and T. Putnam (eds) (1996) *Future Natural: Nature, Science, Culture* (London: Routledge).

Davis, M. (1990) City of Quartz: Excavating the Future in Los Angeles (London: Verso).

Davis, M. (2000) *Magical Urbanism: Latinos reinvent the US city* (London: Verso).

Davis, M. (2002) *Dead Cities: A Natural History* (London: New Press).

Dawson, J. and Dawson, D. III (1998) *Living in Shanghai* (Hong Kong: Pacific Century Publishers).

Deal clinched with architect www.thisisplymouth.co.uk/displayNode. jsp?nodeId=98912&command=displayContent&sourceNode=98821& contentPK=3836732.

Dear, M. J. (2000) *The Postmodern Urban Condition* (Cambridge: Blackwell).

de Certeau, M. (1984) *The Practice of Everyday Life* (Berkeley, CA: University of California Press).

Degan, M. (2002) "Regenerating Public Life? a sensory analysis of regenerated public spaces in el Raval, Barcelona", pp. 19–36 in J. Rugg and D. Hinchcliffe (eds) *Recoveries & Reclamations* (Bristol: Intellect Books).

Demianyk, G. (2002) Historic naval dockyard to become luxury apartments in £30M scheme http://www.thisisplymouth.co.uk/displayNode.jsp? nodeId=98912&command=displayContent&sourceNode=98821&content PK=1498403.

Deutsche, R. (1988) "Uneven Development: public art in New York city", *October*, 47, pp. 3–52; reprinted pp. 49–107 in R. Deutsche (1996) *Evictions: Art and Spatia Politics* (Cambridge (Mass); MIT Press).

Dodd, D. (1999) "Barcelona, the making of a cultural city", pp. 53–64 in D. Dodd and A. van Hemel (eds) *Planning Cultural Tourism in Europe: A Presentation of Theories and Cases* (Amsterdam: Boekman Stichting).

Donald, J. (1999) *Imagining the Modern City* (London: Athlone).

Donnovan, P. (2000) Las Vegas is example for urban growth, www.buffalo.edu/ reporter/vol31/vol31n26/n4.html.

Dore, E. (1992) "Debt and ecological disaster in Latin America", *Race and Class*, 34, 1: 73.

Douglas, M. [1966] (1970) *Purity and Danger: An Analysis of Concepts of Pollution and Taboo* (Harmondsworth: Penguin).

Douglas, M. and Isherwood, B. (1979) *The World of Goods* (London: Allen Lane).

Doyle, M. W. (2002) "Staging the revolution: guerrilla theatre as a counter-cultural practice, 1965–68", pp. 71–98 in P. Braunstein and M. W. Doyle (eds) *Imagine Nation: The American Counterculture of the 1960s and '70s* (London: Routledge).

Drew, B. (1998) *Crossing the Expendable Landscape* (St Paul (MN): Greywolf Press).

Dubet, F. and Lapeyronnie, D. (eds) (1994) *Im Aus der Vorstädte* (Stuttgart: Klett-Cotta).

Duncan, C. (1995) *Civilizing Rituals: Inside Public Art Museums* (London: Routledge).

Duncan, J. (1993) "Sites of representation: place, time, and the discourse of the other", pp. 39–56 in J. Duncan and D. Ley (eds) (1993) *Place/Culture/Representation* (London: Routledge).

Dunn, R. (1998) *Identity Crises: A social Critique of Modernity* (Minneapolis: University of Minnesota Press).

Dürrschmidt, J. (1999) "The local versus the global? Individualised milieux in a complex risk society: the case of organic food box Schemes in the South West", pp. 131–154 in J. Hearn and S. Roseneil (eds) (1999) *Consuming Cultures: Power and Resistance* (Basingstoke: Macmillan).

Eade, J. (1989) *The Politics of Community: The Bangladeshi Community in East London* (Aldershot: Avebury).

Eade, J. (ed.) (1997) *Living the Global City* (London: Routledge).

Eadington, W. (2000) *Trends 2000: Trends in casinos and tourism for the twenty-first century*, www.unr.edu/gaming/Papers/TRENDS%202000.htm.

Eckardt, F. and Hassenpflug, D. (eds) (2003) *Consumption and the Post-Industrial City* (Berlin: Peter Lang).

Eisenschitz, A. (1997) "The view from the grassroots", pp. 150–176 in M. Paccione (ed.) (1997) *Britain's Cities: Geographies of Division in Urban Britain* (London: Routledge).

Elkington, J. and Hailes, J. (1988) *The Green Consumer Guide* (London: Gollancz).

Elliott, J. (1999) *An Introduction to Sustainable Development*, 2nd edition (London: Routledge).

Evans, J. (2002) *"Consuming Children": A Sociological Analysis of Children's Relationship with Contemporary Consumer Culture*, unpublished PhD thesis, University of Plymouth.

Featherstone, M. (1987) "Lifestyle and Consumer Culture", *Theory, Culture and Society* 4, pp. 55–70.

Featherstone, M. (1991) *Consumer Culture and Postmodernism* (London: Sage).

Featherstone, M. (1992) "Postmodernism and the aestheticization of everyday life", pp. 265–290 in S. Lash and J. Friedman (eds) *Modernity and Identity* (Oxford: Blackwell).

Fernandes, E. and Varley, A. (1998) *Illegal Cities: Law and Urban Change in Developing Countries* (London: Zed Books).

Finn, M. C. (2001) "Scotch drapers and the politics of modernity: gender, class and national identity in the Victorian tally trade", pp. 89–107 in

M. Daunton and M. Hilton (eds) (2001) *The Politics of Consumption: Material Culture and Citizenship in Europe and America* (Oxford: Berg).

Forty, A. (1986) *Objects of Desire: Design and Society since 1750* (London: Thames and Hudson).

Foucault, M. [1975] (1991) *Discipline and Punish: The Birth of the Prison* (Harmondsworth: Penguin).

Frantz, D. and Collins, C. (1999) *Celebration USA – Living in Disney's Brave New Town* (New York: Henry Hott & Co.).

Frantz, D. and Collins, C. (2000) *Celebration, U.S.A.: Living in Disney's Brave New Town* (New York: Henry Holt).

Freedom Ship www.freedomship.com/overview.html.

Freud, S. [1910 and 1926] (1962) *Two Short Accounts of Psycho-Analysis* (Harmondsworth: Penguin).

Frisby, D. and Featherstone, M. (eds) (1997) *Simmel on Culture* (London: Sage).

Gabriel, Y. and Lang, T. (1995) *The Unmanageable Consumer* (London: Sage).

George, S. [1976] (1991) *How the Other Half Dies: The Real Reasons for World Hunger*, revised edition (Harmondsworth: Penguin).

Ghirardo, D. (1996) *Architecture After Modernism* (London: Thames & Hudson).

Gilloch, G. (1996) *Myth and Metropolis: Walter Benjamin and the City* (Cambridge: Polity).

Goffman, E. (1961) *Asylums* (New York: Anchor Books).

Goldberger, P. (1996) "The rise of the private city", pp. 135–149 in J. Vitullo-Martin (ed.) *Breaking Away: The Future of Cities* (New York: Twentieth Century Fund Press).

Goldman, R. and Papson, S. (1998) *Nike Culture* (London: Sage).

Gonzalez, J. M. (1993) "Bilbao: culture, citizenship and quality of life", pp. 73–89 in F. Bianchini and M. Parkinson *Cultural Policy and Urban Regeneration: The West European Experience* (Manchester: Manchester University Press).

Gottdiener, M. (1999) "The consumption of space and the spaces of consumption", pp. 264–285 in M. Gottdiener (ed.) *New Forms of Consumption: Consumers, Culture and Commodification* (Oxford: Rowman & Littlefield).

Gottdiener, M. (ed.) (2000) *New Forms of Consumption: Consumers, Culture, and Commodification* (Lanham, MD: Rowman & Littlefield).

Gottdiener, M., Collins, C. and Dickens, D. (1999) *Las Vegas: The Social Production of an All-American City* (Cambridge: Blackwell).

Gratz, R. B. (1989) *The Living City* (New York: Simon & Schuster).

Gregson, N. and Crewe, L. (2003) *Second Hand Cultures* (Oxford: Berg).

Grunenberg, C. (1994) "The politics of presentation: the Museum of Modern Art, New York", pp. 192–211 in M. Pointon (ed.) *Art Apart: Art Institutions and Ideology Across England and North America* (Manchester: Manchester University Press).

Grunenberg, C. (2002) "Wonderland: spectacles of display from the Bon Marché to Prada", pp. 17–38 in C. Grunenberg and M. Hollein (eds) *Shopping: A Century of Art and Consumer Culture* (Liverpool: Hatje Cantz).

The Guardian, Organic sales boom but most still imported, 15 October 2002, p. 8.

Hajer, M. A. (1993) "Rotterdam: redesigning the public domain", pp. 48–72 in F. Bianchini and M. Parkinson (eds) *Cultural Policy and Urban Regeneration: The West European Experience* (Manchester: Manchester University Press).

Hall, T. and Hubbard, P. (eds) (1998) *The Entrepreneurial City* (Chichester: Wiley).

Hamdi, N. [1991] (1995) *Housing Without Houses: Participation, Flexibility, Enablement* (London: Intermediate Technology Publications).

Hannigan, J. (1998) *Fantasy City: Pleasure and Profit in the Postmodern Metropolis* (London: Routledge).

Harloe, M. and Fainstein, S. (1992) "Conclusion: the divided cities" in S. Fainstein, I. Gordon and M. Harloe (eds) *Divided Cities: New York and London in the Contemporary World* (Oxford: Blackwell).

Harrison, C. and Wood, P. with Gaiger, J. (eds) (1998) *Art in Theory 1815–1900: An Anthology of Changing Ideas* (Oxford: Blackwell).

Harvey, D. (1985) *The Urbanisation of Capital* (Oxford: Blackwell).

Harvey, D. (1989) *The Urban Experience* (Baltimore: Johns Hopkins University Press).

Harvey, D. (1996) *Justice, Nature & the Geography of Difference* (Oxford: Blackwell).

Harvey, D. (2000) *Spaces of Hope* (Baltimore: Johns Hopkins University Press).

Harvey, P. (1996) *Hybrids of Modernity: Anthropology, the Nation State, and the Universal Exhibition* (London: Routledge).

Harvey, D. (2003) "Can we build an urban utopia?" pp. 18–19 in *Times Higher Education Supplement*, 14 February.

Häußermann, H. (1997) "The city and urban sociology: urban ways of living and the integration of the stranger", pp. 136–146 in H. Paetzold (ed.) *City Life: Essays on Urban Culture* (Limburg: Jan van Eyck Akademie).

Healey, P. (1998) "Institutional theory, social exclusion and governance", pp. 53–73 in A. Madanipour, G. Cars and J. Allen (eds) (1998) *Social Exclusion in European Cities: Processes, Experiences and Responses* (London: Jessica Kingsley and the Regional Studies Association).

Hearn, J. and Roseneil, S. (eds) (1999) *Consuming Cultures: Power and Resistance* (Basingstoke: Macmillan).

Hebdige, D. (1979) *Subculture: The Meaning of Style* (London: Methuen).

Herald Tribune (2002) www.heraldtribune.com, Engineer from Sarasota planned Freedom Ship, 21 October.

Hess, A. (1993) *Viva Las Vegas: After Hours Architecture* (San Francisco: Chronicle Books).

Highmore, B. (2003) *Everyday Life and Cultural Theory: An Introduction* (London: Routledge).

Horkheimer, M. and Adorno, T. (1973) *Dialectic of Enlightenment* (London: Allen Lane).

Huxtable, A. L. (1997) *The Unreal America* (New York: WW Norton).

Ignatief, M. (1984) *The Needs of Strangers* (London: Chatto & Windus).

Illich, I. (1981) *Shadow Work* (London: Marion Boyars).

Illich, I. [1973] (1990) *Tools for Conviviality* (London: Marion Boyars).

Irvine, S. (1989) "Consuming fashions? The limits to green consumerism", *The Ecologist*, 19, No. 3, pp. 88–93.

Jacobs, J. M. (1996) *Edge of Empire: Postcolonialism and the City* (London: Routledge).

Johnson, P. (1988) "Conspicuous consumption and working-class culture in late-Victorian and Edwardian Britain", *Transactions of the Royal Historical Society*, pp. 27–42.

Keat, R. and Abercrombie, N. (eds) (1991) *Enterprise Culture* (London: Routledge).

Lash, S. and Urry, J. (1994) *Economies of Signs and Space* (London: Sage).

Lawrence, J. C. (1992) "Geographical space, social space, and the realm of the department store", *Urban History*, 19, pp. 64–83.

Lee, M. (1993) *Consumer Culture Reborn: The Cultural Politics of Consumption* (London: Routledge).

Lefebvre, H. [1974] (1991) *Critique of Everyday Life* (volume 1) trans. J. Moore (London: Verso).

Lefebvre, H. (1996) "The right to the city", pp. 147–159 in E. Kofman and E. Labas (eds) *Writings on Cities: Henri Lefebvre* (Oxford: Blackwell).

LeGates, R. T. and Stout, F. (1996) Editors' introduction, pp. 97–98 in R. T. LeGates and F. Stout (eds) *The City Reader* (London: Routledge).

Leigh, R. (1921) *The Human Side of Retailing: A Textbook for Salespeople in Retail Stores and Students of Retail Salesmanship and Store Organisation* (New York: D Appleton).

Leslie, E. (2000) *Walter Benjamin: Overpowering Conformism* (London: Pluto).

Leslie, E. (2001) "Tate modern: a year of sweet success", *Radical Philosophy*, No. 109, pp. 2–5.

Ley, D. (1980) "Liberal ideology and the post-industrial city", *Annals of the Association of American Geographers*, 77, pp. 465–468.

Ley, D. (1997) *The New Middle Class and the Remaking of the Central City* (Oxford: Oxford University Press).

Light, J. (1999) "From cityspace to cyberspace", pp. 109–130 in M. Crang, P. Crang and J. May (eds) *Virtual Geographies: Bodies, Spaces and Relations* (London: Routledge).

Lodziak, C. (1995) *Manipulating Needs: Capitalism and Culture* (London: Pluto).

Lodziak, C. (2002) *The Myth of Consumerism* (London: Pluto).

Loftman, P. and Nevin, B. (1998) "Pro-Growth Local Economic Development Strategies: Civic Promotion and Local Needs in Britain's Second City, 1981–1996", pp. 128–148 in T. Hall, and P. Hubbard (eds) (1998) *The Entrepreneurial City* (Chichester: Wiley).

Light, A. (ed.) (1998) *Social Ecology After Bookchin* (New York: Guildford Press).

Lubove, S. (1996) "Casinos not such a safe bet anymore", p. 56 in *Business Review Weekly*, 18, 32.

Lukes, T. W. (1993) "Green consumerism: ecology and the ruse of recycling", pp. 154–172 in J. Bennett and W. Chaloupka (eds) *In the Nature of Things* (Minneapolis: University of Minnesota Press).

Lunt, P. K. and Livingstone, S. M. (1992) *Mass Consumption and Personal Identity* (Buckingham: Open University Press).

Lury, C. (1996) *Consumer Culture* (Cambridge: Polity).

Lynch, K. (1960) *The Image of the City* (Cambridge, Mass: MIT Press).

MacCannell, D. (1976) *The Tourist: A New Theory of the Leisure Class* (New York: Shocken Books).

MacCannell, D. (1999) "New urbanism and its discontents", pp. 106–138 in J. Copjec and M. Sorkin (eds) (1999) *Giving Ground: The Politics of Propinquity* (London: Verso).

Mack, J. and Lansley, S. (1985) *Poor Britain* (London, Allen & Unwin).

Macnaghten, P. and Urry, J. (1998) *Contested Natures* (London: Sage).

Makimoto, T. and Manners, D. (1997) *Digital Nomad* (Chichester: Wiley).

Malinowski, B. (1944) *A Scientific Theory of Culture and Other Essays* (Chapel Hill: University of North Carolina Press).

Marcuse, H. (1969) *An Essay on Liberation* (Harmondsworth: Penguin).

Marcuse, H. (1970) *Five Lectures* (Harmondsworth: Penguin).

Marcuse, P. (2002) "The Layered City", pp. 94–114 in P. Madsen and R. Plunz (eds) *The Urban Lifeworld: Formation, Perception, Representation* (London: Routledge).

Marx, K. (1990) *Capital: A Critique of Political Economy*, 2nd edition, vol. 1 (Harmondsworth: Penguin).

McCracken, G. (1990) *Culture and Consumption* (Bloomington: Indiana University Press).

McKay, G. (1996) *Senseless Acts of Beauty: Cultures of Resistance since the Sixties* (London: Verso).

McKendrick, N., Brewer, J. and Plumb, J. H. (1982) *The Birth of a Consumer Society: The Commercialization of Eighteenth Century England* (London: Europa).

McMillen, J. (1991) "Casinos and tourism: what's the big attraction?" pp. 153–172 in P. K. Carrol, M. Donohue, K. McGovern and J. McMillen (eds) *Tourism in Australia* (Sydney: HBJ).

McMillen, J. (1996) "From glamour to grind: the globalization of casinos", pp. 263–287 in J. McMillen (ed.) *Gambling Cultures* (London: Routledge).

McRobbie, A. (2002) "From Holloway to Hollywood: happiness at work in the new cultural economy?" pp. 97–114 in P. du Gay and Pryke (eds) *Cultural Economy: Cultural Analysis and Cultural Life* (London: Sage).

Massey, D. (1994) *Space, Place and Gender* (Cambridge: Polity).

Maxwell, K. (2002) "Lisbon: the earthquake of 1655 and urban recovery under the Marquês de Pombal", pp. 20–45 in J. Ockman (ed.) *Out of Ground Zero: Case Studies in Urban Invention* (Munich: Prestel Verlag).

Meethan, K. (2001) *Tourism in Global Society: Place, Space, Consumption* (Basingstoke: Palgrave).

Miles, M. (2000) *The Uses of Decoration: Essays in the Architectural Everyday* (Chichester: Wiley).

Miles, M. (2003) "Strange Days", pp. 33–59 in M. Miles and T. Hall (eds), *Urban Futures: Critical Commentaries on Shaping the City* (London: Routledge).

Miles, S. (1998) *Consumerism as a Way of Life* (London: Sage).

Miles, S. (2003) "Resistance or Security? Young People and the Appropriation of Urban, Cultural and Consumer Space", pp. 65–75 in M. Miles and T. Hall (eds), *Urban Futures: Critical Commentaries on Shaping the City* (London: Routledge).

Miles, S. and Paddison, R. (1998) "Urban consumption: an historiographical note", *Urban Studies*, 35, 5/6, pp. 815–824.

Miller, D. (1998) *A Theory of Shopping* (Ithaca: Cornell University Press).

Miller, D. (2001) *The Dialectics of Shopping* (Chicago: University of Chicago Press).

Miller, T. (2002) "The Sixties-Era Communes", pp. 327–352 in P. Braunstein and M. W. Doyle (eds) *Imagine Nation: The American Counterculture of the 1960s and '70s* (London: Routledge).

Mitchell, K. (1999) "What's culture got to do with it?" *Urban Geography*, 20, 7, pp. 667–677.

Mitchell, W. J. (1995) *City of Bits: Space, Place and the Infobahn* (London: MIT Press).

Mole, P. (1996) "Fordism, post-Fordism and the contemporary city", pp. 15–48 in J. O'Connor and D. Wynne (eds) *From the Margins to the Centre: Cultural Production and Consumption in the Post-Industrial City* (Aldershot: Ashgate).

Mullings, B. (2000) "Fantasy tours: exploring the global consumption of Caribbean sex tourism", in M. Gottdiener (ed.) *New Forms of Consumption: Consumers, Culture, and Commodification* (Boulder, Co: Rowman & Littlefield Publishers).

Mulvey, L. (1989) *Visual and Other Pleasures* (Basingstoke: Macmillan).

Mumford, L. (1938) *The Cultures of Cities* (London: Secker & Warburg).

Murray, R. (1989) "Fordism and post-Fordism", pp. 38–53 in S. Hall and M. Jacques (eds), *New Times: The Changing Face of Politics in the 1990s* (London: Lawrence & Wishart).

Myerscough, J. (1988) *The Economic Importance of the Arts in Britain* (London: Policy Studies Institute).

Myrvoll, S. (1999) "Cultural heritage tourism in Norway, with the focus on Bergen", pp. 44–52 in D. Dodd and A. van Hemel (eds) *Planning Cultural Tourism in Europe: A Presentation of Theories and Cases* (Amsterdam: Boekman Stichting).

Naess, A. (1989) *Ecology, Community and Lifestyle*, trans. D. Rothenberg (Cambridge: Cambridge University Press).

Nava, M. (1992) *Changing Cultures: Feminism, Youth and Consumerism* (London: Sage).

Nava, M. and O'Shea, A. (eds) (1997) *Modern Times: Reflections on a Century of English Modernity* (London: Routledge).

O'Connor, A. (1989) *Raymond Williams: Writing, Culture, Politics* (Oxford: Blackwell).

O'Connor, J. (1998) "Popular culture, cultural intermediaries and urban regeneration", pp. 225–240 in T. Hall and P. Hubbard (eds) *The Entrepreneurial City* (Chichester: Wiley).

O'Connor, J. and Wynne, D. (eds) (1996) *From the Margins to the Centre: Cultural Production and Consumption in the Post-Industrial City* (Aldershot: Ashgate).

Oh, M. and Arditi, J. (2000) "Shopping and postmodernism: consumption, production, identity, and the Internet", in M. Gottdiener, M. (ed.) (2001) *New Forms of Consumption: Consumers, Culture, and Commodification* (Lanham: MD: Rowman & Littlefield).

OMSCO (n.d.) [leaflet on organic dairy farming] www.omsco.co.uk.

Orbist, H. L. and Koolhaas, R. (2001) "Relearning from Las Vegas", pp. 509–617 in C. J. Chung, J. Inaba, R. Koolhaas and S. T. Leong (eds) *Harvard Design School Guide to Shopping* (Cambridge, MA: Taschen).

Paddison, R. (1997) "Politic and governance", pp. 317–334 in M. Pacione (ed.) *Britain's Cities: Geographies of Division in Urban Britain* (London: Routledge).

Paetzold, H. (1997) "The philosophical notion of the city", pp. 15–37 in H. Paetzold (ed.) *City Life: Essays on Urban Culture* (Limburg: Jan van Eyck Akademie).

Papanek, V. [1984] (1991) *Design for the Real World: Human Ecology and Social Change*, revised edition (London: Thames & Hudson).

Papanek, V. (1995) *The Green Imperative: Ecology and Ethics in Design and Architecture* (London: Thames & Hudson).

Park, R. E., Burgess, E. W. and McKenzie, R. D. (1925) *The City* (Chicago: Chicago University Press).

Parker, R. (1995) "Las Vegas, Lotteries and the New Buffalo: Gambling and community development", *Halycon* 17, pp. 223–249.

Paterson, A. (1983) *The price paid for Plymouth's new city centre*, unpublished dissertation, Part II RIBA (Plymouth: Plymouth Polytechnic).

Paton-Watson, J. P. and Abercrombie, P. (1943) *A Plan for Plymouth 1943*, Plymouth.

Peet, R. and Watts, M. (eds) (1996) *Liberation Ecologies: Environment, Development, Social Movements* (London: Routledge).

Pepper, D. (1996) *Modern Environmentalism: An Introduction* (London: Routledge).

Phillips, P. (1988) "Out of order: the public art machine", *Artform*, December, pp. 92–96.

Philo, C. and Kearns, G. (1993) Culture, history, capital: a critical introduction to the selling of places, in G. Kearns and C. Philo (eds) *Selling Places: The City as Cultural Capital, Past and Present* (Oxford: Pergamon).

Pile, S., Brook, C. and Mooney, G. (eds) (1999) *Unruly Cities?* (London: Routledge and Buckingham: Open University Press).

Piore, M. and Sabel, C. (1984) *The Second Industrial Divide* (New York: Basic Books).

Pollan, M. (1998) *A Place of My Own: The Education of an Amateur Builder* (London: Bloomsbury).

Pollock, G. (1994) "Territories of desire: reconsiderations of an African childhood", pp. 63–89 in G. Robertson, M. Mash, L. Tickner, J. Bird, B. Curtis and T. Putnam (eds) *Travellers Tales: Narratives of Home and Displacement* (London: Routledge).

Popular Mechanics "Heavy Cruiser" http://popularmechanics.com/science/transportation/2001/5/heavy_cruiser/index2.phtml.

Porter, R. (1990) *English Society in the Eighteenth Century* (Harmondsworth: Penguin).

Raban, J. (1974) *Soft city* (London: Fontana).

Rendell, J. (1999) "Thresholds, passages and surfaces: touching, passing and seeing in the Burlington arcade", pp. 168–191 in A. Coles (ed.) (1999) *The Optic of Walter Benjamin* [de-, dis-, ex-, vol. 3] (London: Black Dog).

Rendell, J. (2002) *The Pursuit of Pleasure: Gender, Space and Architecture in Regency London* (London: Continuum).

Reynolds, G. and Alferoff, C. (1999) "Junk mail and consumer freedom: resistance, transgression and reward in the panoptic gaze", pp. 241–261 in J. Hearn and S. Roseneil (eds) *Consuming Cultures: Power and Resistance* (Basingstoke: Macmillan).

Ritzer, G. [1993] (revised 2000) *The McDonaldization of Society* (Thousand Oaks: Pine Forge Press).

Ritzer, G. (1999) *Enchanting a Disenchantized World: Revolutionizing the Means of Consumption* (Thousand Oaks: Pine Forge).

Riverford (2003) *This Week's Riverford Box*, 27 January 2003 [weekly leaflet distributed with organic veetable box, including Watson, G. There has to be a better way, not paginated].

Rojek, C. (2000) "Mass tourism or the re-enchantment of the world? Issues and contradictions in the study of travel", pp. 51–70 in M. Gottdiener (ed.) *New Forms of Consumption: Consumers: Culture and Commodification* (Oxford: Rowman and Littlefield).

Rothman, H. (2002) *Neon Metropolis: How Las Vegas Started the Twenty-First Century* (London: Routledge).

Ryan, R. (2001) Urban Generations, *Tate* 24, Spring 2001, pp. 22–31.

Sack, R. D. (1992) *Place, Modernity and the Consumer's World* (London: Johns Hopkins University Press).

Safdie, M. (1997) *The City after the Automobile: An Architect's Vision* (New York: HarperCollins).

Sassen, S. (1991) *The Global City: New York, London, Tokyo* (Princeton: Princeton University Press).

Saunders, P. (1981) *Social Theory and the Urban Question* (London: Hutchinson).

Schein, L. (1997) "Urbanity, cosmopolitanism, consumption", pp. 225–241 in *China Urban: Ethnographies of Contemporary Culture* (Durham: Duke University Press).

Seabrook, J. (1993) *Victims of Development: Resistance and Alternatives* (London: Verso).

Seabrook, J. (1996) *In the Cities of the South: Scenes From a Developing World* (London: Verso).

Selwood, S. (1992) "Art in public", pp. 11–27 in S. Jones (ed.) *Art in Public* (Sunderland: AN Publications).

Scott A. J. (2000) *The Cultural Economy of Cities* (London: Sage).

Seiler, C. (2000) "The Commodification of rebellion: rock culture and consumer capitalism", pp. 203–226 in M. Gottdiener (ed.) *New Forms of Consumption: Consumers, Culture and Commodification* (Oxford: Rowman and Littlefield).

Sennett, R. (1970) *The Uses of Disorder* (New York: Norton).

Sennett, R. (1998) *The Corrosion of Character: The Personal Consequences of Work in the New Capitalism* (New York: Norton).

Shepley, S. (1991) "Planning for Plymouth's future", pp. 210–230 in B. Chalkley, D. Dunkerely and P. Gripaios (eds) *Plymouth: Maritime City in Transition* (Newton Abbot: David and Charles).

Shields, R. (ed.) (1992) *Lifestyle Shopping: The Subject of Consumption* (London: Routledge).

Shields, R. (1999) *Lefebvre, Love & Struggle* (London: Routledge).

Shiva, V. (1999) "This round to the citizens", *The Guardian*, 8th December, G2, pp. 4–5.

Shiva, V. (2000) *Stolen Harvest: The Highjacking of the Global Food Supply* (London: Zed Books).

Shriver, J. (2002) For sale: condos afloat http://usatoday.com/travel/vacations/detinations/2002/2002-05-10-floating-condo.htm.

Short, J. R. (1996) *The Urban Order* (Oxford: Blackwell).

Sibley, D. (1995) *Geographies of Exclusion* (London: Routledge).

Simmel, G. (1950) "The metropolis and mental life", pp. 324–339 in K. Wolff (ed.) *The Sociology of Georg Simmel* (London: Collier-Macmillan).

Simmel, G. (1990) (2nd edition), *The Philosophy of Money*, translated by T. Bottomore and D. Frisby edited by D. Frisby (London: Routledge).

Smith, M. P. (2001) *Transnational Urbanism: Locating Globalization* (Oxford: Blackwell).

Smith, N. (1996a) "The production of nature", pp. 35–54 in G. Robertson, M. Mash, L. Tickner, J. Bird, B. Curtis and T. Putnam (eds) (1996) *Future Natural: Nature, Science, Culture* (London: Routledge).

Smith, N. (1996b) *The New Urban Frontier: Gentrification and the Revanchist City* (London: Routledge).

Soja, E. (1989) *Postmodern Geographies* (London: Verso).

Soja, E. (1998) *Thirdspace: Journeys to Los Angeles and Other Real-Imagined Places* (Oxford: Blackwell).

Soja, E. (2000) *Postmetropolis: Critical Studies of Cities and Regions* (Oxford: Blackwell).

Soria y Puig, A. (ed.) (1999) *Cerdà: The Five Bases of the General Theory of Urbanization* (Madrid: Electa).

Sorkin, M. (1992) "See you in Disneyland", pp. 205–232 in M. Sorkin (ed.) *Variations on a Theme Park* (New York: Noonday Press).

Sorkin, M. (ed.) (1992) *Variations on a Theme Park* (New York: Noonday Press).

Spanier, D. (1992) *All Right, OK, You Win: Inside Las Vegas* (London: Mandarin).

Spitzer, T. M. and Baum, H. (1995) *Public Markets and Community Revitalization* (Washington DC: Urban Land Institute and Project for Public Spaces).

Stearns, P. (2001) *Consumerism in World History: The Global Transformation of Desire* (London: Routledge).

Steiner, C. B. (1994) *African Art in Transit* (Cambridge: Cambridge University Press).

Stewart, S. (1993) *On Longing: Narratives of the Miniature, the Gigantic, the Souvenir, the Collection* (Durham, NC: Duke University Press).

Storey, J. (1999) *Cultural Consumption and Everyday Life* (London: Arnold).

Sudjic, D. (1993) *The 100 Mile City* (London: Flamingo).

Swartz, D. (1997) *Culture and Power: The Work of Pierre Bourdieu* (London: University of Chicago Press).

Sydney Morning Herald (2002) High life on the High Seas, 7 September, http://www.smh.com.au/articles/2002/09/06/1031115933080.html.

Taylor, B. (1994) "From penitentiary to temple of art: early metaphors of improvement at the Millbank Tate", pp. 9–322 in Pointon, M. (ed.) *Art Apart: Art Institutions and Ideology Across England and North America* (Manchester: Manchester University Press).

Taylor, W. R. (1989) "The evolution of public spaces in New York City: The commercial showcase of America", pp. 287–309 in S. J. Bronner (ed.) *Consuming Visions: Accumulation and Display of Goods in America 1880–1920* (London: W. W. Norton).

Thrift, N. (1993) "The urban impasse?", *Theory, Culture, Society*, 10: 229–236.

Thrift, N. and Glennie, P. (1993) "Historical geographies of urban life and modern consumption", pp. 33–48 in G. Kearns and C. Philo (eds)

Selling Places: The City as Cultural Capital, Past and Present (Oxford: Pergamon).

Todd, R. (2001) Las Vegas, 'Tis of thee, *The Atlantic Monthly*, www.theatlantic. com/issues/2001/02/todd-p1.htm.

Travel and Tourism Analyst (2002) *World Cruise Market Update*, Travel and Tourism Intelligence, 1, February.

Turner, J. F. C. (1976) *Housing by People* (London: Marion Boyars).

Urry, J. (1990) *The Tourist Gaze* (Bristol, London: Sage Publication).

Urry, J. (1995) *Consuming Places* (London: Routledge).

Urry, J. (1998) Contemporary transformations of time and space, pp. 1–17 in P. Scott (ed.) *The Globalization of Higher Education* (Buckingham: SRHE/ Open University Press).

Urry, J. (2002) *The Tourist Gaze: Leisure and Travel in Contemporary Societies*, 2nd edition (London: Sage).

Vale, B. and Vale, R. (1991) *Green Architecture: Design for a Sustainable Future* (London: Thames & Hudson).

Veblen T. [1899] (1970) *Theory of the Leisure Class* (London: Unwin).

Venturi, R. Brown, D. S. and Izenour, S. (1972) *Learning From Las Vegas* (Cambridge, MA: MIT Press).

Wall, D. (1999) *Earth First! and the Anti-Roads Movement* (London: Routledge).

Warren, S. (1993) "This heaven gives me migraines: the problems and promise of landscapes of leisure", pp. 173–186 in J. Duncan and D. Ley (eds) *Place/Culture/Representation* (London: Routledge).

Webster, F. (2001) Re-inventing place: Birmingham as an information city? *City*, 5, 1, pp. 27–46.

Whiteley, N. (1993) *Design for Society* (London: Reaktion Books).

Wildt, M. (1995) "Plurality of taste: food and consumption in West Germany during the 1950s", *History Workshop Journal*, 39, pp. 23–41.

Willett, J. (1967) *Art in a City* (London: Methuen).

Williams, R. (1958) *Culture and Society, 1780–1950* (London: Chatto and Windus).

Williams, R. (1976) *Keywords: Am Vocabulary of Culture and Society* (London: Fontana).

Williams, R. H. (1982) *Dream Worlds: Mass Consumption in Late Nineteenth-Century France* (Oxford: University of California Press).

Wilson, E. (1991) *The Sphinx in the City* (Berkeley: University of California Press).

Wilson, E. (2001) *The Contradictions of Culture: Cities, Culture, Women* (London: Sage).

Wilson, E. (2003) *Bohemianism: The Glamorous Outcasts*, London, Taurus Pale Paperbacks [first edition 2000, I. B. Taurus].

Wirth, L. (1964) *Urbanism as a way of Life* (Chicago: Chicago University Press).

Witkin, R. W. (2003) *Adorno on Popular Culture* (London: Routledge).

Wolin, R. (1994) *Walter Benjamin: An Aesthetic of Redemption* (Berkeley: University of California Press).

Wood, R. E. (2000) "Caribbean cruise tourism: globalization at sea", *Annals of Tourism Research*, 27, 2, pp. 345–370.

Young, L. (1999) "Marketing the modern: department stores, consumer culture, and the new middle class in interwar Japan", *International Labour and Working-Class History*, 55, pp. 52–70.

Young, S. (2000) "Gambling in Atlantic City: The Human Toll", *Executive Intelligence Review*, 27, 40, pp. 59–61.

Zhen, Z. (2000) "Mediating time: the 'rice bowl of youth' in fin de siècle urban China", pp. 131–154, in A. Appadurai (ed.) *Globalization* (Dursam, NC: Duke University Press).

Zhen, Z. (2001) "Mediating time: the 'rice bowl of youth' in fin de siècle urban China", pp. 131–154 in A. Appadurai (ed.) (2001) *Globalization* (Durham, NC: Duke University Press).

Zukin, S. [1982] (1989) *Loft Living: Culture and Capital in Urban Change* (New Brunswick, NJ: Rutgers University Press [2nd edition]).

Zukin, S. (1991) *Landscapes of Power: From Detroit to Disney World* (Oxford: University of California Press).

Zukin, S. (1995) *The Cultures of Cities* (Oxford: Blackwell).

Zukin, S. (1996a) "Space and symbols in an age of decline", pp. 43–59 in A. King (ed.) (1996) *Re = Presenting the City: Ethnicity, Capital and Culture in the 21st Century Metropolis* (Basingstoke: Macmillan).

Zukin, S. (1996b) "Cultural strategies of economic development and the hegemony of vision", pp. 223–243 in A. Merrifield and E. Swyngedouw (eds) (1996) *The Urbanisation of Injustice* (London: Lawrence & Wishart).

Further Reading

Provide or Divide?

Georg, S. (1950) "The metropolis and mental life", pp. 324–339 in K. Wolff (ed.) *The Sociology of Georg Simmel*, London: Collier-Macmillan.
John, S. (1993) *An Introductory Guide to Cultural Theory and Everyday Life*, Hemel Hempstead: harvester Wheatsheaf.
Louis, W. (1964) *Urbanism as a Way of Life*, Chicago: Chicago University Press.
Mauel, C. (1977) *The Urban Question: A Marxist Approach*, London: Edward Arnold.

Consuming the Past: Cities, Shopping and Supermarkets

Lee, M. (1993) *Consumer Culture Reborn: The Cultural Politics of Consumption*, London: Routledge.
McKendrick, N. Brewer, J. and Plumb, J. H. (1982) *The Birth of a Consumer Society: The Commercialization of Eighteenth Century England*, London: Europa.
Williams, R. H. (1982) *Dream Worlds: Mass Consumption in Late Nineteenth-Century France*, Oxford: University of California Press.
Young, L. (1999) "Marketing the modern: department stores, consumer culture, and the new middle class in interwar Japan", *International Labour and Working-Class History*, 55, pp. 52–70.

Consuming Cultures: The Symbolic Economies of Cities

El-Khoury, R. and Robbins, E. (eds) (2003) *Shaping the City*, London: Routledge.
O'Connor, J. and Wynne, D. (eds) (1996) *From the Margins to the Centre: Cultural Production and Consumption in the Post-Industrial City*, Aldershot: Ashgate.
Williams, R. (1976) *Keywords: A Vocabulary of Culture and Society*, London: Fontana.

Zukin, S. (1995) *The Cultures of Cities*, Oxford: Blackwell.
Zukin, S. (1996) "Cultural strategies of economic development and the hegemony of vision" in Merrifield, A. and Swyngedouw, E. (1996) *The Urbanisation of Injustice*, London: Lawrence and Wishart.

Consuming Place: Cities and Cultural Tourism

Bianchini, F. and Parkinson, M. (1993) *Cultural Policy and Urban Regeneration: The West European Experience*, Manchester: Manchester University Press.
Boyer, C. (1992) "Cities for Sale: Merchandising History at South Street Seaport", in M. Sorkin (1992) (ed.) *Variations on a Theme Park*, New York: Noonday Press.
Dodd, D. and van Hemel, A. (1999) *Planning Cultural Tourism in Europe: A Presentation of Theories and Cases*, Amsterdam: Boekman Foundation.
Fennel, D. A. (2003) *Ecotourism*, London: Routledge.
Smith, M. K. (2003) *Issues in Cultural Tourism*, London: Routledge.

Consuming Space: The Architectures of Consumption

Benjamin, W. (1999) *The Arcades Project*, Cambridge (Mass): Harvard.
Crawford, M. (1992) "The World in a Shopping Mall", in M. Sorkin (ed.) (1992) *Variations on a Theme Park*, New York: Noonday Press.
Low, S. (2003) *Behind the Gates: Life, Security and the Pursuit of Happiness in Fortres America*, London: Routledge.
MacCannell, D. (1999) "New Urbanism and its Discontents", in J. Copjec and M. Sorkin (eds) (1999) *Giving Ground: The Politics of Propinquity*, London: Verso.
Shields, R. (1992) (ed.) *Lifestyle Shopping: The Subject of Consumption*, London: Routledge.

Consuming Chance: The Gambling City

Gottdiener, M., Collins, C. and Dickens, D. (1999) *Las Vegas: The Social Production of an All-American City*, Cambridge: Blackwell.
Hannigan, J. (1998) *Fantasy City: Pleasure and Profit in the Postmodern Metropolis*, London: Routledge.
Ritzer, G. (1999) *Enchanting a Disenchantized World: Revolutionizing the Means of Consumption*, Thousand Oaks: Pine Forge.
Rothman, H. (2002) *Neon Metropolis: How Las Vegas Started the Twenty-First Century*, London: Routledge.

Reinventing the Consuming City

Donald, J. (1999) *Imagining the Modern City*, London: Athlone.
Light, J. (1999) "From cityspace to cyberspace", pp. 109–130 in M. Crang, P. Crang and J. May (eds) *Virtual Geographies: Bodies, Spaces and Relations*, London: Routledge.
Urry, J. (1995) *Consuming Places*, London: Routledge.
Wood, R. E. (2000) "Caribbean cruise tourism: globalization at sea", *Annals of Tourism Research*, 27, 2, pp. 345–370.

Alternative Consumption

Gold, J. and Revill, G. E. (2004) *Representing the Environment*, London: Routledge.
Gregson, N. and Crewe, L. (2003) *Second-Hand Cultures*, Oxford: Berg.
Macnaghten, P. and Urry, J. (1998) *Contested Natures*, London: Sage.
Power, M. (2003) *Rethinking Development Geographies*, London: Routledge.
Zimmerer, K . S. and Basett, T. J. (2003) *Political Ecology*, London: Routledge.

Index